THE DARK TRIAD OF PERSONALITY

THE DARK TRIAD OF PERSONALITY

Narcissism, Machiavellianism, and Psychopathy in Everyday Life

MINNA LYONS

ELSEVIER

ACADEMIC PRESS

An imprint of Elsevier

Academic Press is an imprint of Elsevier
125 London Wall, London EC2Y 5AS, United Kingdom
525 B Street, Suite 1650, San Diego, CA 92101, United States
50 Hampshire Street, 5th Floor, Cambridge, MA 02139, United States
The Boulevard, Langford Lane, Kidlington, Oxford OX5 1GB, United Kingdom

Library of Congress Cataloging-in-Publication Data
A catalog record for this book is available from the Library of Congress

British Library Cataloguing-in-Publication Data
A catalogue record for this book is available from the British Library

ISBN 978-0-12-814291-2

For information on all Academic Press publications visit
our website at https://www.elsevier.com/books-and-journals

Publisher: Nikki Levy
Acquisition Editor: Nikki Levy
Editorial Project Manager: Megan Ashdown
Production Project Manager: Bharatwaj Varatharajan
Cover Designer: Christian J. Bilbow

Typeset by SPi Global, India

Contents

CHAPTER ONE

Introduction to the Dark Triad

Chapter Outline

1.1 The Dark Triad: What Is It?

Jack/Jodie is a player. S/he likes to gamble with money, and juggle multiple romantic relationships at the same time with several wo/men. S/he has a cynical view of the world, and other people in it. Jack/Jodie feels that it is best to take advantage of others before they try to take advantage of you. Jack/Jodie thinks that s/he is great at everything that s/he does, and deserves best things in life. S/he has very little empathy for others, and treats people as tools for achieving his goals. Jack/Jodie is easily insulted, and longs for revenge when things don't go his/her way.

The Dark Triad of Personality
https://doi.org/10.1016/B978-0-12-814291-2.00001-2

Jack and Jodie are fictional characters, but they could easily exist in real life. Characters like them have qualities that typify features of malignant personality traits, also known as the Dark Triad of personality. In the past few decades, the socially aversive Dark Triad of personality has captured the attention of both researchers and the general public alike. Since the conception of the construct by Paulhus and Williams in 2002, it has been studied intensively in thousands of academic publications. Without a doubt, we have a fascination for people who are antagonistic, selfish, and exploitative, to the extent that these people are often portrayed with admiration in the popular culture (Jonason, Webster, Schmitt, Li, & Crysel, 2012). This book is the first attempt to bring together the wealth of research on the topic, evaluating the significance of the Dark Triad in everyday life ranging from romantic relationship to workplace behavior.

The Dark Triad consists of three overlapping, yet distinctive personality traits: Machiavellianism, narcissism, and psychopathy. The traits share a core of manipulation, callousness, and selfishness (Jones & Figueredo, 2013). All of the three traits are characterized by a disregard of social norms, which often leads to social transgressions in terms of lying, cheating, manipulating, and stealing. Individuals who are high in the dark traits are untrustworthy and uncaring romantic partners, backstabbing work colleagues, and cold and controlling as parents. In short, the Dark Triad can have toxic consequences for others who are in the radar of those high in these traits. However, Dark Triad traits do have positive sides too. Especially in circumstances where there is a possibility to gain something for oneself, individuals with Dark Triad traits can be loyal friends, effective leaders, and heroic rescuers (e.g., Hart, Richardson, & Tortoriello, 2018; Patton, Smith, & Lilienfeld, 2018; Smith, Hill, Wallace, Recendes, & Judge, 2018).

As well as the toxic core, the three traits have some unique characteristics. Machiavellianism is distinctive in the flexible, chameleon-like use of strategies from defection to cooperation to suit the demands of the situation, with the ultimate aim of gaining benefits for the self. Interestingly, a study on a sample of Polish participants found that out of the three traits, Machiavellianism was a significant positive predictor of fluid intelligence (Kowalski et al., 2018). In essence, individual high in Machiavellianism are skillful political maneuvers, with an eye for opportunities to exploit in order to achieve personal gain. The features of psychopathy include impulsivity, reckless risk-taking, and very shallow empathy toward other people. Those high in psychopathy may be less flexible and more opportunistic in their behaviors than high Machiavellian individuals. Narcissism, in turn, is characterized by vanity and grandiosity, and by an inflated self-assessment. Individuals high in narcissism believe that they have superior abilities in comparison to other people, but these beliefs are rarely grounded in reality. All the Dark Triad traits relate to dysfunctional interpersonal relationships, stemming from selfish behavior and lack of care for others. In this book, I will discuss the research on the Dark Triad traits in romantic relationships in Chapter 4 and evaluate dark traits among friends and friendship networks in Chapter 5. Unfortunately, the influence of the Dark Triad within families is less studied, especially in terms of the impact of having a parent with a toxic personality. Therefore parenting and families are only briefly considered later in this chapter, as part of the discussion of the origins (i.e., etiology) of the Dark Triad.

In the personality disorder literature, especially psychopathy and narcissism are often researched in "clinical" samples. Participants in these studies are individuals who are under the supervision of clinical or forensic facilities, and have received a personality disorder diagnosis. In contrast, research on "subclinical" or "nonclinical" populations consists of people in the community, often using students or diverse internet samples. In these samples, the Dark Triad is investigated as a continuum, without making a distinction between "normal" and "abnormal." In Chapter 2, I will provide an overview of the Dark Triad within the clinical framework, and in Chapter 3, forensic implications will be discussed.

In most personality research, the continuous distribution of the scores on the Dark Triad questionnaires is correlated with the continuous distribution of other variables of interest. So far, the Dark Triad has been explored widely in thousands of studies in relation to a large number of intra- and interpersonal variables, including crime, bullying, risk-taking, deception, a host of mating behaviors, morality, racism, empathy, gossip, interoceptive awareness, chronotypes, and social cognition. The list goes on forever. In this book, I will give special consideration to workplace behaviors (Chapter 6), as well as to a rapidly burgeoning field of research, the Dark Triad in the cyberworld (Chapter 7).

The terminology used in clinical psychology/psychiatry is different to that utilized in personality psychology research. Because clinical research often utilizes diagnostic categories, individuals are referred to as "narcissists" or "psychopaths." This terminology implies that there are distinctively different categories of people and relies on arbitrary thresholds for drawing a line between "normal" and "abnormal." In personality literature, these kinds of terms are normally avoided, and people are referred to as being "narcissistic" or "psychopathic," or even more commonly, being "high or low" in a trait narcissism and psychopathy. Throughout this book, I will attempt to use the terminology associated with personality literature rather than with diagnostic categories.

Although all the Dark Triad traits have been conceptualized as dispositional, stable features in an individual, there is some evidence that especially for narcissism, situations may play a part in the manifestation of the trait. For instance, levels of narcissism can be experimentally manipulated to some extent. Narcissism can be increased by asking participants to think about their own achievements (Sakellaropoulo & Baldwin, 2007), or even by thinking of oneself as being a prince or a princess (Li et al., 2016). In a diary study, Giacomin and Jordan (2016) looked at fluctuations in narcissism on daily basis. They found that feeling stressed reduced levels of narcissism and having power over others/doing something positive to other people increased narcissism. This findings is similar to that of Piff (2014), who discovered that although wealthier individuals were more narcissistic, their narcissism scores were lowered when they were primed to think about the benefits of egalitarianism (i.e., the idea that all people are equal to others). Thus although there are baseline levels of narcissism that differ between individuals, narcissism can also be considered as a temporary state which fluctuates in different circumstances. The stability of Machiavellianism and psychopathy is less studied, and although we know that the questionnaire scores on these traits decline with age, the findings are based on cross-sectional, rather than longitudinal studies. To my knowledge, there is no published research reporting experiments manipulating levels of Machiavellianism and psychopathy.

There has been some debate and discussion of the exact nature and relationship between the three traits. Researchers have proposed that narcissism is distinct from the other two, and Machiavellianism and psychopathy should form a "Dark Dyad" (Egan, Chan, & Shorter, 2014; Rogoza & Cieciuch, 2018; Vize, Lynam, Collison, Miller, 2018). Indeed, a meta-analysis of 91 research papers showed that psychopathy and Machiavellianism were more highly correlated with each other than either one is with narcissism (Muris, Merckelbach, Otgaar, & Meijer, 2017), and that Machiavellianism scales should be considered as alternative measures for psychopathy (Vize, Lynam, et al., 2018). Finally, Bertl, Pietschnig, Tran, Stieger, and Voracek (2017) analyzed the factorial structure of popular Dark Triad measures in a community sample of over 2000 participants, and concluded that the Dark Triad is best understood as a single trait, rather than three separate traits. However, an abundance of studies have found that the three traits do correlate differently with several psychosocial variables, and it is useful to study all the three traits together.

Fig. 1.1 demonstrates the relationship between the three Dark Triad traits. The darker colored areas in the middle show the proportion of variance shared between all three traits and between the individual traits. The small section in the middle, where all the three circles meet, shows the proportion of shared variance between the traits. Psychopathy and Machiavellianism share more features with each other than either does with narcissism. The lowest correlations are found between Machiavellianism and narcissism (Furnham, Richards, & Paulhus, 2013).

As will be discussed in the following sections, all of the three traits have different correlates with behaviors. Rather than constructing a single measure of Dark Triad, it is useful to analyze the traits separately when conducting research. Previous research has used cross-correlations with the Dark Triad and the behaviors of interest, followed by regression analyses where the shared variance between the Dark Triad traits is controlled for by entering them as simultaneous predictor variables. This allows the researcher to investigate what the unique contribution of each trait is to the behavior under investigation (however, see Vize, Collison, Miller, Lynam, 2018 for a cautionary tale).

Despite thousands of publications over the past few decades, there are some notable shortcomings in the research, outlined in Table 1.1. Overall,

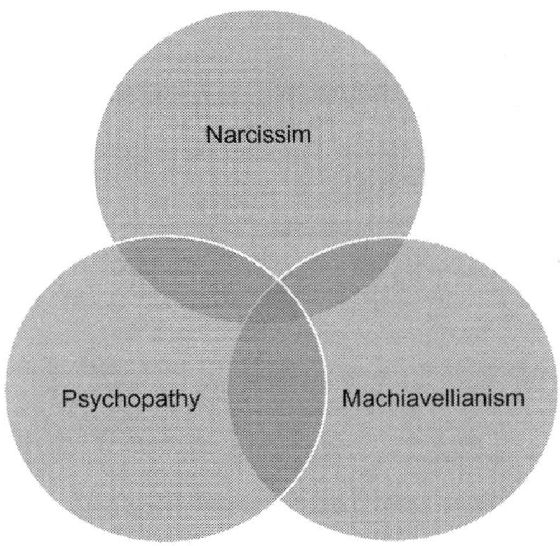

Fig. 1.1 A diagram outlining the relationship between the Dark Triad variables.

Table 1.1 Shortcomings and Suggestions for Dark Triad Research

Criticism	Explanation	Problem	Solution
Sample characteristics	Most studies are conducted using WEIRD samples (Henrich, Heine, & Norenzayan, 2010)	Lack of knowledge on how universal/situation specific Dark Triad and associated behaviors are	Conduct studies on people from all socioeconomic backgrounds (including very poor and very rich), in both Western and other cultures
Reliance on cross-sectional questionnaire design	Bulk of the research utilizes cross-sectional, correlational questionnaire designs	Difficulty in establishing causality, lack of experimental control, or ecological validity	Expand methodology to include more experiments, observations, and interview studies
Lack of replication	Researchers focus on new ideas rather than aiming to replicate existing research	Are the findings real, or just a random artifact or something else?	Systematic replication of existing research from teams that were not previously involved in the research
Post hoc invention of hypotheses/ p-hacking	Researchers trawl through their data to find significant findings and formulate their hypotheses around these findings	Nonsignificant relationships are often unreported	Preregistration of studies and hypotheses
Neglecting multidimensional nature of the Dark Triad	The Dark Triad is collapsed into one composite score/individual Dark Triad traits are studied as one-dimensional constructs	Heterogeneity within the Dark Triad traits is ignored	Use longer measures that allow investigating multidimensional nature of the Dark Triad
Conflating measures with constructs/ "jingle fallacy"	Reliance on the validity of the questionnaire measures as true representation of the traits/Trusting two measures to assess the same construct	The questionnaires may not be valid/mask the multidimensional aspects of the traits	Prioritize using the "gold standard" measures/use multiple measures to study the traits

Analytical strategies partialling out shared variance between the traits	Using analyses such as multiple regression in taking into consideration the influence of each trait on the outcome variable after the shared variance between the traits is controlled for statistically	Unsure what the Dark Triad trait represents after the shared variance between the two other traits has been controlled (e.g., Machiavellianism is no longer the same trait it was prior to statistically controlling for psychopathy)	Using zero-order analytical strategies (e.g., correlating each Dark Triad trait individual with an outcome variable, and comparing the strength of the correlations).

Asendorpf, J. B., Conner, M., De Fruyt, F., De Houwer, J., Denissen, J. J., Fiedler, K., … & Perugini, M. (2013). Recommendations for increasing replicability in psychology. *European Journal of Personality*, *27*, 108–119.
Henrich, J., Heine, S. J., & Norenzayan, A. (2010). The weirdest people in the world? *Behavioral and Brain Sciences*, *33*, 61–83.
Vize, C. E., Collison, K. L., Miller, J. D., & Lynam, D. R. (2018). Examining the effects of controlling for shared variance among the dark triad using meta-analytic structural equation modelling. *European Journal of Personality*, *32*, 46–61.
Watts, A. L., Waldman, I. D., Smith, S. F., Poore, H. E., & Lilienfeld, S. O. (2017). The nature and correlates of the dark triad: The answers depend on the questions. *Journal of Abnormal Psychology*, *126*, 951–968.

most studies have utilized questionnaire designs on relatively wealthy and educated participants from Western cultures, making it hard to generalize the findings to all people. There are also problems with the questionnaire measures, analytical strategies, and lack of replication of findings. Table 1.1 also presents suggestions on how to rectify these shortcomings in future research.

1.1.1 Machiavellianism

Machiavellianism has been a widely researched concept in social and personality psychology since the 1970 publication of "Studies in Machiavellianism" by Christie and Geis. The term originates from the 16th century philosopher, diplomat, and political theorist Niccolo Machiavelli, who advised leaders to use tactics of deceit in achieving their goals. In Fig. 1.2, Machiavelli is portrayed by Santi di Tito, painted in the mid-part of the 16th century.

In one of Machiavelli's most famous essay, "The Prince" ("Il Principe"), Machiavelli discussed "conquest by criminal virtue," where he advised the prince that it would be wise to calculate the costs and benefits of cruel deeds (such as the execution of rivals) in an attempt to achieve more power. In one of his famous quotes, Machiavelli advised the prince to "... appear to be

Fig. 1.2 Sixteenth century portrait by Santi di Tito (with permission of Wikimedia commons licence).

compassionate, faithful to his word, guileless, and devout. And indeed he should be so. But his disposition should be such that, if he needs to be the opposite, he knows how." This quote crystallizes the core of Machiavellianism as a personality trait—use of strategic manipulation flexibly in order to achieve one's own goals.

Indeed, individuals who score high on Machiavellianism (so-called High-Machs) are sensitive to social context and can switch between tactics of cooperation and competition when it is useful to do so (Czibor & Bereczkei, 2012). High-Machs endorse emotional manipulation, for example, playing two people off against each other, paying compliments to others in order to get in their "good books," or using emotional skills to make others feel guilty (Austin, Farrelly, Black, & Moore, 2007). It is of no surprise that individuals high in this trait can be successful in careers such as marketing, business, and sales—fields of work where cool-headed decision making and strategic manipulation would help individuals to further their careers.

There is some confusion about what Machiavellianism consists of, and the theoretical base for this trait is not clear (e.g., Rauthmann, 2013). Some researchers have claimed that Machiavellianism is not qualitatively different from psychopathy. Rather than a distinctive personality trait, Machiavellianism could be a subclinical manifestation of psychopathy, only different in the degrees of severity (Mealey, 1995). However, many studies have found distinctive differences between psychopathy and Machiavellianism, suggesting that they are better treated as separate personality traits. Further, it is possible that Machiavellianism is not a unidimensional, monolithic personality trait, but it may consist of several interrelated subcomponents. For example, Christie and Geis (1970) proposed that Machiavellianism consists of two traits: interpersonally manipulative tactics, and a cynical view of human nature. The tactics and views were confirmed in a recent large-scale cross-cultural study which also found that the tactics, but not the views dimension of Machiavellianism related to psychopathy (Monaghan, Bizumic, & Sellbom, 2018). Most studies on the Dark Triad have considered Machiavellianism as just one trait, which may have masked important differences between actual behavior and perceptions of others.

1.1.2 Narcissism

Narcissism is a well-studied concept in clinical, forensic, and personality literature. Individuals high in narcissism are vain and grandiose. They have a heightened sense of entitlement, thinking that they deserve more than others because they are better than anybody else. The term "narcissism" derives from the story of Narcissus in Greek mythology, depicting Narcissus, a young man, who fell in love with his own reflection after seeing it in water. In the context of psychology literature, the idea came popular with the psychoanalytical movement, and the publication of Sigmund Freud's essay "On Narcissism" in 1914.

According to Keith Campbell and colleagues (2011), it is useful to consider narcissism from three different points of view—the self, the interpersonal, and the strategies for self-regulation. First, the self-view of narcissistic individuals is characterized by feeling unique and special. The self-view relates to a sense of entitlement and a will to have power over others. Second, because of the uniqueness of the self, the interpersonal relationships of high narcissists are characterized by low empathy for others. Narcissistic individuals use other people as a tool for achieving their goals, resulting in shallow and exploitative interpersonal relationships. Third, narcissistic individuals use strategies for maintaining their grandiose self-views. They seek for attention and praise, ride on other people's achievements, and put themselves on the center of everything. When these strategies fail, narcissistic individuals may react with aggression and vengeance. When successful, narcissist thrives and may even achieve great goals in life.

Over the years, narcissism has been conceptualized in many different ways, depending partially on the instruments that have been used to measure it. For example, according to one idea, there are two, distinctive types of narcissism: grandiose and vulnerable (e.g., Miller et al., 2011). Individuals who are high on grandiose narcissism have elevated self-esteem, and aggressive, forceful, and dominant interpersonal styles. Those who are high on vulnerable narcissism feel insecure and inadequate, and try to mask it from themselves and the rest of the world by faking grandiosity. Needless to say, those who have the features of domineering grandiose narcissism fare better than vulnerable narcissists.

Indeed, aspects of narcissism relate to leadership, charisma, and a willingness to dominate, which could lead to (at least) temporary career success. For example, studies on achievements of US presidents have indicated that those who are perceived as having traits of grandiose (but not vulnerable) narcissism have successful profiles in terms of crisis management, popularity, and number of initiatives (Watts et al., 2013). However, the authors also warned about the double-edged sword of narcissism, as the same presidents also engaged in detrimental unethical decision making. I will review the literature on the Dark Triad and career success in more detail in Chapter 6.

Narcissism has also been widely researched as a clinical construct, narcissistic personality disorder (NPD). Often, those who have been stamped with this label have committed a crime, and the mental illness label goes some way to explain why the individuals failed to comply with the societal norms of what is acceptable. The Dark Triad research is not concerned about categorical illness labels, but is more focused on looking at traits such as narcissism as a continuum. Evolutionarily minded researchers view this continuum as adaptive, bringing potential reproductive success to those at the high end of narcissism dimension. The personality and the clinical literature take quite a different view on narcissism, something that will be discussed in more detail in the next chapter.

Although narcissism has been conceptualized as a fairly stable trait-like feature, there are interesting studies into the "narcissism epidemic," a steady increase in narcissism across the generations in the past four or so decades. According to Jean Twenge and Keith Campbell (2009), young college students especially in the United States score higher on narcissism measures than their predecessors did. Indeed, some of this change has been rapid, occurring during a short period of time (e.g., 2002–2007), and is evident across different ethnic groups residing in the United States (Twenge & Foster, 2008). The narcissism epidemic is apparent also in traditionally collectivist cultures, such as China (Cai, Kwan, & Sedikides, 2012). The reasons behind the narcissism epidemic are still debated, but some suggestions are the increase in consumerism, wealth, media, exposure to celebrities, and social media use. Increase in selfishness and vanity are reflected in multiple aspects of life, including song lyrics, and literature.

However, it is good to note that there is also contradictory evidence for the epidemic. In a recent analysis of a large number of individuals from 1990s, 2000s, and 2010s, Wetzel et al. (2017) demonstrated that these different cohorts may have understood the items in the Narcissistic Personality Inventory (NPI) differently, and when this measurement nonequivalence was accounted for in statistical analyses, some aspects of narcissism (e.g., leadership, vanity, and entitlement) may even have decreased across these different generations. Thus the claims about the narcissism epidemic must be treated with caution.

1.1.3 Psychopathy

Psychopathy is perhaps the "darkest" of the Dark Triad traits. Psychopathy, more than the other two traits, has stronger associations with disregard for others, manifesting in disruptive interpersonal behaviors such as bullying (Baughman, Dearing, Giammarco, & Vernon, 2012) and sadism (Carton & Egan, 2017). This disregard for others is especially relevant in the criminal context. Those high on psychopathy are more likely to exhibit criminal activity, varying from small everyday crimes (such as opportunistic shoplifting; Lyons & Jonason, 2015) to having a chronically criminal lifestyle, leading to imprisonment and high levels of recidivism.

The existence of individuals who show deviant behavior and no regard for others has been acknowledged for a long time. Psychopathy was probably noted first within the context of psychology by Philippe Pinel in the 1800s, where he used the term "mania without delirium" to describe individuals who engage in morally questionable, deviant behavior without obvious signs of cognitive disturbances. Cleckley published the "Mask of Sanity," in 1941, which has become a historical landmark outlining case studies on psychopathic personalities. In his book, Cleckley discusses the ability of psychopaths to outwardly mimic a normally functioning individual, having the skill to mask their mental illness. Psychopathy is also acknowledged in other cultures. Anthropologist Jane M. Murphy (1976) interviewed Inuit people in the Bering strait, who had invented the term "kunlangeta" to men who lie, cheat, steal, take sexual advantage of women, and do not care about punishments. Apparently, the Inuit way of dealing with these socially deviant individuals was to quietly push them off the ice.

Psychopathy is unlikely to be a monolith construct but may consist of several subcomponents. There are still debates about what the factors of psychopathy are. The findings vary from study to study, often depending on the scale that is used to assess psychopathy. Theories and empirical evidence has suggested four-, three-, and two-factor models. For example, according to the triarchic model, psychopathy comprises of boldness, meanness, and disinhibition (Patrick, Fowles, & Krueger, 2009). The two-factor model divides psychopathy into primary (Factor 1) and secondary (Factor 2) psychopathy. Primary psychopathy involves interpersonal and affective factors, such as coldness and callous manipulation, whereas secondary psychopathy is more about risky, impulsive behaviors. Primary psychopathy has also been named as the "successful" psychopathy, as having low guilt and empathy could be a great tool for achieving power in the society. Secondary psychopathy, in turn, is the "unsuccessful" psychopathy facet, leading to crime and imprisonment rather than a career in the parliament.

1.2 Dark Triad and Other Personality Traits

There has been a great amount of research trying to establish how the Dark Triad relates to other models of personality, such as the Big Five (or the Five-Factor Model, FFM) and the Big Six (i.e., the HEXACO model, which includes the FFM and Honesty-Humility). In order for the Dark Triad to be a convincing construct, the traits need to be distinctively different from other personality traits.

Briefly, the FFM consist of five stable personality traits: openness, conscientiousness, extraversion, agreeableness, neuroticism. Individuals who score high in openness are inventive and curious, open for adventure and new experiences. Those who have low levels of this trait are more conventional, prefer routine, and are not bothered about widening their horizons. Conscientious individuals are organized, reliable, and self-disciplined, whereas low conscientiousness relates to carelessness, disorganization, and low reliability. Highly extraverted people thrive on meeting others. They like the company of people and are often upbeat, energetic, and talkative. Individuals low in this trait prefer their own company and act more shy and reserved in social situations. Agreeableness is related to being warm, compassionate, and helpful. Low agreeableness is associated with being antagonistic and unhelpful toward others. Neuroticism is characterized by anxiousness and the tendency to feel negative emotions more often and more intensively. People low in neuroticism (and high in its opposite pole, emotional stability) are calm, stable, and not easily worried. The HEXACO model includes the FFM and honesty-humility. Individuals high in honesty-humility are sincere, fair, modest, and humble. Individuals at the opposing end are dishonest, big-headed, and unfair.

The FFM and the HEXACO models have been some of the most researched personality paradigms in the past few decades, and the Dark Triad literature has received its fair share of studies. Unfortunately, research findings have not always been consistent from one study to another, which could partially be due to different questionnaires that are used in research (Vize, Lynam, et al., 2018). For example, some studies have found that all the three traits link with low agreeableness, suggesting that individuals high in the Dark Triad are unfriendly, cold, and argumentative (Jakobwitz & Egan, 2006; Paulhus & Williams, 2002). However, other studies have found that only Machiavellianism and psychopathy relate to low agreeableness (Lee &

Ashton, 2005). A meta-analysis of 22 studies that correlated the Big Five with the Dark Triad traits found that although all the three traits were negatively correlated with agreeableness, the strength of correlation was much stronger for psychopathy and Machiavellianism than for narcissism (Muris et al., 2017). These studies suggest that psychopathy and Machiavellianism are similar to each other, sharing the core of low agreeableness, whereas narcissism is different. Nevertheless, low agreeableness alone does not explain many of the characteristic of the individual Dark Triad traits, such as the narcissistic grandiosity, Machiavellian strategic manipulation, and impulsivity of psychopathy. Thus the Dark Triad is more than just a component of low agreeableness.

In several studies, Kibeom Lee and colleagues (Lee & Ashton, 2014; Lee et al., 2013) have demonstrated that the common variance in the Dark Triad traits, as well the unique variance in each trait, shows a meaningful relationship with low honesty-humility. The authors have suggested that the common core between narcissism, Machiavellianism, and psychopathy resides in the lack of sincerity, fairness, greed avoidance, and modesty. However, a meta-analysis by Muris et al. (2017) concluded that there are differential associations between the Dark Triad and honesty-humility, depending on the aspects of the trait. For example, narcissism had a strong, negative correlation between modesty and lack of greed avoidance, whereas Machiavellianism and psychopathy were associated with lack of fairness and low sincerity.

With regards to neuroticism, the findings are somewhat confusing. A meta-analysis has proposed that all the traits are related to low neuroticism, which means that individuals high in the Dark Triad are less likely to express anxiety, fear, and worry (Muris et al., 2017). However, these associations are dependent on the scales that the studies are utilizing in measuring the Dark Triad. For example, in research that has used longer rather than shorter questionnaires, Machiavellianism (Muris et al., 2017) as well as primary and secondary psychopathy (Jakobwitz & Egan, 2006) was positively correlated with neuroticism scores. Yet, other studies have found that secondary (rather than primary) psychopathy is the more neurotic psychopathy variant (e.g., Ross, Lutz, & Bailley, 2004). Thus although the status of trait neuroticism in relation to the Dark Triad needs more clarification, it is probably safe to say that at least Machiavellianism and secondary psychopathy are related to proneness to feel anxious and worried.

In addition to a relationship to low agreeableness and honesty-humility, psychopathy has been linked to low conscientiousness, being disorganized, and careless. However, this could be more typical of the antisocial, impulsive aspects of secondary psychopathy, rather than the cold, callous aspects of primary psychopathy (Jakobwitz & Egan, 2006). Low conscientiousness could partially explain why secondary psychopathy is the "unsuccessful" psychopathy facet, as conscientiousness has been identified as an important factor for achieving career success (e.g., Judge, Higgins, Thoresen, & Barrick, 1999).

The findings of a recent meta-analysis of over 150 studies (Vize, Lynam, et al., 2018) suggested that psychopathy and Machiavellianism share very similar profiles, characterized by low agreeableness and low conscientiousness. Narcissism, in turn, had a weak positive association with openness and weak to moderate positive relationship with extraversion. This suggests that the Dark Dyad of Machiavellianism and psychopathy relate to unreliability, disorganization, carelessness, and coldness, whereas narcissism is characterized by striving to be with other people, and enjoying new experiences. Table 1.2 summarizes the findings of zero-order correlations between the Dark Triad and the Big Five from four studies that used longer measures for assessing the Dark Triad.

Table 1.2 Brief Summary of Relationship Between the Dark Triad and the Big Five

Trait	Nomological Network Zero-Order Correlations
Machiavellianism	Low agreeableness[a–d] High neuroticism[a,b] Low conscientiousness[a–d]
Psychopathy	Low Agreeableness[a–d] High neuroticism[a] High extraversion[b] Low conscientiousness[b,d] High openness[b]
Narcissism	Low agreeableness[a,b,d] Low conscientiousness[a] High extraversion[b–d] High openness[b]

[a]Jakobwitz and Egan (2006).
[b]Paulhus & Williams (2002).
[c]Lee and Ashton (2005).
[d]Vernon et al. (2008).

1.3 Emotion, Cognition, and Behavior

The Dark Triad traits have distinctive correlates with how individuals feel, act, and perceive the world. In this section, I will briefly discuss aspects of the traits that have an impact on interpersonal functioning, namely, empathy and emotional intelligence, as well as risk-taking and impulsivity.

1.3.1 Empathy, Emotional Intelligence, and Experiencing Emotions

One of the core facets of the Dark Triad is selfishness and coldness. Individuals high in the Dark Triad traits show very little care for others, having a priority in looking out for number one, their own selves. It is possible that low empathy and lack of pro-social emotions facilitate the exploitative nature of those high on the Dark Triad. Having shallow feelings and lack of guilt can be a great tool for exploiting others.

Several studies have investigated the link between the Dark Triad and traits that are important in interpersonal interactions. Some of the traits of interest in this regard are those that increase our understanding of ourselves and others, acting as a social lubricant in making interactions easier. Some of the variables of interest are empathy, emotional intelligence, alexithymia, and Theory of Mind. Although these are somewhat different from each other, the unifying theme is that they are associated with how individuals understand other people. Emotional intelligence and alexithymia are also concerned with how well people understand their own emotions, which is important in regulating social interactions. Table 1.3 has a brief description of these variables.

Emotional intelligence consists of distinctive subcategories that relate to how accurately people perceive and manage the emotions and mood of others and themselves. Empathy has an overlap with emotional intelligence in the interpersonal aspect, ability to accurately perceive emotions in others. Empathy consists of two components: cognitive and affective. Cognitive empathy involves having an understanding of why other people feel the way they do. For example, if someone is crying, a person who has cognitive empathy may be accurate in identifying what has made that individual feel so bad that they cry. Affective empathy, in turn, is about feeling what others feel. Those who are high in affective empathy may feel despair and sorrow while observing someone crying. Affective and cognitive empathy are viewed as mutually exclusive. Those who understand others emotions

Table 1.3 Description of Traits Related to Understanding Self and Others

Trait	Description
Empathy (cognitive)	Ability to understand the sources of others feelings
Empathy (affective)	Ability to feel what others feel
Empathy (global)	Cognitive + affective empathy
Emotional intelligence	Understanding and managing the emotions of self and other people
Theory of Mind	Attributing mental states to others
Alexithymia	Inability to identify and describe feelings

(i.e., have cognitive empathy) don't necessarily feel what others feel, and those who can feel for others (i.e., have affective empathy) don't necessarily understand the causes of others emotions. A related construct to empathy is Alexithymia, which translates literally to "no words for mood." Alexithymia is about the inability to identify and describe feelings and emotions to the self, as well as avoiding thinking about emotions. Theory of Mind is a closely related ability, which is about attributing mental states (feelings, emotions, intentions, and beliefs) to other people. There is some confusion on the terminology related to these concepts, their relationships, and the instruments that are used to investigate them.

A large number of studies have looked at the Dark Triad (both individual traits separately, and the Dark Triad as a whole) in relation to the concepts before. Here, I will only discuss those studies that have researched all the three traits together. In this way, it is easier to assess the relative contribution of each trait to inter- and intrapersonal abilities that are important in social relationships. Remember that the traits share a moderate amount of variance, and by looking at each trait individually, it is impossible to judge whether the relationships are driven by unique aspects of the trait, or by aspects of the trait that are shared with one or two of the other Dark Triad traits.

Overall, most studies have found that Machiavellianism and psychopathy (but not necessarily narcissism) are characterized by low empathy/emotional intelligence. Petrides, Vernon, Schermer, and Veselka (2011) investigated the relationship between emotional intelligence and the Dark Triad, using a trait emotional intelligence questionnaire. The authors reported that narcissism was associated with higher, and Machiavellianism and psychopathy with lower self-assessed emotional intelligence. These findings are echoed in the study of Jonason and Krause (2013), who discovered that especially psychopathy had a negative correlation with empathy, and even more so in women than in men. In one of our earlier studies, we explored how emotional quotient (an index for empathy) relates to the Dark Triad in sex-specific ways (Jonason, Lyons, Bethell, & Ross, 2013). We found that all of the Dark Triad variables were related to lower empathy. However, we also found sex-specific associations, such that primary psychopathy (cold and callous predisposition) had a stronger negative relationship with empathy in men, and aspects of narcissism had a stronger negative relationship with empathy in women. A study by Jauk and colleagues (Jauk, Freudenthaler, & Neubauer, 2016, Jauk et al., 2016) found pretty much opposing results, reporting that in their sample, psychopathy had a negative relationship with trait (i.e., self-report measure) and ability (i.e., experimental measure) empathy in women. In men, narcissism was related to low ability emotional intelligence and psychopathy to low trait emotional intelligence. All these studies have used different measures, which probably partially explain the differences in the findings. Further, there is a lack of experimental research, which is problematic especially in terms of overclaiming of abilities by those who score high on narcissism measures.

There is a general consensus in research that those high on the Dark Triad have impaired affective empathy, inability to feel what others feel. However, these traits are not necessarily related to low cognitive empathy, understanding the source of other's emotions. For instance, Wai and Tiliopoulos (2012) found that although all the three traits had negative correlations with a measure of affective empathy, they were not related to cognitive empathy. In order to successfully manipulate others, it would be expected that the ability to understand others emotions would be beneficial. Although Dark Triad is not necessarily related to superior cognitive empathy, there do not seem to be any deficits in this area either.

Studies that have looked at the ability to read other's emotions based on facial cues have mixed results. For example, one of the items from the NPI states that "I can read people like a book." An interesting question is that do individuals who are high in the Dark Triad (especially narcissism) actually have a superior emotion recognition ability, or are they just overclaiming and exaggerating their capability. On the one hand, ability to read emotions is related to higher empathy, which enhances prosocial tendencies and reduces the exploitation of others. On the other hand, emotion recognition ability can be channeled toward antisocial purposes. Individuals who have low empathy and exploitative attitude toward others would benefit from understanding how their victim is feeling. Indeed, Nagler, Reiter,

Furtner, and Rauthmann (2014) found that those who are high on Dark Triad may possess "dark emotional intelligence," abilities that are used for the purpose of manipulation. Being able to read the emotions of others may be important in planning the next step in manipulating them.

The research on the Dark Triad and emotion recognition has mixed results. Wai and Tilipolous (2012), for example, demonstrated that narcissism related to increased recognition of anger, but not sadness, fear, or happiness. Primary psychopathy had an association with poorer recognition of happy, sad, and angry facial expressions. Konrath, Corneille, Bushman, and Luminet (2014) found similar for narcissism, suggesting that exploitative facet of the trait related to better recognition of emotions in a picture of pairs of eyes, but only for negative emotion states. These studies suggest that narcissists may be tuned into negative aspects of emotions, and psychopaths may lack emotion recognition for a wider range of emotions. However, they used still photographs of faces or pairs of eyes. It is possible that this stimulus lacks ecological validity, as in the real life, we are exposed to moving, rather than static stimulus.

Indeed, in a study by Demetrioff, Porter, and Baker (2017), undergraduate students were shown short videos depicting microexpressions, minute movement of the face revealing a true felt emotion. They found that those who were high in psychopathy had an increased recognition for moving facial expressions of sadness. Furthermore, those who were high in the interpersonal manipulation facet of psychopathy were worse at detecting microexpressions relating to happiness. These results suggest that when exposed to a more realistic stimulus, those who score high on psychopathy have an advantage with regards to identifying negative emotion states.

It is possible that the poorer emotion recognition ability stems from how individuals themselves react to emotion-evoking events. In a study conducted with one of my undergraduate students, Charlotte Brockman, we asked our participants to view video clips that normally produce happiness, sadness, or fear. The clip that elicited happiness had contagiously laughing babies, the video inducing sadness had a dog trying to console a dead friend, and the fear-inducing clip had a horror film knife attach scene. After viewing each clip, participants were shown photographs of faces that presented emotions of happiness, sadness, and fear. Participants were asked to indicate how strongly they related to the faces as a result of viewing the video clips. Interestingly, we found some discrepancies in the felt emotion and the emotion that was supposed to be evoked. Those who were high in narcissism identified more strongly with happy faces after watching the fearful clip, and those who were high in psychopathy identified more strongly with sad and fearful faces after watching a happy clip (Lyons & Brockman, 2017). It is possible that individuals high in narcissism and psychopathy feel emotions differently, which could affect the way they recognize emotions in other people too.

The inability to understand one's own emotions, and avoiding thinking about them are characteristics of Alexithymia, and could be at the crux of failing to understand the emotions of others. Those who struggle to identify their own emotions also have low empathy for others. A few studies that have investigated the association between the Dark Triad and Alexithymia have, indeed, found that those at the higher end of the Dark Triad traits have higher scores in a measure for Alexithymia. A study by Jonason and Krause (2013) found that psychopathy was associated with a difficulty in describing feelings to oneself and narcissism with a difficulty in identifying feelings. Both psychopathy and Machiavellianism had an association with externally oriented thinking, which is about avoiding to think about one's own emotions. Cairncross, Veselka, Schermer, and Vernon (2013) found that psychopathy and Machiavellianism had a positive, and narcissism a negative correlation with Alexithymia. Their results suggest that those high in narcissism may have the ability to use their own emotions as social cues. This ties in with other research that has demonstrated that narcissism is the least malevolent out of the three traits.

1.3.2 Risk-Taking and Impulsivity

There has been significant amount of interest in the Dark Triad in relation to impulsivity and risk-taking behaviors. Some of this stems from evolutionarily informed research, which often has a focus on testing whether aversive personality traits are a manifestation of a fast Life History Strategy (LHS; discussed later in this chapter). In brief, evolutionary behavioral scientists posit that as a response to environmental insecurity, risk-taking behaviors could (together with the Dark Triad) be part of an adaptive package, which has a function in reaping immediate benefits from the environment without a concern of future consequences.

Many decisions in life contain some element of risk. Risk is multidimensional, ranging from social (i.e., criticizing a friends choice of clothing), physical (i.e., crossing a busy road), sexual (i.e., having unprotected sex with multiple unknown partners), and health (i.e., ingesting an unknown pill for thrills) to financial (i.e., gambling a week's wages in blackjack game) risk-taking. The costs and payoffs of risks are varied and depend on the individual and the circumstances. The payoffs are mainly associated with losing or gaining status or resources, and ultimately, could contribute to reproductive success (i.e., evolutionary fitness).

Impulsivity is associated with risk-taking, although the relationship between the two is not well defined. According to Hamilton, Felton, Risco, Lejuez, and MacPherson (2014), the difference is that risk-taking is activated as a response to cues of rewards, whereas impulsivity is about acting without thinking of the consequences, without potential rewards. Studies have found a nonlinear relationship between impulsivity and indicators of risk-taking. Individuals can be high in impulsivity but low in risk-taking, and vice versa.

With regards to empirical research on the Dark Triad and risk, the overall consensus is that psychopathy and narcissism are related to higher risk-taking, whereas individuals high in Machiavellianism have a more cautious approach to life. Further, it appears that all the three traits have a relationship with impulsivity, acting without thinking of future consequences. However, the research findings are slightly different across different studies and participants, which are probably due to differences in the sample characteristics, and the measures used in the studies.

For example, in an adolescent sample in Germany, Malesza and Ostaszewski (2016) found that narcissism and psychopathy (but not Machiavellianism) were linked to both self-reported and laboratory measurement of risk behaviors. Slightly different findings were reported by Crysel, Crosier, and Webster (2013), who investigated both impulsivity (as a questionnaire measure) and risk-taking (experimental measures of gambling), using a short questionnaire for the Dark Triad. The authors discovered that although all the three traits were positively correlated with self-reported impulsivity, only narcissism was related to risky gambling decisions. Jones and Paulhus (2011) explored both functional (being socially adventurous) and dysfunctional (lacking self-control) impulsivity, and found that psychology and narcissism were associated with both types of impulsivity, but Machiavellianism was related to neither. However, their findings did not concur with those of Jonason and Tost (2010), who reported that Machiavellianism and psychopathy (but not narcissism) were related to aspects of impulsivity (low self-control and lack of consideration of future consequences). Based on these results, it is safe to say that individuals high in narcissism and psychopathy may thrive on taking risks, whereas all Dark Triad traits could have an association with an impulsive approach to life (i.e., acting without thinking of the future).

Other behaviors that are closely related to impulsivity and risk-taking are substance use and gambling. Again, research demonstrates that psychology and narcissism are connected to higher incidence of risky substance abuse, whereas Machiavellianism is not (Stenason & Vernon, 2016). The evidence is much stronger for psychopathy than it is for narcissism. For instance, a study that investigated a wide range of societal misconducts found that only psychopathy was a significant predictor for self-reported drug use (Azizli et al., 2016). Similar results were reported by Jonason, Baughman, Carter, and Parker (2015), who found that psychopathy was related to more risk-taking in terms of smoking and drinking. It is no wonder that in the same study, psychopathy was also associated with a lower life expectancy. Based on these findings, it is safe to conclude that psychopathy has the strongest associations with risky health behaviors (i.e., drinking, smoking, and drug use). Narcissism may be related to substance abuse, but this is not a consistent finding across different studies. Machiavellianism, in turn, is not related to risk-taking in terms of substance use.

With regards to dysfunctional gambling behavior, psychopathy, again, emerges as the most significant predictor. Trombly and Zeigler-Hill (2016) found that although all three traits were individually correlated with gambling, in a regression analysis where shared variance was controlled for, only psychopathy was a significant predictor. In an online experiment, Jones (2014) gave participants bonuses that they could gamble, including gambling with other participants' bonuses with the risk of being punished. Again, only psychopathy emerged as a significant predictor of persistent gambling, even in the face of retribution from other players. In a review of different types of pathological gamblers, Milosevic and Ledgerwood (2010) identified a typology of gamblers characterized by antisocial impulsivity. These gamblers exhibit many characteristics of secondary psychopathy, including impulsivity and chronical understimulation. It is safe to assume that gambling is most related to secondary psychology and could be partially caused by impulse control issues.

1.4 Etiology

An important question for anybody interested in personality is the development of individual differences. What is most important, nature, nurture, or both? What proportion of personality can be attributed to social experiences? What proportion is due to inherited genetic predisposition? How does the experience throughout the lifetime (including prenatally) interact with the genetic predispositions to produce individual differences in personality? Although the etiology of the Dark Triad has been relatively little investigated, there has been some advancement in the field into the origins of the Dark Triad traits.

1.4.1 The Dark Triad Within Evolutionary Framework

Evolutionary psychologists are interested in WHY, ultimately, individual differences exist. The theory of evolution has provided one of the most powerful frameworks for understanding personality variation across different species of animals, including humans. Although initially evolutionary psychologists considered personality as nonadaptive random genetic noise, there has been a surge of more recent theorizing and empirical work analyzing personality from middle-level evolutionary theory perspectives (e.g., Life History Theory (LHT), Frequency Dependent Selection, Costly Signaling Theory). In short, evolutionary researchers are interested in investigating whether different levels of personality variation are adaptive in terms of increased reproductive success and survival. Reproductive success is measured in terms of passing on genes to the next generation, and producing offspring that is in turn able to pass their genes on. Although relatively little research on human personality has investigated actual reproductive success (i.e., number of children and grandchildren), research has used different proxies for reproduction, such as the number of sexual intercourses or sex drive.

The Dark Triad has been a popular topic of research among evolutionarily minded researchers. Socially deviant behaviors have traditionally been considered as maladaptive, evolutionary psychologists have reconsidered these traits as potentially adaptive mechanisms for increasing reproductive success. One of the most prevalent ideas is that variation in the Dark Triad is related to individual differences in their LHS. According to the LHT, individuals vary in a continuum in the amount of time and effort that they invest in current reproduction (i.e., seeking for partners and copulating with them) and in future reproduction (i.e., maturation and growth; providing for their offspring; maintaining stable relationships). Those who invest little effort in future reproduction (i.e., parenting), and focus more on seeking for multiple partners are thought to follow a fast LHS, resulting in a higher total number of children. There are certain traits (e.g., superficial charm, risk-taking, impulsivity) that may facilitate reproductive efforts of those on the fast end of the LHS continuum. On the other end of the continuum, individuals who follow a slow LHS have fewer sexual partners, stable relationships, and fewer children. Low impulsivity and hesitation to take risks may be features that help in investing in the future.

It is possible that fast LHS is partially contingent on the environment an individual finds themselves in. In unpredictable environments with high mortality, it may be adaptive to speed up reproduction, prioritizing in having offspring when still young. Early reproduction and a large quantity of children could function as an insurance policy against the risk of early death. Ultimately, evolution is concerned about successful reproduction, and those who live in high-risk environments will benefit from early reproduction. In this view, the Dark Triad is a condition-dependent strategy for fast life history, developing as a personality trait that has a function in speeding up reproduction. Indeed, there is some evidence that those high in the Dark Triad traits (especially Machiavellianism and psychopathy) have grown up in harsh, unstable environments (Jonason, Icho, & Ireland, 2016), suggesting that the traits have evolved as adaptations for fast LHS.

One of the replicated findings from several studies is that individuals at the higher end of the continuum have an elevated interest in short-term mating with multiple partners, rather than investing in stable pair-bonds (Koladich & Atkinson, 2016). This suggests that all of the Dark Triad traits are related to a fast LHS. I will review the literature on mating strategies in more detail in Chapter 3. For now, it is good to know that most studies have focused on investigating different proxies of fast LHS, including interest in short-term mating. Fewer studies have looked at the actual reproductive success of individuals high in these traits, including the number of surviving and reproducing offspring.

Other studies have demonstrated that especially psychopathy is positively associated with other measures aimed at tapping into the fast LHS (Jonason, Koenig, & Tost, 2010). However, it has also been suggested that only some aspects of the Dark Triad are related to a fast LHS. Melissa McDonald and colleagues (McDonald, Donnellan, & Navarrete, 2012) found that the Machiavellianism, entitlement/exploitativeness facet of narcissism, and impulsive antisocial facet of psychopathy related to a fast LHS, whereas fearless dominance facet of psychopathy and leadership and grandiose facet of narcissism had an association with a slow LHS. It is clear that more work is needed on measuring the differences between the subcomponents of the Dark Triad, as these have not been studied in most research.

Another evolutionarily relevant framework for understanding the Dark Triad is the notion of the Cheater Strategy, which has been discussed in terms of frequency-dependent selection. According to the frequency-dependent selection idea, a behavioral strategy is adaptive depending on what strategies other individuals in the population are following. A cheater strategy is a behavioral strategy geared toward enhancing reproductive success by gaining rewards from the environment without contributing to others welfare. This kind of strategy is beneficial only in an environment where majority of individuals are not cheaters.

In a still timely review paper, the late Linda Mealey (1995) suggested that psychopathy fits the characteristics of a frequency-dependent cheater strategy. Psychopaths (i.e., those at the very extreme upper end on a psychopathy continuum) appear to be relatively low in frequency, forming approximately 1% of the population. Psychopaths are exploitive, lack guilt and shame, and try to benefit from others without paying any costs. This only works in a population where psychopaths are relatively rare, as if they became more prevalent, the strategy would no longer be adaptive.

1.4.2 Genetics

As for much of human behavior and personality, the genetics of the Dark Triad is still relatively poorly understood. Personality is a complicated process, and how it is manifested depends on a convoluted interplay between prenatal, postnatal, genetic, and epigenetic influences. There have been some attempts to unravel the contribution of genes to the Dark Triad, mainly in the form of twin studies. For example, using heritability estimates, Vernon, Villani, Vickers, and Harris (2008) found that about 31% of variance in Machiavellianism, 64% of in psychopathy, and 59% in narcissism were attributable to genetics. This implies that a large proportion of these traits (especially psychopathy and narcissism) are genetically predetermined.

However, the twin study methodology is not without its problems. According to the twin study method, correlates for behavior are measured from pairs of monozygotic (i.e., identical) and dizygotic (i.e., nonidentical) twins. If the identical twins are more similar to each other than nonidentical twins, the similarity is attributed to genes, as identical twins share more of their genes with each other than nonidentical twins do. The twin study method relies on the Equal Environment Assumption (EEA). The EEA assumes that identical twins are treated in a similar manner by their environment as nonidentical twins are. Nevertheless, there is evidence that identical twins (who are more similar to each in how they look and behave) are treated more like the same person than nonidentical twins are. The evidence for the EEA is biased (Felson, 2014), and the twin study results should be treated with a pinch of salt. Based on the few twin studies on the genetics of the Dark Triad, it is difficult to draw any definitive conclusions.

Other methods include trying to identify genetic contribution at a molecular level. These studies may either focus on looking at differences (polymorphism) in genes known to be relevant in affective-behavioral regulation (single-nucleotide polymorphism studies), or scan the whole genome in an attempt to find locations that differ between groups of people (genome-wide association studies). These methods, to my knowledge, have not yet been utilized for studying the Dark Triad constellation as a whole. The existing studies have mostly focused on psychopathy, probably due to its relevance in the forensic context.

Several genes, especially those active in transporting and synthetizing neurotransmitters and enzymes (such as dopamine, serotonin, oxytocin, and monoamine oxidase A) have already been implicated in the development of psychopathy (e.g., Wu & Barnes, 2013), and many of the contemporary research is studying the interplay between genetics and environment (G × E) in the development. For example, Sadeh et al. (2010) found that the callous aspects of psychopathy had an association with lower socioeconomic status, but only in individuals who had two long alleles for a serotonin transporter gene. To my knowledge, there currently are no studies investigating the interplay between genes and environment in the development of all the Dark Triad traits. Humans are biological creatures, living in intricate socio-ecological environments. The development of personality is a complex process, and although genetics are likely to play at least some role in this, there are many more factors that have yet to be unraveled.

1.4.3 Environmental Influences

The environment that an individual is born to exerts a powerful influence on subsequent development, including personality differences. According to the evolutionary life history paradigm, signs of resource scarcity and insecurity contribute to the development of fast LHS. This makes intuitive sense, as in high mortality environments it makes sense to start reproduction early. All that evolution cares about is passing on genes to the next generation, and individuals across different species are likely to be harnessed with subconscious mechanisms that monitor their environment for cues of the environmental quality. It is not certain what these cues are, but some possibilities are quality of parental care, crime and disorder in the environment, and availability of resources.

Parenting, for instance, can provide a proxy for the socioecological environment that the child is growing up in. In harsh environments where resources are scarce and unpredictable, parents may decrease their investment in their children. This has been found to be the case for especially unpredictability in early life, manifested by chaotic households (e.g., changes in employment, status, residency, cohabitation). The effects of unpredictability in childhood exert influence in adulthood, for example, in reduced paternal investment in men (Szepsenwol, Simpson, Griskevicius, & Raby, 2015). Indeed, a study that investigated childhood resource scarcity vs unpredictability found that unpredictable childhood conditions had an association with higher scores in all the Dark Triad traits (Jonason et al., 2016). Interestingly, those who were high on Machiavellianism reported that they had financially privileged but stressful, unpredictable childhoods. Thus it is possible that rather than scarcity of resources, unpredictability in childhood is a better determinant of the Dark Triad personalities in adulthood.

There is a wealth of studies investigating how parenting that a child receives influences adult personality. Many of these studies are retrospective in nature, asking adults to try to recall how their parents treated them when they were children. Studies on the Dark Triad and parenting indicate that recollections of a cold, uncaring mother may lead to the lack of secure attachment, which could influence the development of Machiavellian strategies and some aspects of narcissism as an adult (Jonason, Lyons, & Bethell, 2014). Further, recollections of uncaring mothers have an association with high primary psychopathy in women and high secondary psychopathy in men (Blanchard, Lyons, & Centifanti, 2016a, 2016b). It is possible that one of the pathways to a fast LHS and the Dark Triad is via parental care and resources as a child. For example, Lukaszewski (2015) found that those who experiences resource scarcity also had less supportive parents, which may lead to the development of fast LHS.

1.5 Sex Differences in the Dark Triad

Overall, men are more risk-taking (Byrnes, Miller, & Schafer, 1999), aggressive (Archer, 2004), and less empathetic (Christov-Moore et al., 2014) than women are. These sex differences emerge in childhood, potentially as a product of sexual selection acting on fundamental reproductive differences between the sexes (Martel, 2013). In short, in species with internal fertilization, males can increase their reproductive success by mating with multiple partners, whereas females can increase theirs by choosing their partners wisely, and by providing good quality parental care for the offspring. The higher risk-taking and lower empathy could be useful in intrasexual competition for mates. It has been suggested that the Dark Triad has evolved as a male-typical mating adaptation, facilitating a fast LHS (Jonason, Li, Webster, & Schmitt, 2009). Interestingly, especially psychopathy has been associated with more male-typical features, and also shows more characteristics related to fast LHS.

Research has found consistent sex differences in the Dark Triad, demonstrating that these traits are more prominent in men than in women. In a meta-analysis, Muris et al. (2017) brought together findings from 50 publications reporting sex differences in the Dark Triad. They found medium sex differences for psychopathy, and small differences for narcissism and Machiavellianism. When they analyzed the sex differences controlling for the shared variance between the Dark Triad traits, only psychopathy emerged as having significant differences. Thus psychopathy seems to be the only male-prominent trait within the Dark Triad constellation.

However, most of the studies have been conducted utilizing relatively young college age samples. Greg Carter, Campbell, and Muncer (2014) tested the Dark Triad composite and several sexual and thrill-seeking related behaviors in a large community sample with an average age of 39.5 years. Contrary to most research, the authors did not find any sex differences in the short composite measure they used for the Dark Triad. They suggested that "Future work could usefully consider manifestations of the Dark Triad in women and give greater consideration to the benefits of DT personality beyond the domain of mating strategies" (p. 163). As well as investigating the adaptiveness of the Dark Triad to women, it is clear that research needs more diverse samples from different cultures, ages, and socioeconomic backgrounds. The tentative conclusion is that sex differences are more likely to occur for psychopathy, where men score higher on this trait than women do, which could be function of biological processes such as the male hormone testosterone (Welker, Lozoya, Campbell, Neumann, & Carré, 2014).

1.6 Measurement

There are a growing number of questionnaire measures for the composite Dark Triad, as well as for the individual traits. The questionnaires vary in their length, reliability, and validity, as well as in their utility in different samples (e.g., community versus forensic/clinical populations). There have been several attempts to extract factor structures from the existing measures, and many of the studies have different results. Thus some of our understanding of what the Dark Triad is has been derived from what factors different studies have found for the questionnaires, rather than from a clear theory explaining what the traits are.

When conducting research on the Dark Triad, it is important to choose carefully which questionnaires to use. The longer, traditional questionnaires should be employed if the study design does not have serious time constraints. If the study is a lengthy one, the shorter composite measures can be used as a reasonable substitute for the longer questionnaires.

In this section, I will provide a brief overview of the most popular instruments that have been utilized in the Dark Triad research. It is good to keep in mind that there are plenty of other instruments out there as well, which are often used in research on clinical/forensic samples, but not necessarily when investigating the Dark Triad continuum. The characteristics of the most common instruments are summarized in Table 1.4.

1.6.1 Measuring Machiavellianism

The most commonly used questionnaire for studying Machiavellianism is the 20-item MACH-IV scale, developed by Richard Christie and colleagues in an attempt to capture the duplicitous and scheming nature of individuals with Machiavellian traits (Christie & Geis, 1970). It is good to note that some of the questions in this instrument may seem a little outdated, but better alternatives are yet to be developed. Although most studies have investigated Machiavellianism as a unidimensional measure, various analyses have extracted different factor structures from the scale, suggesting that Machiavellianism may consist of several, interrelated components. Indeed, studies have extracted between one and five factors, each with different labels and different questions (see Rauthmann, 2013). Although the MACH-IV has been hailed as the "Golden Standard" measure for Machiavellianism, it is not without its problems.

For instance, there are disputes about what Machiavellianism consists of, and whether the MACH-IV scale can be used to measure the trait accurately. Christie and Geis (1970) suggested that Machiavellianism has two main domains: interpersonal tactics and views of human nature. Those high on Machiavellianism have a very cynical view on human nature, perceiving others as vicious, untrustworthy, weak, or lazy. They also endorse behavioral tactics that are centered around flattery and deceit. According to

Table 1.4 The Most Commonly Used Measures for the Dark Triad

Questionnaire	Number of Items	Trait Measured	Times Cited	Example Items and Response Scale
The Short Dark Triad questionnaire (SD-3; Jones & Paulhus, 2014)	27	All three traits	+200	Machiavellianism: Avoid direct conflict with others because they may be useful in the future Narcissism: Many group activities tend to be dull without me Psychopathy: People often say I'm out of control 1 = Strongly Disagree 5 = Strongly Agree
Dirty Dozen (DD; Jonason & Webster, 2010)	12	All three traits	+400	Machiavellianism: I tend to manipulate others to get my way Narcissism: I tend to want others to admire me Psychopathy: I tend to be callous or insensitive 1 = Disagree Strongly 9 = Agree Strongly
Narcissistic Personality Inventory (NPI) (Raskin & Terry, 1988)	40	Narcissism (various factor structures)	+2200	Forced choice between two statements: A: Modesty doesn't become me B: I'm essentially a modest person
Self-report psychopathy (SRP-III) (Paulhus et al., 2009)	64	Psychopathy (primary and secondary)	+400	I think I could beat a lie detector (primary psychopathy) I enjoy driving at high speeds (secondary psychopathy) 1 = Strongly Disagree 5 = Strongly Agree

Levenson's self-report psychopathy scale (LSRPS) (Levenson, Kiehl, & Fitzpatrick, 1995)	26	Psychopathy (primary and secondary)	+1100	Success is based on survival of the fittest: I am not concerned about the losers (primary psychopathy) I find myself in the same kind of trouble, time after time (secondary psychopathy) 0 = Disagree Strongly 4 = Agree Strongly
MACH-IV (Christie & Geis, 1970)	20	Machiavellianism	+2000	It is hard to get ahead without cutting corners here and there 1 = Strongly Disagree 5 = Strongly Agree

Christie and Geis (1970), both of these traits are captured by the MACH-IV scale. However, further factor analyses have extracted more than two components. For instance, Hunter, Gerbing, and Boster (1982) suggested that there are four factors: tactics, which can be divided into deceit and flattery, and views of human nature, which can be divided into immorality and cynicism. More recently, John Rauthmann proposed that the "core" of Machiavellianism can be measured with only five items from the MACH-IV scale, which represent the cynicism and misanthropy associated with the trait (Rauthmann, 2013). It may be that that the endorsement of negative views of other people leads to immoral and manipulative behavior, but that these views are more central to the concept of Machiavellianism than the actual behavior is. The problem with Machiavellianism is that it lacks a clear theoretical background (Fehr et al., 1992), and much of the theorizing is about trying to find explanations for the factor structures extracted from the MACH-IV questionnaire.

1.6.2 Measuring Narcissism

There are several self-reported measures for narcissism, and there are still debates into which one is the best measure to use in nonclinical populations. The measures have been born out of the DSM diagnostic category for NPD, as well as using theories of narcissism in scale construction.

One of the most used scale for the Dark Triad narcissism is probably the 40-item forced-choice NPI (Raskin & Hall, 1981), used in approximately 70% of social and personality psychology studies (Cain, Pincus, & Ansell, 2008). This instrument has its origins in the DSM-III diagnostic category for NPD, and the purpose for its construction was to facilitate the investigation of narcissism continuum in community samples. The instrument consist of 40 pairs of statements (e.g., When people compliment me I sometimes get embarrassed/I know that I am good because everybody keeps telling me so). Participants score a point every time they choose the narcissistic item over the nonnarcissistic one. Although there have been different versions of the NPI (e.g., 16- and 13-item ones), the longer version probably remains the most popular one in the Dark Triad literature.

Factor analyses have found different factor structures for the NPI, and the factor structures may partially be dependent on what scoring systems are used (e.g., forced-choice, Likert scale, or true/false formats; Wetzel, Roberts, Fraley, & Brown, 2016). For instance, the initial analyses of Raskin and Terry (1988) proposed a 7-factor model, whereas subsequent research has identified 2, 3, 4, and 5 factors (see Wetzel et al., 2016 for a summary). Most studies have identified intrapersonally adaptive (e.g., vanity, leadership, authority) and interpersonally maladaptive (e.g., exploitativeness, entitlement) facets that seem pertinent to the NPI. Although it is clear that narcissism and the NPI are multidimensional, most studies on the Dark Triad have failed to take this into consideration, which makes it difficult to judge the role of adaptive and maladaptive narcissism in different behaviors.

There are also a number of other questionnaires for narcissism, for example, NPD Scale (NPDS; Ashby, 1978), O'Brien Multiphasic Narcissism Inventory (O'Brien, 1987), Hyper-sensitive Narcissism Scale (Hendin & Cheek, 1997), and Minnesota Multiphasic Personality Inventory (MMPI; Morey, Waugh, & Blashfield, 1985). However, these are used less in the Dark Triad research and will not be reviewed further here.

1.6.3 Measuring Psychopathy

Much of the current psychopathy assessment is derived from Robert Hare's Psychopathy Checklist-Revised (PCL-R; Hare, 1991). For the past few decades, this measure has been used as the "Golden Standard" for assessing psychopathic personalities. The checklist consists of 20 statements, for which a clinician is rating the strength that the items apply to the individual who is being diagnosed. However, PCL-R is a measure that is used in clinical and forensic populations, and it is not suitable for use as a self-rated measure. In order to have a tool that can be utilized as a self-reported tool for community samples, the PCL has been used in creating new measures. For example, the PCL-R was used as a template for creating the Self-Report Psychopathy Scale (SRP-III, Paulhus, Neumann, & Hare, 2009) for use in nonclinical, nonforensic populations.

1.6.4 Composite Questionnaires

As a response to the increasing popularity of research into the Dark Triad, there has been a recent development of composite questionnaire measures. These are the Dirty Dozen (DD; Jonason & Webster, 2010) and the Short Dark Triad (SD3; Jones & Paulhus, 2014). The benefit of shorter composite measures is a massive reduction in the number of items respondents have to answer. Using the longer, more traditional instruments requires the participants to answer up to 124 questions, which can be time consuming, and result in high dropout rates in surveys. The shorter instruments can be useful especially if other aspects of the study require time-consuming input from the participants. However, the shortfall is that the brevity may compromise construct validity of the questionnaire. In brief, the risk with shorter instruments is that they may no longer measure what they are supposed to measure. This can be especially problematic for psychopathy and narcissism, which are multidimensional in nature. The short measures fail to capture the subtleties of these traits.

Despite their young age, both the DD and the SD3 have already been used widely in the Dark Triad literature, and the validity and reliability of these questionnaires has been under careful scrutiny (see, e.g., Maples, Lamkin, & Miller, 2014). DD is a very brief, 12-item measure, consisting of four questions/trait. The measure has been demonstrated to have good internal reliability (i.e., the four questions for each trait are measuring the same thing), but the convergent validity has been more limited (i.e., the correlations with more established, longer measures can be relatively weak). SD3 has 27 questions, nine/trait, and has good internal reliability, and stronger convergent validity than the DD measure.

The intercorrelations between the Dark Triad traits are partially dependent on the instruments that are used, and the DD has been criticized for having a larger overlap between narcissism and Machiavellianism (0.57) than the SD3 (0.26) or the longer instruments do (Muris et al., 2017. This could be due to similarity between the questions asked for narcissism and Machiavellianism. Muris et al. (2017) noticed that the four questions for Machiavellianism and narcissism are "other-oriented," consisting of statements as "I tend to want *others* to admire me" (narcissism), or "I tend to manipulate *others* to get my way" (Machiavellianism). The four psychopathy questions in the DD are solely "self-oriented" (e.g., "I tend to lack remorse"), describing personal attributes rather than what the individual may want from other people. This unintentional commonality between narcissism and Machiavellianism questionnaires may have inflated the correlations between these traits.

In summary, the short Dark Triad measures are a reasonable substitute to the longer questionnaires and can be used when there are time constraints with the research. The SD3 is more preferable, as it has higher convergent validity (i.e., higher correlations with the conventional measures). Further, in the SD3, psychopathy can be divided into subscales representing risky behaviors as well as callous affect, whereas the DD only measures the callous affect aspect.

1.7 The Dark Tetrad

Recently, researchers have suggested that the Dark Triad should be accompanied by a fourth related trait, sadism. Those who are high in sadism get a "kick" out of inflicting unnecessary pain on others. O'meara, Davies, and Hammond (2011) defined sadistic personality as "... a person who humiliates others, shows a longstanding pattern of cruel or demeaning behavior to others, or intentionally inflicts physical, sexual, or psychological pain or suffering on others in order to assert power and dominance or for pleasure and enjoyment" (p. 523). Although sadism per se does not feature in the classification systems for mental disorders, it is mentioned in the DSM where sexual paraphilias are discussed. However, it is good to note that sexual sadism is not necessarily related to everyday sadism. Individuals can be sadistic in their everyday interactions with others (e.g., in the workplace), without getting sexual gratification from cruelty.

Sadism is different from the Dark Triad traits, as not all of those who are high on Machiavellianism, narcissism, and psychopathy necessarily enjoy hurting others. This has led to the development of the Dark Tetrad, including sadism as the fourth trait in the Dark Triad. There has been a surge of studies on the Dark Tetrad, and the outcomes of the research show that the concept is, indeed, worthwhile investigation.

How does sadism relate to the Dark Triad? Chabrol, Melioli, Van Leeuwen, Rodgers, and Goutaudier (2015) gave questionnaires on the Dark Tetrad to a group of over 600 high school students, in an attempt to classify them into personality types. First, the authors found that all the four traits correlated with each other, suggesting that they share at least some variance. Those who scored high on the Dark Triad also obtained high scores on a sadism questionnaire. Second, they also found four distinctive clusters of personalities in their sample: Those who scored low on all the four traits, those who scored high on Machiavellianism and sadism, those who were high on psychopathy and narcissism, and finally, those who were high on all the four traits. The sample that was high on all of the four traits constituted were a significant minority, around 15% of the sample. These individuals also demonstrated the highest levels of antisocial behavior and suicidal ideation (without depressive symptoms). This study shows that in a nonclinical sample of adolescents, more than one in ten are high on the Dark Tetrad, and those individuals may also account for much of antisocial behaviors observed in young people.

Međedović and Petrović (2015) analyzed sadism in relation to the Dark Triad, and found that it is, indeed, a related construct. With regards to the Big Five personality traits, they found that sadism was negatively associated with low agreeableness, honesty-humility, and conscientiousness. Although sadism is similar to the Dark Triad traits, all of the traits are sufficiently different to warrant the idea of the Dark Tetrad as a personality construct.

Erin Buckels, Jones, and Paulhus (2013) devised a set of experiments investigating "everyday sadism," behaviors that not too extreme or illegal. The authors set out to investigate how sadism and the Dark Triad link to the willingness to kill bugs and hurt people. The experimenter asked people to choose their favorite from a list of occupations, one of which was about exterminating insects (killing them in a coffee grinder; no bugs were actually harmed during this experiment). Those who were high on sadism were more likely to choose the exterminator job and also reported getting more pleasure out of crunching bugs. Sadism (but not the other three Dark Tetrad traits) also had an association with a higher likelihood of aggressing toward an innocent victim (i.e., blasting white noise at a confederate). This study confirmed that indeed, sadism (but not Machiavellianism, narcissism, or psychopathy) relates to the willingness and enjoyment in inflicting pain without any additional rewards.

Other studies that have investigated everyday sadism have found that it does, indeed, have an association with getting pleasure from cruelty. More sadistic individuals have a higher frequency of playing violent video games than those who are high on the Dark Triad (Greitemeyer, 2015), indicating that sadistic tendencies extend to hurting others in the virtual worlds of gaming. Also, those who troll (i.e., leave negative and derogative comments, often anonymously) others are high on the Dark Tetrad, especially sadism (Craker & March, 2016; Buckels, Trapnell, & Paulhus, 2014). Especially sadism and psychopathy seem to be a toxic combination with regards to trolling, as a study found that both these traits were typical of internet trolls (Sest & March, 2017). van Geel, Goemans, Toprak, and Vedder (2017) investigated the Dark Tetrad and traditional bullying and bullying in the cyber-environment. They found that when the other three traits were controlled for, sadism emerged as a significant predictor of both traditional and internet bullying.

Everyday sadism has been measured using questionnaires such as the 10-item Short Sadistic Impulse Scale (SSIS; O'meara et al., 2011) or the 9-item Assessment of Sadistic Personality (ASP; Plouffe, Saklofske, & Smith, 2017). Both questionnaires have been used in investigations into everyday nonsexual sadism and are appropriate for use with the Dark Triad measurements.

1.8 Conclusion

The research on the Dark Triad has grown exponentially in the past few decades, with much of the literature focusing on establishing the profiles of socially aversive personalities. Studies investigating the Dark Triad within the nomological network with other personality traits have suggested that all the three relate to low honesty and low agreeableness. This suggests that the core of the Dark Triad lies in dishonestly, coldness, and manipulation. Narcissism seems to be "brightest" of the dark traits, with extraverted approach-oriented attitude to life. Research has suggested that especially psychopathy relates to low empathy and emotional intelligence, which could facilitate exploitation of others. Psychopathy and narcissism relate to higher risk-taking and impulsivity, whereas individuals high in Machiavellianism have a more cautious approach to life.

The exploitative, selfish nature of those high in the Dark Triad has led to theories trying to explain the existence of these traits from evolutionary perspective. Some of the most commonly applied theories are the LHT, which posits that these traits are adaptive in the context of fast strategies, prioritizing mating over parenting. The Dark Triad traits could also facilitate a Cheater strategy, which could be adaptive in extracting resources from the environment by the means of using others.

Despite thousands of publications in the past few decades, there are still many gaps in the literature, some of which will be identified in the following chapters. Although there is a wealth of good-quality research attempting to improve our understanding of socially aversive personalities, the literature suffers from several shortcomings which should be addressed in future studies (see Table 1.1). The following chapters present a summary of the literature so far, exploring the Dark Triad in the framework of clinical (Chapter 2) and forensic (Chapter 3) psychology, within mating (Chapter 4) and friendship (Chapter 5) literature, as well as in the realms of workplace (Chapter 6) and the cyberworld (Chapter 7) behaviors.

Further Reading

Book, A., Visser, B. A., & Volk, A. A. (2015). Unpacking "evil": Claiming the core of the dark triad. *Personality and Individual Differences*, *73*, 29–38.

Muris, P., Merckelbach, H., Otgaar, H., & Meijer, E. (2017). The malevolent side of human nature: a meta-analysis and critical review of the literature on the dark triad (narcissism, Machiavellianism, and psychopathy). *Perspectives on Psychological Science*, *12*, 183–204.

Paulhus, D. L., & Williams, K. M. (2002). The dark triad of personality: narcissism, Machiavellianism, and psychopathy. *Journal of Research in Personality*, *36*, 556–563.

CHAPTER TWO

The Dark Triad Within a Clinical Framework

Chapter Outline

2.1 Introduction

> *"Mr. A" is a 42-year-old married man presenting to a private-practice psychotherapist complaining of problems with his wife. He is a successful entrepreneur, highly competitive, who describes enjoying social gatherings, where he tends to be the center of attention, as well as challenges at work, where he believes that he has a superior ability to solve problems. He comes to treatment because he is wondering whether or not to stay in his marriage. Mr. A described having lost all sexual interest in his wife during their early years together. Throughout the marriage, he has maintained a series of lovers whom he has housed, supported, and then cut off and replaced. He feels that this arrangement has had no impact on his relationship with his wife but wonders if he would do better with someone else (Caligor, Levy, & Yeomans, 2015, p. 415)*

The earlier clinical case study was presented by Caligor et al. (2015) as an example of the type of problems that are typical to individuals who have

The Dark Triad of Personality
https://doi.org/10.1016/B978-0-12-814291-2.00002-4

a diagnosis of a Narcissistic Personality Disorder (NPD). Due to the extreme interpersonal difficulties that sometimes stems from the behavior of those who are at the high end of the Dark Triad continuum, these traits have received great amount of attention in the context of clinical and forensic psychology. The Dark Triad relates to the violation and bending of social and moral norms, including a lack of interest in maintaining monogamous pair-bonds, something that many (especially) Western societies cherish. Individuals who suffer from these actions are not always the perpetrators themselves, but the people around them: lovers, spouses, friends, relatives, and colleagues. Indeed, people who are "survivors" of a toxic relationship with a high Dark Triad person are more likely to feel like they are in a need of psychological interventions than those who are high on these traits themselves.

The interpersonal damage caused by dark personalities could imply that individuals high on these traits are not "mad" (i.e., mentally ill, needing some kind of interventions), but simply "bad" (i.e., obnoxious individuals, which is something that cannot be helped). This has also been the topic of public discussions about the personality and behavior of the US president Donald Trump (see also Box 2.1). However, interpersonal toxicity does have health (whether mental or physical) consequences to those at the upper end of the dark continuum and is not irrelevant to research and theories on psychopathology. The focus of this chapter will be on theoretical and practical links with clinical psychology, and the health consequences of the Dark Triad will be discussed in Chapter 6.

Some of the current debates in the clinical literature are around the use of terminology and diagnostic categories. Should we call people "a narcissist or a psychopath" or "narcissistic or psychopathic"? Does categorizing individuals into distinctive types (e.g., psychopaths vs. nonpsychopaths) serve a purpose in understanding aversive personalities? How does labeling influence people—does it become a self-fulfilling prophecy? Are people with labels stigmatized by others? According to many personality researchers, categories are artificial clinical entities, based on arbitrary thresholds between normal and abnormal. It may be better to investigate personality (including socially aversive personalities) as a normal continuum of individual differences rather than as separate "illness" categories.

In the latest editions of both the Diagnostic and Statistical Manual (DSM-5; published in 2013 by the American Psychiatric Association) and the International Classification of Disease (ICD-11; published by the World Health Organisation in 2018), psychopathy (under the antisocial personality

BOX 2.1 Does Donald Trump possess traits of malignant narcissism?

In the field of psychology, it is rare for professionals to make a diagnosis of a public figure without directly dealing with the individual. This is based on the American Psychiatric Association's Goldwater rule (named after a 1964 US presidential candidate, Barry Goldwater), stating that it is not ethical for psychiatrist to discuss public figures and their mental health without examining the individual in person. However, psychologists have made a rare exception in case of Donald Trump, the 45th president of the United States of America. Indeed, the sentiment about the "duty to inform" citizens about potentially harmful public figures has prompted prominent psychology researchers to suggest that the Goldwater rule should be turned over, and that in select cases such as Trump, informed opinions about public figure's mental health should be allowed (Lilienfeld, Miller, & Lynam, 2018).

Examination of Trump's public figure in the light of the latest version of the Diagnostic and Statistical Manual (DSM-V) certainly suggests striking similarities between NPD diagnosis and Trump's persona. According to DSM-V, individuals who have a NPD diagnosis are characterized, among other things, by grandiosity, attention seeking, unawareness of one's own motivations, and excessive attunement to reactions of others (but only if perceived as relevant to self). By analyzing the speech content and Twitter behavior of Mr. Trump, researchers have come to the conclusion that his communication is grandiose, simplistic, impulsive, and uncivil (Ahmadian, Azarshahi, & Paulhus, 2017; Ott, 2017). Trump's tweets are characterized by lavish statements about his achievements, coupled by vicious attacks toward anyone who dares to criticize him, or his administration. The fragile nature of Trump's ego (typical to vulnerable narcissism) is reflected in the large number of offending remarks directed toward others. The New York Times maintains a list of people, companies, and places that Trump has insulted since becoming a president. These insults paint a picture of a person who is impulsive, aggressive, and easily offended. Trump's communication style suggests features that are common in patients who have received a NPD diagnosis.

Around Trump' s inauguration in January 2017, prominent psychologists and psychiatrists sent out public letters of warning, discussing the likelihood that Mr. Trump possesses a severe form of NPD. This would imply that his decision making is impeded and make it questionable whether he is fit for service. Due to the many malicious features in Trump's interpersonal style, there have been serious concerns about his ability to lead a country. Prior to Trump's inauguration, three leading psychiatrists wrote a public letter to President Barak Obama, warning him about the lack of mental stability of Trump, and calling for a full psychiatric evaluation by a team of impartial investigators. More specifically, they tapped into traits "...including grandiosity, impulsivity, hypersensitivity to slights or criticism, and an apparent inability to distinguish between fantasy and reality" (Greene, 2016).

Continued

BOX 2.1 Does Donald Trump possess traits of malignant narcissism?—cont'd

Since then, there has been a public petition launched by John Gartner, a clinical psychologist, titled "President Trump is mentally ill and must be removed." The petition had over 62,000 signatures in 2017, although it is not clear how many of these are mental health professionals (Lilienfeld et al., 2018). Further, in an open letter to the New York Times in February 2017, a group of 35 mental health professionals expressed their concerns about the ability of Trump to lead a country, stating that "... emotional instability indicated by Mr. Trump's speech and actions makes him incapable of serving safely as president" (Dodes & Schachter, 2017).

In contrast, there are others who think that labeling Mr. Trump as mentally ill is an insult to those who actually suffer from mental illnesses. In a letter to New York Times, Allen Frances wrote that "Bad behavior is rarely a sign of mental illness, and the mentally ill behave badly only rarely. Psychiatric name-calling is a misguided way of countering Mr. Trump's attack on democracy. He can, and should, be appropriately denounced for his ignorance, incompetence, impulsivity and pursuit of dictatorial powers" (Frances, 2017).

Other experts have suggested that rather than a mental illness, Trump could be going through a cognitive decline caused by frontotemporal dementia. His spontaneous speech has seen a decrease in fluency, complexity, and vocabulary, which could be an indication of a neurogenerative disease (Begley, 2017). Other symptoms of dementia include acting inappropriately or impulsively, getting distracted easily, struggling to make correct sounds when uttering a word, and appearing to be selfish or unsympathetic. Thus another possibility is that the inappropriate, obnoxious behavior of the President is not caused by personality disorder or an abhorrent personality, but by a cognitive decline related to dementia or normal aging.

Sources

Ahmadian, S., Azarshahi, S., & Paulhus, D. L. (2017). Explaining Donald Trump via communication style: Grandiosity, informality, and dynamism. *Personality and Individual Differences, 107*, 49–53.

Begley, S. (2017). *Trump wasn't always so linguistically challenged. What could explain the change?* Retrieved from: https://www.statnews.com/2017/05/23/donald-trump-speaking-style-interviews/.

Dodes, L., & Schachter, J. (2017). Mental health professionals warn about Trump (Letter to the editors). *New York Times*, Retrieved from: https://www.nytimes.com/2017/02/13/opinion/mental-health-professionals-warn-about-trump.html?mcubz=0&;_r=0.

Frances, A. (2017). Letter to editor. *New York Times*, Retrieved from: https://www.nytimes.com/2017/02/14/opinion/an-eminent-psychiatrist-demurs-on-trumps-mental-state.html.

Greene, R. (2016). Is Donald Trump mentally ill? 3 professors of psychiatry ask President Obama to conduct a "full medical and neurological examination" *Huffington Post blog*,https://www.huffingtonpost.com/richard-greene/is-donald-trump-mentally_b_13693174.html.

Lilienfeld, S. O., Miller, J. D., & Lynam, D. R. (2018). The Goldwater Rule: perspectives from, and implications for, psychological science. *Perspectives on Psychological Science, 13*(1), 3–27.

Ott, B. L. (2017). The age of Twitter: Donald J. Trump and the politics of debasement. *Critical Studies in Media Communication, 34*, 59–68.

disorder (ASPD)) and narcissism are classified as personality disorders. In both diagnostic manuals, personality disorders are organized into distinctive clusters, which are supposed to be based on the similarities in the underlying psychopathology associated with the disorders in each cluster. NPD and ASPD, for example, are under the Cluster B personality disorders in the DSM. Cluster B disorders are characterized by problems with impulse control and emotion regulation, leading to dramatic, emotional, and erratic behavior. The latest DSM edition was supposed to bring an improved diagnostic accuracy by also including a rating scale for the severity of the personality disorder, as well as whether a disorder is present or not. Nevertheless, the system has been under much criticism. In fact, the whole concept of personality disorders as mental illnesses is hotly debated for several reasons which will be outlined later in this chapter.

Diagnostic manuals such as the DSM are claimed to serve multiple purposes for different users. They can help clinicians and researchers to communicate by having a shared language and understanding of the underlying problems people may be experiencing. Diagnoses can provide a tool for insurance companies, schools, and educational systems for helping, training, and dealing with people. However, the diagnostic categories can also be misused, especially in the legal system. The DSM was never created as a tool for the needs of courts and attorneys in legal decision-making process, but nevertheless, it is often freely used in determining "mental abnormalities" in a defendant.

The tempestuous development of the DSM-5 personality disorder diagnosis leaves one doubtful about the utility of the manual in research or clinical practice. During the creation of the proposals for diagnosing personality disorders, there was little agreement within the working group on the nature of the disorders, and indeed, what even classifies as a disorder. The process saw the removal, and subsequent reentering of the NPD diagnosis, and a movement from a complete overhaul of the diagnoses by using only dimensional model to the creation of a hybrid model (including both categorical diagnosis and continuous rating of personality functioning). According to Zachar, Krueger, & Kendler (2016), the development of the hybrid model "... is a story of shifting expectations, conflicting goals, and fractured alliances" (p. 1). The disagreements in the attempts to restructure personality disorder diagnosis is reflecting the problems within the overall concept of personality disorders and their existence as separate, independent entities.

The notion of disordered personalities and their diagnosis is problematic for several reasons. First, the definition of personality disorder circles around impairments in personality functioning. This description is awkward, because it is not clear what the opposite is—how are individuals with "ordered" (as opposed to "disordered") personalities supposed to behave (Leising, Rogers, & Ostner, 2009)? Second, there are no clear-cut biological causes for personality disorders, which imply that they are not "illnesses" in the traditional sense. The definition of personality disorder as an illness is not based on the biomedical model, but on the idea that individuals with the diagnoses divert from the socially acceptable norms in Western Europe and America. Socially acceptable norms differ from one culture and historical period to another. It doesn't make much sense to stamp a person with a personality disorder label if their behavior could be classified as abnormal in one, but quite normal in another culture. Third, the diagnostic approach stems from the idea that individuals can be categorized into those who have and those who do not have a mental illness. The categories are based on arbitrary thresholds rather than on sound scientific evidence. Although the DSM-5 tried to address this issue by having a rating scale as well as a diagnostic classification, there is little agreement among the personality and personality disorder working group on whether the new classification is sensible or not (Zachar et al., 2016). Fourth, personality disorder diagnoses are associated with tremendous stigma, and those who are labeled are often perceived as difficult and dangerous. Stigma not only influences general well-being, but can also lead to discrimination, and disadvantage in the legal system, employment, and relationships. For all these reasons, the utility of the personality disorder label has to be considered carefully. In the personality psychology research, the Dark Triad is seldom treated as a disorder.

2.2 Machiavellianism as a Clinical Construct

Although Machiavellianism does not directly feature in the classification systems, some consider it as part of the psychopathy continuum. The cold, detached interpersonal style of individuals high in Machiavellianism has been proposed as a nonclinical manifestation of psychopathy, exhibited in individuals who have not been incarcerated and institutionalized (McHoskey, Worzel, & Szyarto, 1998). For example, McHoskey (2001) analyzed the MACH-IV scale in relation to a host of clinical symptoms, and concluded that those who score high on the questionnaire are also high on a number of other scales indicating personality dysfunction. More specifically, Machiavellianism had links to antisocial personality, which is currently classified as a mental disorder. It would be easy to conclude that

Machiavellianism is pretty much the same as psychopathy, but to a lesser degree, and would be at least a predisposing factor for vulnerability to mental illnesses. Indeed, research that has investigated the Dark Triad and a host of physical and mental health difficulties have demonstrated that Machiavellianism and psychopathy are associated with worse health outcomes (Jonason, Baughman, Carter, & Parker, 2015).

However, other studies have found that psychological well-being is negatively associated with psychopathy, but not Machiavellianism (Aghababaei & Błachnio, 2015). In another study, Richardson and Boag (2016) demonstrated that in a heterogeneous internet sample, stress had a positive relationship with Machiavellianism, but not with psychopathy. These studies suggest that Machiavellianism and psychopathy are not similar when it comes to psychological outcomes, and Machiavellianism warrants being treated not just as a lesser degree of psychopathy, but as a personality trait in its own right. Although Machiavellianism does not have a clear place in the clinical literature, it has its utility in understanding several mental health outcomes and a predisposition to vulnerability.

2.3 Psychopathy as a Clinical Construct

Psychopathy has been a subject to much confusion in the clinical field, partially because psychopathy itself is not a diagnosis in the DSM system, but falls under the diagnostic category of ASPD. Although lay people and clinicians alike freely use the term "psychopath," it is not classified as a disorder in the diagnostic manuals. The ASPD diagnosis has a focus on impulsive, norm-violating behaviors. The diagnostic systems have been criticized for not taking into consideration other crucial components of psychopathy, namely, empathy deficits, boldness, and callousness associated with it. This is a serious shortcoming as not all individuals who inflict harm on others have problems with controlling their behavior. For example, many of those who commit financial crimes may have empathy deficits associated with primary psychopathy, but they would not classify for a psychopathy diagnosis using the diagnostic manuals.

In order to patch this shortcoming, the latest version of the diagnostic and statistical manual, DSM-5, has tried to address the issue. In addition to having a section for diagnosing ASPD ("criterion A"), it also includes a new, alternative section ("criterion B") for assessing the levels of functioning and maladaptive personality traits in an individual. This "hybrid model" tries to take into account the dimensional, continuous nature of personality (disorder) features, and the severity of malfunctioning of personality.

In order to assess the presence/absence of ASPD, one first has to consult Section II in the DSM-5, which is exactly similar as it was in the previous edition of the manual. ASPD diagnosis requires four criteria to be met for a person to classify for a diagnosis. The first criteria are disregard for, and violation of other people's rights, where one of the following subfeatures has to be present: (i) failure to obey laws, (ii) lying, deception and manipulation, (iii) impulsivity, (iv) aggression, (v) disregard of the safety of self and others, (vi) irresponsibility, and (vii) lack of remorse. The other criteria are age (has to be over 18), history (features of conduct disorder (CD) prior to age of 15), and comorbidity (absence of schizophrenia or bipolar disorder). This means that the diagnosis can be based solely on behavioral aspects tapping into secondary psychopathy, and an individual with a cold, callous feature of primary psychopathy may not qualify for a diagnosis.

In the alternative, emerging model in DSM-5 (Section III), the degree of ASPD can be measured in several continuous domains: disinhibition (impulsivity, risk-taking, irresponsibility) and antagonism (deceitfulness, hostility, manipulativeness, callousness). Researchers have welcomed this addition as sensible, as it taps more onto the continuous nature of ASPD. The hybrid diagnostic model allows to identify important aspects of psychopathy, namely, boldness (i.e., interpersonal efficacy, emotional resiliency, glibness/superficial charm, fearlessness, and grandiose sense of self-worth). Individuals who exhibit high levels of boldness can be distinctively different from those who qualify for an ASPD diagnosis. Boldness is related to the concept of primary psychopathy, which probably is how most people conceptualize psychopathy as a trait—successful, fearless manipulators who are not easily stressed about things that would normally make people nervous.

The main advantage of the DSM-5 Section III is, then, that it allows (to some extent) the identification of individuals who are high in primary psychopathy. Psychopathy (also called "Psychopathy Specifier") can be assessed by adding low anxiousness, low withdrawal, and high attention seeking into the mix. Studies that have investigated the DSM-5 psychopathy specifier in relation to existing psychopathy measures have found significant positive relationships (e.g., Anderson, Sellbom, Wygant, Salekin, & Krueger, 2014; Strickland, Drislane, Lucy, Krueger, & Patrick, 2013). Although psychopathy is not an official diagnosis, following 50 years of diagnostic debates, it is finally accepted as a component of ASPD in the DSM-5 alternative model. An individual can, as a result of a clinical interview and assessment with the maladaptive trait model questionnaire, receive a diagnosis of "ASPD with Psychopathic Personality Traits." I will review the maladaptive trait model with regards to all the three Dark Triad traits later in this chapter.

Although not officially recognized as a diagnostic tool for mental disorder, the Psychopathy Checklist-Revised (PCL-R), developed by Robert Hare (2003), has been used widely in the forensic settings. This manual is a licensed, validated assessment tool, recommended for use by only experienced, trained clinicians. The 20-item inventory is completed as a result of a semistructured interview and some detective work, trying to construct a case study of the person using all the information available on the individual. The process may use police and court records, military service records, health information, and informant reports (e.g., statements from parents, school, employer, friends). The interviewer determines the absence (0 = definitely does not apply) and presence (1 = somewhat applies, 2 = definitely applies) of each item. The questions that are scored are assessing things like callousness, lack of guilt, parasitic lifestyles, and impulsivity, tapping to the Factor 1 (primary) and Factor 2 (secondary) psychopathy. The person whose psychopathy is assessed can score anything between 0 and 40. The cutoff point for psychopathy is 25 + in the UK and 30 + in the United States. In essence, a person has to be "more psychopathic" in order to receive the label of psychopath in the United States, indicating that cultural norms play a part in the psychopathy construct.

How do clinicians deal with children who exhibit behaviors that are psychopathic in nature? There has been a surge of interest in investigating psychopathy-like features in children and adolescents, partially due to the need to identify those who might be at risk of turning into adult offenders. Children and young people who use calculated aggression against others, lack empathy, and exhibit delinquent behaviors are often of interest if they have been detained for criminal activities. Prior to the age of 18, children cannot be given an ASPD diagnosis, due to constant development, maturation, and changes in their personality. The diagnostic label reserved for children who show features of psychopathy and ASPD is CD. When the child matures, they will get reassessed, and the diagnosis sometimes changes to ASPD diagnosis.

During the revisions of the diagnostic criteria, CD diagnosis was left unchanged in the new edition. In order for a child to receive a diagnosis, they have to show pervasive behaviors that violate either the rights of others or major societal norms, and cause significant impairment in social, academic, or occupational functioning. In addition, one of the following has to be present: aggression to people or animals, destruction of property, deceit or theft, and serious violation of rules. In addition to this, DSM-5 has a "specifier" to take into account the callous and unemotional features of some young people. The "Limited Prosocial Emotions" (LPEs) specifier consists of lack of remorse or guilt, callousness or lack of empathy, lack of concern for own performance, or shallow affect.

The LPE specifier is important in many respects, especially when trying to deal with children who are callous and unremorseful, but do not necessarily show any signs of the behavioral aspects related to ASPD. A feature article in New York Times (Can you call a 9 year old a psychopath?) outlined a case study of a 9-year-old boy who threw a 3 year old into a swimming pool, and took a chair by the side of the pool to sit down, and calmly watched him drowning (Kahn, 2012). In later police interviews, the boy was cheerfully telling about his curiosity to see someone drowning. He did not show an iota of remorse, basking excitedly in the glory of the attention he was getting. The lack of regret for cruel actions is a major concern when assessing the risk of future violence. Thus the LPE specifier may have some clinical utility above what the CD diagnosis can offer.

Can you call a 9 year old a psychopath? It is necessary to carefully consider the implications of diagnosis and terminology when treating children. Some of the issues that have been raised are (i) lack of stability in psychopathy-like behaviors (children may still "grow out of it"), (ii) differences in structure of child and adult psychopathy, and (iii) lack of predictive validity of psychopathy traits in predicting future behavior. Alongside these concerns, another serious problem is around the misuse of psychopathy instruments in labeling some children as "untreatable."

The concept of psychopathy as a lifelong, untreatable condition can have damaging effect of children who have committed delinquent acts and have been taken to court. Viljoen, MacDougall, Gagnon, & Douglas (2010) assessed over one hundred court cases in the United States and Canada, investigating the use of psychopathy-related terminology in cases where the children were assessed by a mental health professional. They found that evidence relating to psychopathy was present in a sizeable number of the cases. Although the judges did not usually refer to psychopathy evidence when making their decisions, when psychopathy was mentioned, it was in the context of difficulty of treatment of the young person (i.e., the idea that psychopathy is immutable, and children who exhibit the traits of it cannot be changed). The cases where psychopathy was mentioned, but the young person was determined as not having it, the sentencing was more lenient, and the court reports included statements about beliefs that the defendant is amenable to change. In the case of diagnosis and children, extreme caution should be applied, as the terminology can influence the likelihood of the child receiving help in the future.

2.4 Narcissism as a Clinical Construct

Narcissism as a clinical construct is not without its controversies either. Some of the difficulties spawn from inconsistencies within and across the disciplines of clinical psychology, psychiatry, and social/personality psychology. There are major disparities in how narcissism is defined, and subsequently, how it is measured in different studies. Most experts agree that narcissism has both pathological and normal expressions. "Normal" narcissism is manifested by a healthy self-image and self-esteem, which does not fall apart when faced with threats to the self. "Pathological" narcissism, in turn, is characterized by fragile self-image, which can easily crumble under criticism from others. Theorists disagree about the relationship between normal and pathological narcissism. According to some, pathological and normal vary in a continuum, where pathological is just a more severe manifestation of the normal (e.g., Watson, 2005). According to others, pathological and normal are distinctively different manifestations of narcissism, forming two separate dimensional personality traits (e.g., Pincus et al., 2009).

The DSM-5 personality and personality disorder working group initially recommended the removal of NPD diagnosis from the diagnostic manual together with several other PD diagnoses. The vague rationale for this decision was based on the wish to reduce the number of PD diagnoses and to decrease the comorbidity (i.e., overlap) between the diagnoses. However, after an outcry from several prominent researchers in the field (e.g., Miller et al., 2010), the working group decided to retain the NPD diagnosis in DSM-5 without changes from the previous manual.

The DSM-5 Section II diagnosis of NPD states that there has to be a presence of a pervasive pattern of grandiosity, a need for admiration, and a lack of empathy, together with five or more of the following: grandiose sense of self-importance; preoccupation with fantasies of unlimited success, power, brilliance, beauty, or ideal love; beliefs of being special and unique; requirements of excessive admiration; a sense of entitlement; interpersonal exploitativeness; lack of empathy; envy of others; arrogant, and haughty behaviors or attitudes. The NPD diagnostic category has been criticized for excessive focus on grandiose aspects of narcissism. The Section III dimensional model (which is used more in research than in clinical practice) also allows to determine vulnerable aspects of narcissism by assessing, for instance, the levels of negative affectivity.

2.5 The Dark Triad and DSM-5 Maladaptive Personality Model

The DSM-5 proposed an alternative model for personality disorders, which included the "maladaptive trait model," measured by a continuous Personality Inventory for the DSM-5 (also called PID-5). The maladaptive personality idea is very similar to dimensional models in personality literature—individuals are not categorized as having a disorder, but rather, they differ in the degree that they have the characteristics of maladaptive personalities. The new model is used to supplement the classical system of diagnosis. As well as determining the presence of a personality disorder (i.e., classical diagnosis), clinicians can also measure the degree and nature of personality dysfunction (i.e., the new maladaptive trait model).

The PID-5 has five, broad, polar categories determining how personality can cause a social dysfunction. These domains can be mapped onto the Big Five personality framework as well, suggesting that maladaptive personality is just an extreme variant of "normal" personality traits. The PID-5 domains are the following: negative affect vs. emotional stability (frequency and intensity of experiencing negative emotions), detachment vs. extraversion (withdrawal of socioemotional experience, including avoidance of close bonds with others), disinhibition vs. conscientiousness (orienting toward immediate gratification, disregarding future consequences), antagonism vs. agreeableness (callousness, disregard for others, exaggerated self-importance), and psychoticism vs. lucidity (expressing odd, eccentric, and unusual behaviors and thoughts). These five domains consists of several different facets. Different forms of the PID-5 (e.g., long, short, adult, child) can be downloaded for research and clinical use from this website https://www.psychiatry.org/psychiatrists/practice/dsm/educational-resources/assessment-measures#Personality

Since the publication of the DSM-5 and the alternative model to personality disorder diagnosis, there have been several studies investigating the relationship with the maladaptive model and components of the Dark Triad. The pertinent question in this research is that how well the abnormal personality variation represented in the DSM-5 map onto the Dark Triad traits.

Which components of the model (if any) are typical of those who are on the higher end of the Dark Triad continuum? For example, antagonism is a key feature of all three Dark Triad traits, leading to major dysfunction in social relationships, sometimes at levels that could be described as "psychosocial disability." Those who are high in antagonism are callous toward others and often view other people as instruments for achieving their own goals. Needless to say, this kind of behavior leads to short-lived social relationships or much misery for those who for some reason (e.g., children of antagonistic parents) have to endure the connections with the highly antagonistic individual. In the DSM-5 alternative personality disorder model, antagonism consists of several facets (i.e., manipulativeness, grandiosity, attention seeking, hostility, callousness, and deceitfulness). The interesting question is that how do the different Dark Triad traits map onto antagonism and its different facets, and is it possible to identify high levels of the trait in the clinical context?

Grigoras and Wille (2017) investigated the maladaptive trait model in a sample of Romanian law enforcement officers (e.g., police, firefighters). They found that beyond the Big Five of personality, antagonism in the PID-5 questionnaire was a significant predictor of Machiavellianism and narcissism, but not psychopathy. Antagonism consists of manipulativeness, deceitfulness, and grandiosity, which can be detrimental in interpersonal relationships. However, narcissism also had associations with lower negative affect and low detachment, which indicates that narcissism also relates to experiencing positive emotions, and seeking to be in contact with others. Psychopathy was associated with disinhibition, which could lead to impulsive, maladaptive behaviors driven by present, rather than future needs. The PID-5 associations with the Dark Triad suggest that the three traits have unique profiles with regards to clinically maladaptive traits. What is interesting is that in a more fine-grained analyses, only grandiosity (a facet of antagonism) was a shared facet between all the three dark traits. All the Dark Triad traits related to high levels of grandiosity, the belief that one is greater than other people, and hence, deserves special treatment. Grandiosity has been traditionally considered as a central feature of narcissism, but not necessarily of psychopathy or Machiavellianism.

Other studies have investigated psychopathy or narcissism individually, correlating questionnaire measures/personality disorder assessments to PID-5 facets. In a review of some of these studies, NPD and ASPD were most consistently related to antagonism and disinhibition (Al-Dajani, Gralnick, & Bagby, 2016), although there were inconsistencies across samples, and different questionnaires that were used in the research.

When investigating the maladaptive trait model in clinical samples who under therapeutic intervention, the patterns of relationships with narcissism are completely different from community populations. Pincus, Dowgwillo, and Greenberg (2016) presented a series of case studies drawn from mental health outpatient clinics and clinical psychology trainee case loads. The clinical cases exhibited high degree of antagonism, disinhibition, detachment, presenting profiles that are very different to studies from nonclinical samples. One of the key features of the clinical case studies was that the individuals referred themselves to mental health services due to depressive mood, suicidal thoughts, and difficulties in adjusting to changing life circumstances. The features of narcissistic grandiosity emerged only later, during therapeutic interventions with the clinicians. Moreover, grandiosity was characterized by vulnerability, resulting in personal attacks (in both private lives and against the therapist) when feeling that the ego was under a threat. Pincus and colleagues discussed the case studies in terms of vulnerable narcissism, which is an ignored element in the NPD diagnosis, but does feature in the hybrid model.

One line of studies has focused on looking at the degree of psychosocial dysfunction in individuals who have high levels of antagonism, as measured by the PID-5. For instance, Ro, Nuzum, and Clark (2017) investigated different facets of antagonism in a sample of psychiatric outpatients and informants, collecting information from the patients, clinicians, and people who are close to the patients. The authors were interested in studying how diverse aspects of antagonism relate to psychosocial functioning, such as work problems, money, relationships, and satisfaction with life. They also explored the possibility that antagonism could be classified as a psychosocial disability, preventing people from living their everyday lives. Interestingly, their results suggested that out of all the antagonism facets, hostility came out as the largest predictor of impaired psychosocial functioning. It is not a surprise, as previous research as established strong links between hostility and poor health, unhealthy lifestyles, and dysfunction in social relationships.

Although the hybrid model has brought some improvement to the diagnosis of PDs, there are still considerable question marks over the DSM system. The PID-5 dimensional model has been used more extensively in research, rather than in clinical practice. Most researchers agree that the categorical diagnostic models (i.e., diagnosing a presence or an absence of a PD) are outdated and not based on empirical research on difficulties that may stem from personality functioning. However, there is still hope for future improvements in the diagnostic systems. In the words of Krueger and

Markon (2014), "Research involving the DSM-5 trait model will be useful in shifting the DSM further away from categorical diagnoses derived through political processes and presumed authority and toward an empirically based dimensional model of personality and psychopathology for use in diverse research and clinical settings" (p.486).

2.6 The "Vulnerable" Dark Triad

The Dark Triad constellation includes a bewildering array of strengths and vulnerabilities. For instance, some of the aspects of narcissism, including grandiosity and leadership, seem to be beneficial in terms of well-being and life outcomes. However, there may be other aspects of narcissism that impair the functioning of the individual in their everyday lives. This constellation of strengths and vulnerabilities seems contradictory and led Miller et al. (2010) to propose that as well as the traditionally researched Dark Triad, there is a second triad which constitutes of vulnerable aspects of aversive personality constellation. The vulnerable Dark Triad is especially relevant in the clinical context, although it is not integrated clearly with the diagnoses of ASPD and NPD.

The "darkness" of the Dark Triad consists simply of disagreeableness (antagonism, deceitfulness, dishonesty, and selfishness). As well as the aversive "core," some individuals high on the Dark Triad also present profiles that are characterized by psychological vulnerability—neuroticism, negative emotionality, and the inability to control emotions, which may lead to vulnerability to mental distress. Furthermore, some aspects of the Dark Triad are also associated with impulsivity and inability to wait for rewards, which can result in rash decisions that may put the individual in a risky position (e.g., crossing a busy road without a care for the traffic or having unprotected sex with a stranger).

According to Miller et al. (2010), it makes sense to think of the Dark Triad as two constructs. In addition to a more adaptive constellation (i.e., Factor 1 psychopathy, and grandiose narcissism as measured by the Narcissistic Personality Inventory), there is a second Dark Triad, characterized by features of Borderline Personality Disorder (BPD), vulnerable narcissism (e.g., fragile self-esteem, insensitivity), and Factor 2 psychopathy (e.g., risk-taking and impulsivity). All the three aspects of the vulnerable Dark Triad are linked to neuroticism and have associations with insecure attachment, suboptimal parenting as a child (i.e., low warmth and high intrusiveness from the parents), as well as childhood trauma (i.e., sexual, verbal, physical, and emotional abuse). Further, vulnerable Dark Triad is associated with difficulties in current functioning, including nonsuicidal self-harming behaviors. These etiological factors that are present in the vulnerable Dark Triad are absent from the adaptive dyad of grandiose narcissism and Factor 1 psychopathy. Despite the differences in etiological factors, both types of dark personality constellations have a positive relationship with antagonistic behaviors such as crime and substance use.

2.7 Treatment Implications

Providing help and support individuals who have received an NDP or ASPD diagnosis is challenging. The treatment suggestions don't often come from the individual themselves, but from relatives, or the legal system. The patients themselves often view the treatment plans as useless, failing to see why they would need professional help in the first place.

Historically, narcissism has been considered as untreatable by several clinical writers (e.g., Freud, Abraham, Kohut), partially stemming from the resistance to change one's grandiose self-image. One of the factors that makes psychological therapies difficult is the influence of narcissistic features in the therapist–patient relationship. Earlier writers such as Kohut and Kernberg stated that due to the power imbalance in the therapeutic relationship, the narcissistic patient may be plagued by feelings of envy toward their therapist, resulting in resistance to change as a protest against the therapy. Any positive change could be threatening to the narcissistic individuals, as it would require admitting that they had flaws in the first place. Pincus, Cain, and Wright (2014) discussed case studies of individuals with features of narcissistic vulnerability, and noted the remarkable resistance to receiving psychological help. The inability to recognize faults in oneself coupled with the tendency to put blame on others can result in a breakdown in the therapeutic alliance. Pincus et al. describe Mr. A, a single man in his late 30s, who had terminated therapies with two different therapists after a number of sessions.

"In treatment, Mr. A's narcissistic vulnerability was identifiable through the dominant affects of unrelenting resentment, anger, and envy, which he clearly could not regulate effectively. However, his therapists' efforts to empathize with his emotions and developmental history were consistently met with increased grandiosity and denigration. In therapy he regularly belittled, mocked, and challenged therapists, "I know I'm narcissistic and there's nothing you can do about it," "You can do your empathy thing, but it will have no effect on me," "You're just a trainee, you don't know enough to help me," and "I'm only here to get medication because the VA requires too much paperwork and makes me wait too long" (Pincus et al., 2014, p. 441). Indeed, such levels of hostility can evoke the clinician to have negative attitudes toward the patient (Tanzilli, Colli, Muzi, & Lingiardi, 2015), which sometimes leads to the clinician-initiated termination of the therapeutic sessions.

There are surprisingly few studies investigating the psychological treatment outcome associated with narcissistic features. Ellison, Levy, Cain, Ansell, and Pincus (2013) studied a sample of outpatients receiving a wide variety of therapies at a University-based mental health clinic, looking at the relationship between grandiose and vulnerable narcissism on treatment outcomes. They found that those who had grandiose features were more likely to terminate their psychotherapy and were also less likely to seek for help from a national helpline or from a hospital. This indicates that grandiose individuals do not think that there is anything wrong with them, refusing to get help in order to change. Patients with high levels of vulnerable narcissism also had a host of other maladaptive features, such as depression, panic, and psychosis. Narcissism did not influence the change in mental distress over the course of the therapy. The findings corroborate with other studies using clinical samples, suggesting that vulnerable narcissism is related to more maladaptive outcomes than grandiose narcissism, and should be included more clearly in the diagnostic criteria for NPD.

Narcissism is not only problematic in psychological treatment settings, but can also present a major problem for healthcare providers who deliver care for physical health problems. Narcissistic patients that seek help for physical ailments can be demanding, threatening, superior, and refuse to comply with their treatment. They have the tendency to become the "experts" in their condition, and either idolize or denigrate the healthcare professionals who try to help them. Magidson et al. (2012) suggested that "Temporarily allying with a patient's need for self-enhancement and feelings of superiority can be an effective technique with patient's exhibiting signs of narcissism, particularly in the context of brief interventions" (p. 202).

There is relatively little research with regards to the treatment of ASPD, CD, or psychopathy. Rather than empirical literature, the field is plagued by a wealth of opinions about treatability. Can a leopard change its spots? Is it possible to make people "less psychopathic" by therapeutic interventions? These are important questions, especially in the legal settings. If judges and juries have the perception of psychopathic behaviors as unchangeable, the sentencing decisions can be harsher in an attempt to mitigate future recidivism. In the demoralizing words of Suedfeld and Landon (1978), "review of the literature suggests that a chapter on effective treatment should be the shortest in any book concerned with psychopathy. In fact, it has been suggested that one sentence would suffice: No demonstrably effective treatment has been found" (p. 347). Actually, according to Harris and Rice (2006), treatments could even make psychopathic individuals worse, rather than better.

However, these negative views about treatability of psychopathy have been accused of "therapeutic nihilism" (Wong & Olver, 2015), based on research that is outdated and methodologically flawed. Indeed, studies have found that treatment is effective especially for Factor 2 (i.e., antisocial, impulsive behavior) psychopathy. Factor 1 (i.e., cold, callous predisposition) may be less malleable to change, but does not predict violence and recidivism either. Thus the efforts should be on programs that are directed to the modifiable criminogenic features of the individual, those factors that cause violence. These programs may be in the form of intensive therapies (e.g., cognitive behavioral therapy), helping offenders to "... learn, practice, and generalize offense-reducing thoughts, feelings, and behaviors to replace offense-producing behaviors in day-to-day functioning" (Wong & Olver, 2015, p. 307). The programs that are recommended for treating psychopathic offenders are tailor-made to suit the individuals' learning and response styles.

2.8 Mental Illness Labeling and Stigma

Out of all mental disorder diagnoses, PDs are among the most stigmatized (Sheehan et al., 2016), probably because PD labels imply badness as well as madness, possibly due to the associations with criminal behavior in ASPD and psychopathy. Stigma comes dressed in different guises. Public stigma is linked to the belief that people with PD diagnoses are difficult, dangerous, and should be avoided at any cost. These beliefs could lead to social isolation in forms of denial of opportunities in work, education, housing, and social contact. Self-stigma encompasses the feelings that the diagnosed individual has toward themselves, where the stereotype associated with the label is internalized by the person. Self-stigma relates to issues with identity and could lead to a self-fulfilling prophecy, acting the part that has been assigned by the diagnosis. With regards to NPD, ASPD, and psychopathy diagnoses, there is some research into public stigma, but hardly any studies

Table 2.1 Types of Stigma

Type of Stigma	Definition	Outcome	Example Study
Self-stigma	Individuals identify with their label and allow the label to define them as a person	Behave in a way expected by the label (self-fulfilling prophecy)	Children who thought that others perceived them as "trouble makers and rule breakers" were subsequently more likely to be engaged in delinquency later in life (Adams, 1996)
Public stigma	Others perceive the individual in a certain way and identify them through the stereotype created by the label	Avoid contact with those who have the label or treat them differently Deny employment, housing, treatment, education, social contact	ASPD vignette evoked most social distance (e.g., not wanting to be friends with the person) out of 40 DSM mental disorder vignettes (Feldman & Crandall, 2007)

(Feldman, D. B., & Crandall, C. S. (2007). Dimensions of mental illness stigma: What about mental illness causes social rejection? *Journal of Social and Clinical Psychology*, *26*, 137–154; Adams, M. S. (1996). Labeling and differential association: toward a general social learning theory of crime and deviance. *American Journal of Criminal Justice*, *20*, 147–164.)

on self-stigma. This could be due to the often involuntary nature associated with these diagnoses, which are given as a result of a psychiatric assessment during legal procedures (Table 2.1).

The media has a major contribution to the formation of stigma. Film and TV characters categorized as psychopaths are often depicted as dangerous, merciless, sadistic murderers (Hesse, 2009). The lay public has the (mis)conception that "psychopaths" are dangerous, rare, and responsible for their actions. Several researchers have investigated jury perceptions of psychopathy, their understanding of what it is, and how this relates to sentencing decisions. These studies have found that when a defendant is given the label of being a psychopath, the jury is harsher in their decisions, promoting longer sentences and death sentencing (Edens, Colwell, Desforges, & Fernandez, 2005). This shows how public stigma associated with personality disorder diagnosis can have serious, detrimental consequences for the labeled individual.

One interesting question is how stigma is influenced by how people understand the causes of psychopathy. If psychopathy is conceived as a genetic disorder, can the individual be blamed for their own actions, or is their behavior something that is not under their own voluntary control? Biomechanical causal explanations for psychopathy present a double-edged sword when it comes to public perceptions. On the one hand, biology reduces the perceived personal responsibility for actions, increasing sympathy for the offender, leading to more lenient sentences. On the other hand, biological causality evokes feelings of incurability, danger, and a risk of reoffending, which could influence harsher sentencing decisions. It is crucial to understand how labeling influences perceptions of the individual based on the ideas of causality behind the mental illness label.

Worryingly, courtrooms are increasingly resorting to genetic testing and brain imaging in an attempt to prove that the defendant is biologically predisposed to behave violently. For instance, an Italian woman who killed her sister had her sentence reduced from life to 20 years after genetic testing indicated that she had a variant of the MAOA (so-called warrior) gene that has been linked to violence (Feresin, 2011). The use of neuroscientific evidence and genetic testing in the courtroom is controversial due to lack of reliable biological markers for psychopathy and genetic predisposition for violent acts. I will discuss this in greater length in Chapter 6. Nevertheless, this implies that judges may be more lenient if they understand psychopathy as a biological disorder, where the offender has a lesser ability to control their actions.

2.9 The Dark Triad in the Legal System

A concentration camp guard in former Yugoslavia, guilty of sadistic torture and murder, tried to plead diminished responsibility for his actions on the grounds of suffering from a personality disorder. Despite a number of experts testifying that he may indeed suffer from personality distortions, the court did not accept diminished responsibility (Sparr, 2009).

There is an ongoing debate about whether those who inflict harm on others should be dealt within the forensic setting, or whether they should be excused under the insanity plea. If the conclusion is that the perpetrator is insane, s/he may be sent to a psychiatric institution rather than to the prison (see Maibom, 2008).

According to the M'Naghten rule applied in legal cases,

> *... that every man is to be presumed to be sane, and ... that to establish a defense on the ground of insanity, it must be clearly proved that, at the time of the committing of the act, the party accused was laboring under such a defect of reason, from disease of the mind, as not to know the nature and quality of the act he was doing; or if he did know it, that he did not know he was doing what was wrong.*

Thus the arguments are focusing on whether an individual is consciously aware of the wrongness of their actions. This awareness can be challenging to establish, especially in cases where the perpetrators may have different ideas of what is morally right or wrong. Enduring debates in the legal system have centered around the possibility that individuals who commit moral violations are insane. Do they have control over their actions? Do they understand that their actions were wrong? Are they mad (in which case they would not be responsible for their actions), or simply bad? This question has puzzled theorists, researchers, and philosophers and has led to comprehensive research programs trying to understand the moral landscape of people who have disregard for others.

Interestingly, in the legal system, personality disorder diagnosis often fails to lead to more lenient sentences. Indeed, the prevalence of prison inmates with personality disorder diagnosis is high. According to some estimates, over 50% of prisoners have a personality disorder diagnosis (Bland, Newman, Dyck, & Orn, 1990). "Mad or bad" debates have important sentencing and treatment implications for those who have committed a crime. As a consequence, the individual Dark Triad traits (especially narcissism and psychopathy) have received much attention in the clinical and forensic literature. I will review the research on the Dark Triad and crime in Chapter 6.

The awkward relationship between psychiatry and law is evident in the use of the DSM in the forensic settings, especially in the United States. Courts can use mental illness terms any way the like, leading to shoddy use of clinical terms in legal decision making. According to Frances and Halon (2013), "Legal and psychiatric truths are very different animals. Whereas the legal system requires black and white answers, clinical psychiatry and psychology almost always deal in probabilities and shades of gray. The inherent ambiguities of psychiatric diagnosis often make it impossible to meet the legal demand that there be an unambiguously dichotomous yes or no answer" (p. 336).

2.10 Conclusion

Components of the Dark Triad, namely, psychopathy and narcissism, have a long history in the clinical psychology literature. The diagnostic traditions have utilized categories such as NPD, ASPD, and psychopathy in trying to understand and label the difficulties stemming from interpersonally aversive personalities. Machiavellianism fits in this picture either as a subclinical form of psychopathy, or a personality trait in its own regard, distinctively different from psychopathy and narcissism. There are major doubts about the utility of using diagnostic labels, as there is more empirical evidence for antagonistic personalities varying in a continuum rather than existing as separate entities. Although the DSM-5 was an attempt to rectify the misgivings in the diagnostic systems, it was only partially successful. Despite the working group recommendations for a continuous model, DSM-5 retained the NPS and ASPD diagnostic categories from the previous edition. However, the new edition saw an addition of a hybrid, continuous model which allows the assessment of the degree of personality dysfunction.

The Dark Triad is important in the clinical context for many reasons. The aversive aspects of personality can have a negative influence on several aspects of life, including social relationships and violations of rules and social norms, leading to trouble with the law and authorities. These can, in turn, result in physical and mental health difficulties, which may require clinical interventions. There is evidence for vulnerable Dark Triad, which makes individuals more vulnerable to psychopathology. Despite earlier claims that psychopathy (or ASPD) is untreatable, these assertions are without convincing empirical evidence. Especially the behavioral aspects of secondary psychopathy (which have more links to violence and offending) can be reduced in intensive psychological interventions. The future challenge is to understand how the Dark Triad continuum relates to vulnerability to mental distress and how to devise therapies that help to alleviate the distress.

Further Reading

Krueger, R. F., & Markon, K. E. (2014). The role of the DSM-5 personality trait model in moving toward a quantitative and empirically based approach to classifying personality and psychopathology. *Annual Review of Clinical Psychology, 10*, 477–501.

CHAPTER THREE

The Dark Triad and Forensic Implications: Antagonistic, Aggressive, and Criminal Behaviors

Chapter Outline

3.1 Introduction

Criminologists and forensic psychologists have invested considerable time and effort into investigating why people commit crimes, with personality being just one of the many criminogenic determinants of interest. The early development of most of the research on personality and crime took place within the clinical literature, speculating whether people who commit crimes are "mad" or "bad." Many of the attempts to understand what makes up "criminal personality" focused on linking crime with DSM personality disorders, particularly with narcissistic personality disorder (NPD), antisocial personality disorder (ASPD), and psychopathy (Yochelson & Samenow, 1993). Indeed, clinicians have suggested that most people who commit a series of violent crimes or murders have a personality disorder such as

The Dark Triad of Personality
https://doi.org/10.1016/B978-0-12-814291-2.00003-6

NPD (Stone, 2007). You may want to revisit Chapter 2 for a discussion of the Dark Triad in the domains of clinical and forensic psychology.

At the more extreme end of personality variation, personality disorders provide an important predictor of serious, frequent offending, beyond what can be explained by other mental disorder diagnoses (Ogloff, Talevski, Lemphers, Wood, & Simmons, 2015). Personality variation clearly plays a vital role in the proclivity to commit crimes of varying degrees, possibly more so than other "criminogenic factors" such as socioeconomic status. Indeed, in a large, representative sample, O'Riordan and O'Connell (2014) explored the role of the Big Five, and multiple other factors (e.g., family size, intellect, education, father's social class, occupation) with regards to having received a sanction from the criminal justice system in the United Kingdom. They found that out of all the variables, only personality (high extraversion and neuroticism, and low agreeableness and conscientiousness) was a significant predictor of involvement in crime in adults. As well as the Big Five, the Dark Triad provides another important personality paradigm for understanding the role of personality in the forensic context.

The antagonistic core of the Dark Triad is represented by antisocial and deviant behaviors, which can result in catastrophic interpersonal consequences, including loss of resources (e.g., theft) and physical danger (e.g., assault, death) to the targets of these behaviors. People at the higher end of the dark personality spectrum are deceitful, amoral, with shallow empathy and reduced guilt after moral transgressions. All of these features are relevant in the forensic context, making these individuals more likely to be bending social rules, and in some cases, perpetrate crimes of varying degrees. Not only perpetration, but those who put themselves in situations involving high risk may also be at a greater risk of becoming victims of crime themselves.

Crime itself consists of heterogeneous sets of actions. There are several different types of criminal behaviors, all of which could have different relationships with each of the Dark Triad traits. The diverse array of law-breaking behaviors includes property crimes (e.g., theft, robbery, joy-driving), drug-related crimes, identity thefts, fraud, cybercrime (see Chapter 8), interpersonal crime (e.g., rape, assault, murder), and so on. Crimes can also vary in how premeditated or impulsive they are. In this chapter, I will review the relationship between the Dark Triad and other traits and conducts that are related to crime (e.g., self-control, aggression, lying), as well as examining the Dark Triad and crime in incarcerated and nonincarcerated populations.

3.2 Causes and Correlates of Crime?

There are several different theories of what causes crime. Some explain crime as a by-product of other behaviors or traits (e.g., aggression, impulsivity, low empathy) that may predispose individuals to crime. Others view crime as a potentially fitness-enhancing adaptation, evolved in the context of competition for resources or mating opportunities. For evolutionary theorists, it is probably of no surprise that age or biological sex plays a large part in crime (see, e.g., the Young Male Syndrome theory by Wilson and Daly (1985)). Men are more likely to commit crimes of all types, and they also have higher prevalence of ASPD, conduct disorder, psychopathy, and other conditions that have a close relationship with offending. Men also have higher levels of Dark Triad traits, suggesting that personality may be a factor that facilitates evolutionarily adaptive behaviors (such as crime) that could increase reproductive success. Of course, women do commit crimes as well, and an interesting question to ask is whether female crime is a function of the Dark Triad traits. In other words, are those individuals (irrespective of their sex) who are high on the Dark Triad more likely to commit crimes? Similarly, are more likely to commit crime because they are, overall, higher on the Dark Triad traits?

3.2.1 Aggression and Violence

Aggression has been studied widely in the criminal context, especially in prisoners who have been diagnosed as having a personality disorder. Aggressive tendencies can lead to antisocial acts, which also have a strong relationship with criminal behavior. Indeed, longitudinal research has found that early teacher reports of aggression in children are related to lawbreaking in later life (Stattin & Magnusson, 1989), suggesting that proclivity to commit crimes can be identified relatively early. Aggressive behaviors and attitudes in those high on the Dark Triad spectrum extend to animal cruelty (Kavanagh, Signal, & Taylor, 2013), racism (Hodson, Hogg, & MacInnis, 2009), and acceptance of different types of violent acts (Blinkhorn, Lyons, & Almond, 2016). It is possible that aggression is a "criminogenic" factor that can lead to a higher likelihood of committing crimes, especially violent crimes against other people.

It is likely that out of the three Dark Triad traits, psychopathy is the most relevant when it comes to aggression and interpersonal violence. In a recent meta-analysis of over 100 research papers, Muris, Merckelbach, Otgaar, and Meijer (2017) investigated a large number of different psychosocial correlates associated with the Dark Triad, including aggression. All the Dark Triad traits were associated with increased aggression–delinquency, but "psychopathy runs the show" (p.194). When shared variance between the three traits was statistically controlled, psychopathy emerged as a significant predictor for many different kinds of adverse interpersonal behaviors, including the tendency for aggression. In terms of viciousness, psychopathy seems to be the leading Dark Triad trait, followed by Machiavellianism (Pailing, Boon, & Egan, 2014; Westhead & Egan, 2015). Narcissism is more likely to relate to reactive aggression in circumstances where the narcissistic egos or goals are under threat (see Case Study 3.1).

Case Study 3.1 Narcissistic personality disorder and serious crime

At the higher end of the spectrum, many of the maladaptive features of narcissism have the potential to lead to disastrous consequences. Narcissism is associated with fantasies of greatness and grandiosity, which often have no grounding in reality. When these fantasies are under threat, a narcissistic individual may act with rage in order to defend their view of the world. Those high on narcissism also seek admiration and success, which they are willing to pursue almost at any cost. Coupled with low empathy, their wish to maintain an unrealistically lavish lifestyle can lead to ruthless exploitation of others. When the grandiose fantasies of a narcissist are not realized, the consequences can be disastrous. Narcissistic rage can lead to violence and even murder.

In the forensic context, individuals who have violated the rights of others will often be assessed by a psychologist for signs of a personality disorder. Those who exhibit signs of grandiosity and entitlement may end up with a diagnosis of Narcissistic Personality Disorder (NPD; see Chapter 2 for more detail). When NPD diagnosis is linked to an aggressive interpersonal violation, the term "narcissistic rage" becomes relevant in understanding the causes of violence. According to psychoanalyst Heinz Kohut (1972), narcissistic rage is characterized by the need for revenge, in order to undo a hurt or righting a wrong. This need is compulsive, and the payback happens at any cost. The cases of murderers who have killed in a narcissistic rage vary from premeditated murders with the motivation of fame and revenge (e.g., many school shooters who attempt to commit mass murders) to murders that happen in a spur of the moment.

The profiles of murderers who have received an NPD diagnosis make interesting, albeit chilling reading. Brad Bushman (2017) has argued that many of the mass shootings in schools in the United States are fuelled by narcissism, desire for fame, and loss of face (e.g., being dumped by a girlfriend, being excluded from school, or experiencing ostracism from other pupils). When analyzing discussions of young people who have callously planned and executed the killing of their peers, the statements sometimes

CASE STUDY 3.1 Narcissistic personality disorder and serious crime—cont'd

closely resemble items from the Narcissistic Personality Inventory (NPI). For instance, the two young boys who shot dead 13 of their classmates in Columbine, US in 1999 were recoded saying, "Isn't it fun to get the respect that we are going to deserve" (NPI item: "I insist upon getting the respect that is due me") and "Directors will be fighting over this story; Tarantino … Spielberg." (NPI item: "I wish someone would someday write my biography"; from Bushman, 2017). Statements like these suggest that in some extreme cases, the narcissistic desire for fame and respect can lead to premeditated mass murders.

Narcissism can also be related to murders that are evidenced by lack of planning. Narcissistic individuals can be driven to explosive rage as a reaction to an event that may pose a threat to their worldview, self-esteem, goals, or reputation. This kind of reactive anger can also be a factor leading to murder, quite different from murders that are carefully premeditated. An example of the perils of narcissistic rage is the case of Brian Blackwell, 18-year-old schoolboy from Liverpool, UK. Blackwell callously stabbed and bludgeoned his elderly parents to death at their family home in 2004 (Weston, 2017).

Blackwell was an academically successful, private school pupil who was the only son of wealthy elderly parents. In the months leading to the murders, Blackwell created a web of lies to entice his girlfriend, claiming that he was internationally known tennis player with millions of pounds to spare. He bought his girlfriend lavish gifts (including a car), took her on expensive holidays, and gave her a job as his personal secretary. In order to fund this lifestyle, he applied for credit cards under his father's name and drew large sums of money out of his parents' bank accounts. When the parents confronted him, trying to stop him from spending more money on taking his girlfriend on a holiday to the United States, he snapped. In an uncontrollable rage, Blackwell bludgeoned his parents with a claw hammer and stabbed them with a carving knife. He then went on a holiday with his girlfriend, leaving the decomposing bodies of his parents in their family home.

Blackwell was later diagnosed as having NPD and is currently serving a life sentence with little hope of being released. His case was the first in the UK where NPD and narcissistic rage were used by the defense, reducing the charge from murder to manslaughter. At the time of the sentencing, the judge recommended that Blackwell should never be released, and when this book was written in 2018, he was still serving a life sentence.

Of course, narcissism and NPD are neither necessary nor sufficient cause of murder. Not everyone who murders is a narcissist, and not every narcissist is a murderer. However, some of those who exhibit high level of narcissism may murder because of the desire for fame, superiority and grandiosity, and narcissistic rage when things don't go according to their plan.

The violent tendencies also transfer to intimate partner violence (IPV) in close relationships. Carton and Egan (2017) investigated psychological and physical abuse, and found that psychopathy had an association with especially psychological abuse. The same pattern was found in a Japanese sample, indicating that psychopathy (rather than Machiavellianism or narcissism) is an important factor predicting abuse that happens within relationships (Kiire, 2017). Taking together the literature on the Dark Triad and aggression, viciousness, and IPV, it would appear that psychopathy is the most relevant out of the three traits, with the potential for criminal acts in terms of physical damage to others.

3.2.2 Self-control

Another important feature that has been consistently connected to crime is impulsivity, characterized by low self-control/self-regulation. According to Gottfredson and Hirschi's (1990) influential theory, crime is mainly caused by the lack of self-control, which is closely related to self-centered narcissism, impulsivity, aggression, and an inability to delay rewards. Gottfredson and Hirchi assert that other factors such as personality are spuriously correlated with crime via lack of self-control. In their view, personality itself does not matter that much. Indeed, it is possible that the Dark Triad–crime link is moderated by self-control (or the lack of it).

Multiple studies have, indeed, found that low self-control is a convincing explanation for proclivity to commit crimes. Interestingly, longitudinal studies by Terrie Moffitt and colleagues (Moffitt et al., 2011) have demonstrated that almost half of those who exhibited lower levels of self-control in childhood were more likely to have received a criminal conviction in adulthood. This would suggest that lack of self-control can lead to a life path where an individual is more vulnerable to crime as an adult.

However, a study by Flexon, Meldrum, and Piquero (2016) cast doubt on the self-control theory of crime. The authors analyzed data from almost 400 young university students, investigating the role of self-control and the Dark Triad in drug abuse and criminal offenses. They found that lack of self-control was a unique predictor of substance use. They also found that both low self-control and high Dark Triad were independent predictors of criminal offending. This suggests that the Dark Triad is not spuriously correlated with offending. Both personality and self-control are important.

Another study examined self-control, delinquency, and the Dark Triad in a sample of high school students from Saudi Arabia (Wright et al., 2017).

Delinquency was measured with questions asking about drug-related behaviors (i.e., use and distribution) and violent delinquency (i.e., use of physical force, threats, or intent to kill or injure). The researchers found that low self-control alone was not enough to explain violent delinquency. More serious, violent behaviors were typical to those who scored high on the composite Dark Triad and low in self-control. Predatory, instrumental violence does not happen just because of lack of the ability to control one's actions, but requires high levels of malevolent personality traits as well.

3.2.3 Deception

Although deceitfulness is not classified as a crime, it is part of an immoral behavioral toolkit that has implications in the criminal context. The Dark Triad has obvious relevance in the domain of deception. Those who have exploitive interpersonal orientation may benefit from other people by telling them lies, which would be in line with the evolutionary predictions derived from the cheater strategy theory. For obvious reasons, lying and lie detection has received a lot of attention in the field of Forensic Psychology. There seems to be an arms race between offenders lying about their crimes and the police, judges, and detectives trying to catch the liars. If the Dark Triad is a successful cheater strategy, it would be expected that individuals high in these traits are proficient liars, and also good at identifying when others are telling lies.

A few years ago, we wanted to investigate the reasons for why people tell lies, and whether these reasons are different in those who score high on the Dark Triad (Jonason, Lyons, Baughman, & Vernon, 2014). Our participants (a diverse internet sample) answered a large number of questions about the frequency of lying, who they told their lies to, and what the motivations were behind telling lies. We found that psychopathy and Machiavellianism (but not narcissism) were related to telling lies more often. Interestingly, previous research has found that a small proportion of people are prolific liars, telling most of the lies (Serota & Levine, 2015), and our results suggest that these compulsive liars could be those who are more psychopathic and Machiavellian. As well as investigating the frequency of lies, we were interested in the motivation for why people tell lies. Although narcissism was associated with lying in order to gain something for the self, and Machiavellianism with small white lies, psychopathy was related to not needing any reason for telling lies. Those who were high in psychopathy were lying habitually, and were happy to lie for no specific motive, but just for the sake of lying. Further evidence for compulsive lying in psychopathy comes from a study that found that psychopathy was associated with positive emotions when telling lies (Baughman, Jonason, Lyons, & Vernon, 2014).

More evidence for the increased propensity to tell lies comes from Azizli et al. (2016), who investigated lies and crimes in over 400 American undergraduate students. Lying was measured with a questionnaire about general lying behavior (e.g., "How often do you lie"?), as well as with two scenarios depicting a high-stakes academic (i.e., plagiarizing an essay) and mating (i.e., lying to current partner about meeting up with ex-partner) contexts. All the Dark Triad traits were independently, positively correlated with deception. Interestingly, in regression analyses, only Machiavellianism emerged as a significant predictor of overall lying, as well as lying in high-stakes academic context. This suggests that those high in Machiavellianism, possessing a scheming, political nature, could be sensitive to the high-stakes context, and behave in a manner that does not jeopardize their future chances of success.

If the Dark Triad (more specifically, Machiavellianism and psychopathy) have a relationship with increased propensity to tell lies, are they successful also in detecting lies? In order to execute a socially exploitive strategy, it would make sense to have a perceptual sensitivity to recognize when other people are being deceitful. The evidence for the Dark Triad and lie detection is conflicting. For instance, there is some indication that those who produce more lies are also more proficient in lie detection – essentially, you can't kid a kidder (Wright, Berry, & Bird, 2012; Wright, Berry, Catmur, & Bird, 2015). Due to the deceptive nature of those who are high on especially Machiavellianism and psychopathy, we would expect that these traits also relate to enhanced ability to detect lies. This is especially important in the criminal context and in individuals who are habitual offenders. According to the "feedback hypothesis," people who commit crimes live in environments where crime is common, and hence, should also be sensitive to the possibility that they will be victims of crime. In order to avoid this, those who have a tendency to commit a crime (i.e., individuals high in the Dark Triad) may also have enhanced sensitivity to detect lies (see Hartwig, Granhag, Strömwall, & Andersson, 2004).

High-stakes, emotional lie situations are an especially interesting area of research. In several studies with students and colleagues, we have used TV appeals for missing people, a context that is both highly emotional, and has a lot on stake. Over the years, I have collected a sample of clips of people who are either lying (i.e., guilty of murder), or telling the truth in front of TV cameras. One example is Stuart Hazell, a British man guilty of murdering the granddaughter of his partner, 12-year-old Tia, in 2012. After hiding her body, he paraded in front of TV cameras, crying fake tears and pleading for the girl to come back home. People are often fooled by the crocodile tears, as many of us are inclined to think that others are, generally speaking, honest and genuine. However, it is possible that those who are more callous and unemotional see right through the crocodile tears.

In one study, we investigated the role of primary and secondary psychopathy in detecting lies in TV appeals. In an online study, we asked people to watch 20 video clips (10 lies, 10 truths), and measured their psychopathy with the 64-item Self-Rated Psychopathy III questionnaire. We found that men who were higher in primary psychopathy were better at detecting lies, whereas women who scored higher on the same trait were marginally worse (Lyons, Healy, & Bruno, 2013). These findings provide some support for the idea that primary psychopathy (also called "successful psychopathy") could facilitate a strategy that aims to gain more status and power, which is adaptive especially for men in terms of increased mating opportunities. Referring back to the forensic context, high primary psychopathy has been shown to be an important factor in business (i.e., white collar) crime. If there is a tendency for deceitfulness at the higher level of business organizations, it would be beneficial for those who are deceitful to recognize the same tendencies in others in order not to be cheated. The worse lie detection in high primary psychopathy women is harder to explain and highlights the need to develop more theories and research to investigate adaptiveness of the Dark Triad for women.

In another study, we explored the three Dark Triad traits (using the 27-item SD-3 measure) and lie detection ability in high-stakes, emotional TV appeals (Lyons, Croft, Fairhurst, Varley, & Wilson, 2017). This time, 347 online participants completed the lie detection tasks and the Dark Triad questionnaire. Interestingly, we found that narcissism in men was correlated with worse, and Machiavellianism in women with better lie detection ability. The lower lie detection ability of high narcissistic men is interesting, and could have a link to viewing others as less worthy, impeding the ability to evaluate the veracity of people's statements. The higher accuracy of Machiavellian women is interesting too, suggesting that cunningness and manipulativeness in women could be adaptive in terms of an increased capacity in seeing through fake tears.

Finally, Wright et al. (2015) investigated the Dark Triad in an interactive laboratory task, where people were asked to lie about their opinions. The authors did not find any relationship between the Dark Triad and ability to tell or detect lies. This echoes the findings by Wissing and Reinhard

(2017), who found that the Dark Triad was not related to lie detection in simulated job interview situation. However, both of these studies were conducted in a low-stakes setting, with little emotions attached to the lies. Overall, detecting lies in a high-stakes, emotional situations is easier, and these are also the context where the Dark Triad has been most relevant with significant findings.

3.3 Dark Triad in the Prison

Much of the research on the Dark Triad (namely, psychopathy and narcissism) has been conducted in prison samples, which does not increase our understanding of how normal personality variation relates to the tendency for criminal behavior in everyday life. However, prison research can aid our knowledge of extreme situations, where offending and levels of the Dark Triad can reach heights far beyond what happens in everyday circumstances. Prison research has focused on aspects such as types of offending, premeditation in the crime, and likelihood of reoffending. Although the Dark Triad plays a role in sexual offending, this will be discussed in more detail in Chapter 4.

The proclivity for aggression in high psychopathy individuals implies that they are more likely to commit violent, interpersonal crimes, varying in severity from homicide to harassment. Indeed, psychopathy played a major role in violent offending in a longitudinal study on young Canadian offenders (McCuish, Corrado, Hart, & DeLisi, 2015). The authors followed the offending paths of males and females from the age of 12 to the age of 28 years, and found that those who were high on "psychopathic personality disturbance" committed repeated violent crimes, but were not more likely to commit nonviolent crimes. This suggests that psychopathy may be more relevant in crimes that involve physical threat to others, but not necessarily in crimes that are directed toward property.

In incarcerated violent offenders, psychopathy plays a clear role in how premeditated the crime is. Murderers who are psychopathic kill in order to achieve a goal; homicides are cold-blooded, premeditated, and not preceded by an affective (e.g., anger) reaction. In comparison, homicides committed by nonpsychopathic offenders are more of a reaction to an event (e.g., anger) and can be classified more as "crimes of passion." This was the focus of research by Woodworth and Porter (2002), who studied a sample of imprisoned Canadian convicted for a homicide. They coded the homicides for how reactive (i.e., lack of planning, impulsivity) and instrumental (i.e., motivated by external goals without affective reaction, such as obtaining drugs, money, sex, or revenge) they were. Their findings were in line with the predictions that stem from the idea of "cold blooded" versus "crime of passion" murders. Psychopathic homicide offenders were more likely to commit their crimes in cold blood, with a clear goal in mind, whereas non-psychopathic offenders murdered because of an emotional reaction to an event, without much planning. Interestingly, the cold-blooded murders were more typical to Factor 1 (cold, callous, and unemotional) than Factor 2 (impulsive, risk-taking) aspects of psychopathy. Rather than investigating psychopathy as a homogenous trait, it may be more useful to consider different aspects of psychopathy separately.

But is it really possible to construct a profile of offending based on different types of psychopathy? Boduszek, Debowska, and Willmott (2017) were interested in understanding how the four-factor model of psychopathy relates to homicide, general violent crimes, property crimes, and white-collar crimes in a large sample of over 1100 adult male prisoners from Poland. They investigated affective responsiveness (i.e., the tendency to use empathy to guide decision making), cognitive responsiveness (i.e., putting oneself in other people's shoes when deciding how to treat them), interpersonal manipulation (i.e., attempting to manipulate others in order to get what one wants), and egocentricity (i.e., putting oneself first when making decisions). They identified four distinctive classes of offenders—those who score low on all aspects of psychopathy ("low psychopathy group," more than 40% of the sample), those who obtained moderate scores on affective/cognitive aspects of psychopathy but were low on other aspects ("moderate affective/cognitive responsiveness group," almost 15% of the sample), those who scored high on interpersonal manipulation but low on other aspects of psychopathy ("high interpersonal manipulation group," just over 20% of the sample), and finally, those who scored high on interpersonal manipulation and egocentricity, and moderate on other aspects of psychopathy ("high psychopathy group," 7.1% of the sample).

When they compared types of offending (using the low psychopathy group as the comparison group), they found interesting patterns. For example, both white-collar criminals and property criminals were more likely to belong to the "high interpersonal manipulation group," which somewhat corresponds with the successful psychopathy idea. Individuals who use manipulation and charm to reap financial benefits from others may achieve high societal status if successful, and imprisonment if they get caught.

Prisoners who were in the "high psychopathy group" were more likely to have a conviction for general violent offending. Boduszek et al. explained this by speculating that they may lack a mechanism that inhibits violence, and resort to offending because of lack of engagement with others (both cognitively and empathetically), coupled with a selfish drive to gratify one's own interests. However, this group of prisoners was in the minority. Interestingly, the findings are contrary to some previous research, and indicate that most prisoners in both maximum and medium security prison units do not classify for the criteria for psychopathy diagnoses.

As well as having an association with different types of crimes, the Dark Triad may influence versatility as a criminal. Edwards, Albertson, and Verona (2017) explored the roles of the Dark Triad and Vulnerable Dark Triad (VDT, see Chapter 2). VDT consists of high anxiety, impulsivity, and attachment issues, predisposing the individual for psychopathology. Dark Triad, in turn, is comprised of callous, unemotional, and manipulative predisposition, coupled with grandiose ideas of one's own success. Edwards and colleagues found that in an offender sample, callousness aspect of the Dark Triad related to versatility as a criminal, suggesting that individuals were more likely to commit crimes of all types. VDT, in turn, was associated only to drug offenses and nonplanned property crimes (e.g., thefts and robberies). Violent crimes (e.g., murder and assault) were uniquely related only to the Dark Triad.

Psychopathy has also been related to higher likelihood of reoffending. Próspero-Luis et al. (2017) in a sample of currently incarcerated prisoners, intentions to reoffend (i.e., commit a theft) related to higher psychopathy scores, and that this was because those high on psychopathy had a reduced expectancy of negative outcomes, and increased expectancy of positive outcomes as a result of committing another theft when released from the prison.

Although the prison literature points at the role of psychopathy as a predictor for offending, it is good to keep in mind that not all high psychopathy individuals commit crimes, and not all of those who are in prison for criminal activity are high in psychopathy. Crime is a complicated, multifaceted, and heterogeneous area of research, and as with most psychology research, there are no simple explanations for why crime happens.

3.4 Dark Triad and Crime in the Community

As important as it is to understand extreme manifestations of criminality, it is also imperative to consider the links between personality and more subtle, everyday behaviors of rule-breaking and delinquency. Not every misconduct leads to prison, and most of minor criminal acts are likely to go undetected and/or unpunished. Indeed, everyday small misconduct can skew official crime statistics, leading to a gross underestimation of crime. Or, to borrow a quote from Buonanno, Drago, Galbiati, and Vertova (2014), "by its very nature, crime is a hidden phenomenon and official statistics may not record crime rates correctly because of measurement errors or misreporting" (p. 1). Understanding the personality correlates of criminal tendencies is important and can be useful in tackling the problem of hidden crime.

Minor misconduct comes in many forms, including drug abuse, theft, violence, plagiarism, reckless driving, and vandalism (Nathanson, Paulhus, & Williams, 2006). The terminology used to describe small crimes includes delinquency (minor offenses, often performed by young people), antisocial behavior (acting in a way that causes nuisance to others), and misconduct (acting in an improper manner). In this chapter, I will use the word "delinquency" when talking about minor crimes and antisocial behaviors in people who have not been convicted and imprisoned.

There has been some research interest in the role of the Dark Triad in overall delinquency. Behaviors that break rules and laws (e.g., drug use/dealing, vandalism, assaults), but at levels that are so low they are unlikely to be reported to the police, are typical to individuals at the higher end of the Dark Triad spectrum. Generally, findings from community samples seem to mirror those of the prison research. In groups of people who have low levels of offending (e.g., students), psychopathy has emerged as the most relevant predictor of delinquency.

Henri Chabrol and his team have explored the Dark Tetrad (Dark Triad + sadism) and criminality in young people in France. In an earlier study, they investigated delinquent behaviors in 615 underaged high school students, and found that psychopathy and sadism related to more delinquent acts, but only in boys (Chabrol, Van Leeuwen, Rodgers, & Séjourné, 2009). In another piece of research, the team sampled over 500 young adult college students, a population that traditionally has low levels of crime (Chabrol, Bouvet, & Goutaudier, 2017). In a similar way to the earlier adolescent sample, psychopathy and sadism were positive predictors of antisocial behavior. Similar findings have been replicated by other research teams from other countries. In Netherlands, Muris, Meesters, and Timmermans (2013) gave 12- to 18-year-old children and their parents questionnaires on the Dark Triad, aggression, and delinquency. Again, when the shared variance between the three traits was statistically controlled, psychopathy was the only significant predictor of parent-reported aggression and delinquency.

Chabrol et al. (2017) suggested that sample characteristics (i.e., relatively wealthy college students) could explain the lack of relationship with delinquency, and two other Dark Tetrad traits, narcissism and Machiavellianism. This underscores the more generic problem with research on personality and crime—most of it is conducted either in people who have received a conviction, or in people from middle-class backgrounds. Perhaps delinquency is related to Machiavellianism and narcissism too, but in people who live in more impoverished environment. Socioeconomic status, and how people perceive their place in the society (i.e., subjective status) is important in unethical behavior, aggression, and personality traits such as narcissism (e.g., Dubois, Rucker, & Galinsky, 2015; Greitemeyer & Sagioglou, 2016). For example, criminality is something that potentially leads to increased status (e.g., more money or respect), and individuals who strive for status could be more inclined to use crime in achieving it. It is clear that the Dark Triad (and psychology research more generally) needs to branch out to study individuals from all echelons of society, not just those who are from middle-class backgrounds.

As well as focusing on the general tendency to commit delinquent acts, more specific aspects of delinquency warrant further attention. We know that low-level, unreported thefts are very common within families, workplaces, and businesses, but the majority of these petty crimes are never reported to the police. In fact, many of them may even go unnoticed by the victims of the crime. Taking the relationship between the Dark Triad and overall disingenuous, unethical behaviors, the constellation is highly relevant in trying to understand who the people are who commit small thievery.

Some years ago, we examined everyday small, petty crimes in a student and community sample of over 250 individuals (Lyons & Jonason, 2015). We asked our participants a range of questions, including whether they have ever stolen anything, how often they steal, do they plan the thefts in advance, and who they steal from. Participants who reported having ever stolen something were higher in dysfunctional impulsivity, Machiavellianism, and primary and secondary psychopathy than those who had not stolen. Fig. 3.1 illustrates nicely the differences between high and low Dark Triad individuals in stealing (high and low groups were determined by using the "median split" method). Especially secondary psychopathy (risk-taking and impulsivity) related to more versatile thieving behavior. Those high in secondary psychopathy stole more frequently, stole from strangers and shops, and, interestingly, were also more likely to plan the event of the theft. When we asked what the motivations for thieving was, people high in secondary psychopathy were more likely to steal because they did not have money or food. Thus secondary psychopathy could have an association with small thefts that are related to the need to acquire more resources, rather than stealing for thrill-seeking and fun.

A different picture emerged with regards to primary psychopathy and Machiavellianism. We found a negative correlation between primary psychopathy and stealing because of lack of money, and a near-significant positive correlation with stealing for fun. This indicates that when those who score high on primary psychopathy steal, it is not because they need to get more resources, but because they get enjoyment out of the act. We also asked the participants about how frequently they would steal if there was no

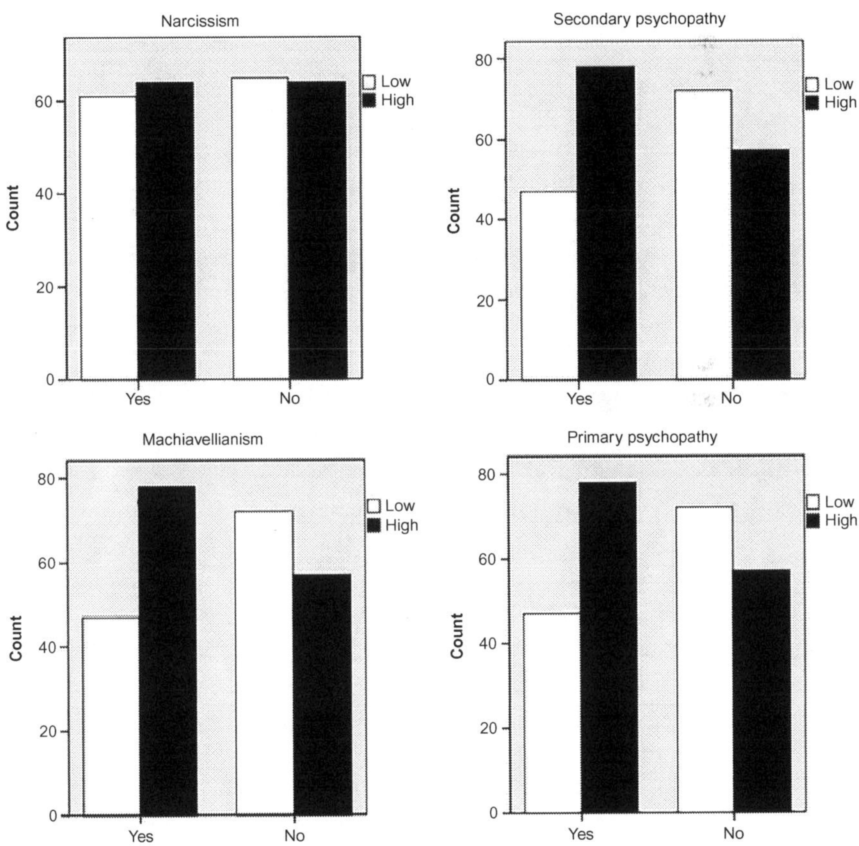

Fig. 3.1 High and low Dark Triad and responses to a question "Have you ever stolen anything". *(Data adapted from Lyons and Jonason (2015)).*

risk of getting caught. Machiavellianism and primary psychopathy were positively related to more frequent thefts if the risk was removed. Perhaps those high in primary psychopathy and Machiavellianism would be happy to commit crimes, but the risk of getting caught acts as a deterrent. Interestingly, those high in primary psychopathy were convicted for stealing marginally more than those high in secondary psychopathy in a community sample of young Finnish men (Drislane et al., 2014). When people high on primary psychopathy claim that getting caught is a deterrent for stealing, it does not necessarily stop from stealing and getting caught.

Another study that looked at misconduct in terms of self-reported crime also found that psychopathy (but not narcissism or Machiavellianism) had a relationship with self-reported crime, both minor and serious (Azizli et al., 2016). The authors gave their undergraduate student participants a questionnaire called "Comprehensive Misconduct Inventory," which has a battery of questions asking how many times the person has engaged in behaviors such as hard/soft drug abuse, minor or serious criminality, driving offenses, bullying/harassment, or acting against authorities. The correlational analyses indicated that all the Dark Triad traits were relevant in most of the categories of misconduct, although Machiavellianism and narcissism lacked an association with hard drug use, and narcissism did not relate to bullying and harassment. When the authors conducted regression analyses, controlling for the shared variance between the traits, psychopathy came out as the only significant predictor of higher frequency of drug abuse and criminality.

As well as predicting violent crimes in incarcerated populations, the Dark Triad has received some interest in violent offending in student samples. Violence (especially that of sexual nature) is unfortunately a common phenomenon and could be perpetrated by students with higher levels of socially aversive personality traits. Fix and Fix (2015) used a sample of young undergraduate men in studying the links between psychopathy and different types of offending. They found that psychopathy was positively related to committing violent crimes, property crimes, and drug-related offenses. The findings suggest that university students high in psychopathy have similar types of criminal proclivities as convicted criminals, the only difference being that the students have not been caught and imprisoned.

In another study using a military sample, Drislane et al. (2014) tested the three-factor (i.e., boldness, meanness, and disinhibition) model of psychopathy in a large sample of young men enrolled in military service in Finland. As a quick reminder from Chapter 1, boldness is characterized by the willingness to dominate others, venturesomeness, and emotional resilience, whereas meanness is about cruelty, use of aggression, and lack of empathy. Boldness and meanness are also considered as components of successful psychopathy. Disinhibition is about impulsivity, lack of patience, and irresponsible behaviors, similar to secondary psychopathy in the two-factor model. The authors were able to distinguish two different types of high psychopathy classes in their sample—primary (high boldness and low anxiety) and secondary (high disinhibition and high anxiety). The authors had access to the Finnish Police Crime Register and were able to access their criminal records. They looked at the information on crimes committed by high primary and secondary psychopathy groups, comparing them to the group consisting of low psychopathy participants. Both psychopathy groups were more likely to have registered offenses, including drunk driving and other traffic crimes, violence, stealing, vandalism, and property crimes. However, when comparing the differences between types of crime in primary and secondary psychopathy groups, only one was found. Individuals in the primary psychopathy group were much more likely to have committed a violent crime (including assaults and robberies) than those in the secondary psychopathy group.

In summary, studies utilizing nonprison samples have found that there is a small proportion of population "at large" in the community, presenting high levels of psychopathy. Across several studies on diverse nationalities, rather than Machiavellianism and narcissism, psychopathy is emerging as the driving force behind the connections with delinquency and different types of crimes. In a similar manner as in incarcerated populations, primary psychopathy is one of the most important factors in criminality in student and community samples. Primary psychopathy is especially related to crimes that are of a violent and instrumental nature (e.g., robberies and assaults). It is possible that the low empathy and selfishness associated with high primary psychopathy can lead to using violence as a tool for gaining financial benefits to oneself.

3.5 White-Collar Crime

Dr. C, born 1948, was a psychiatrist who became famous through his selfless effort in a disaster during a military peacetime exercise. He figured for many years as a trusted specialist of his field in the media. A journalist from a finance newspaper exposed that Dr. C. had a blooming business selling fake medical certificates to criminals, which helped them avoid legal persecution of various kinds. The court found Dr. C. guilty and ruled that he should lose his license to ever issue medical certificates again. Dr. C. also acquired his heroic status before engaging in crime, which only served the purpose of increasing his income (Arnulf, & Gottschalk, 2013, p. 107).

This case study example from Norway illustrates the type of crimes that involve the abuse of one's position or status with the purpose of boosting own income.

"White-collar" or "economic" crime refers to professional, nonviolent criminal acts performed in order to get financial benefits. White-collar crimes include bribery, money laundering, identity thefts, cybercrime, Ponzi schemes, embezzlement, and environmental crimes. Economic crimes are very common, and it is estimated that almost half of larger companies in Europe have been victims of crime leading to financial damage (see Blickle, Schlegel, Fassbender, & Klein, 2006). According to Gottschalk (2018), white-collar criminals belong to the "elites" of the society who have gained enough trust to be given a position of power in an organization. White-collar criminals include business entrepreneurs, managers, heads of department, professionals such as doctors and lawyers, as well as people who invest in markets.

Generally, both the public and law enforcement officers perceive white-collar crime as less serious than other types of crime, probably because it does not have obvious associations with interpersonal violence. However, the idea that white-collar criminals are gentler and kinder offenders is a dangerous myth, and there is evidence that if needed, they can turn to "red" collar. White-collar criminals have been known to commit murders, often in order to hide their financially motivated crime (Alalehto & Azarian, 2018; Perri, 2011). Further, the perceptions of white-collar criminals may depend on their personality traits, especially psychopathy. In a mock jury sentencing experiment, white-collar criminals that were perceived as psychopathic (especially high in callousness) received longer sentences (Rulseh, Edens, & Cox, 2017). Although the jury sentencing is not telling us whether psychopathy leads to white-collar crimes, it does underscore the willingness to punish business criminals who are perceived as psychopathic.

There is scant research into white-collar criminals. This was noticed by Babiak, Neumann, and Hare (2010), who stated that "... there is a dearth of empirical data on the role of psychopathy in fraud, corruption, malfeasance, and other egregious violations of the public trust. This is unfortunate, particularly if we take the view that corruption and financial disasters can be as much the fault of individuals as they are of impersonal economic and social forces. We need research in this area" (p. 175). Despite this statement, there is surprisingly little research into personality factors associated with the propensity to misuse one's occupational position in order to commit a financially motivated crime. There are isolated studies, some of which have utilized nonprison samples, asking about their perceptions of crime, and others that have investigated white-collar criminals who have been imprisoned.

One study that looked at incarcerated white-collar criminals and their neurobiological characteristics indicated superiority in information processing, which could give an advantage in committing financial offenses in the workplace (Raine et al., 2012). This taps into the successful psychopathy idea, highlighting the possibility of cold, manipulative "evil geniuses," striving to get to, or maintain a high position of power by any means necessary, including committing financial crimes on their way to the top. The Dark Triad's associations with deceitfulness and hunger for money, power, and status make it a likely personality constellation relevant in white-collar crimes.

Gerhard Blickle et al. (2006) studied 76 prisoners in Germany, who had committed white-collar crimes, comparing them to 150 managers in companies. The white-collar criminals were mainly men who were in prison for bribery, counterfeiting, embezzlement, forgery, fraud, fraudulent bankruptcy, smuggling, and tax evasion. The business criminals scored high on hedonism, narcissism, and interestingly, also conscientiousness. Hedonists are individuals who crave for material things and instant gratification of their needs, something that is typical to high Dark Triad individuals. Coupled with narcissistic fantasies of greatness and success, hedonism can influence the proclivity to steal money from the company the manager is working for.

In another study, Boduszek et al. (2017) investigated psychopathy in different offender samples, including those who were convicted for homicides, general violent crimes, property crime, and white-collar offenses. Those who scored high on overall psychopathy were more likely to be in prison for general violent offending. However, those who were convicted for white-collar and property crimes were more likely to have high scores on the interpersonal manipulation facet of psychopathy. These results provide further support for the idea that white-collar criminals have characteristics of "successful psychopathy," manipulation without problems with impulse control.

Lingnau, Fuchs, and Dehne-Niemann (2017) used a vignette design in order to find out whether those who score high on psychopathy are more accepting of two common financial crimes—accounting fraud and insider trading. Accounting fraud consists of falsifying financial information of a company in order to create a façade of good financial health. Insider trading is a crime that involves using confidential information in one's own advantage when trading on the stock exchange. They found that those who scored high on coldheartedness and Machiavellian egocentricity were more accepting of insider trading, and coldheartedness was a significant positive predictor of acceptance of accounting fraud. The authors suggested that those who endorse these crimes are more likely to commit it themselves too, indicating that corporate crime is committed by those who are selfish, lack remorse, and have no empathy for others.

3.6 Conclusion

The Dark Triad is a prime candidate for personality traits that are relevant in understanding why people commit crimes. The antagonistic, selfish core of the triad influences involvement in a large number of antisocial and criminal activities, ranging from drug offenses to assaults, robberies, property thefts, and white-collar crimes. Psychopathy is the darkest of the three traits, showing consistent associations with crime across different studies in prison and well as community and student samples. Although there is less research investigating the Dark Triad and involvement in white-collar crimes, the existing data speaks for the importance of psychopathy in business and workplace criminal activity.

Further Reading

Arnulf, J. K., & Gottschalk, P. (2013). Heroic leaders as white-collar criminals: an empirical study. *Journal of Investigative Psychology and Offender Profiling*, *10*, 96–113.

Boduszek, D., Debowska, A., & Willmott, D. (2017). Latent profile analysis of psychopathic traits among homicide, general violent, property, and white-collar offenders. *Journal of Criminal Justice*, *51*, 17–23.

Lyons, M., & Jonason, P. K. (2015). Dark triad, tramps, and thieves. *Journal of Individual Differences*, *36*, 215–220.

Bushman, B. J. (2017). Narcissism, fame seeking, and mass shootings. *American Behavioral Scientist*.

Kohut, H. (1972). Thoughts on narcissism and narcissistic rage. *The Psychoanalytic Study of the Child*, *27*(1), 360–400.

Weston, A. (2017). New documentary sheds light on shocking case of killer schoolboy Brian Blackwell. https://www.liverpoolecho.co.uk/news/liverpool-news/new-documentary-sheds-light-shocking-12899520.

CHAPTER FOUR

Mating Strategies (Mate Competition, Mate Attraction, and Established Relationships)

Chapter Outline

4.1 Introduction

Try a little exercise. Type in on an internet search engine the words "Am I dating ...?." The top options that come up are "... a sociopath," "... a narcissist," and "... a psychopath." The internet is littered with pages offering quizzes and advice on how to spot signs of psychopathy and narcissism in new dating partners. On the other hand, there also are multitudes of sites giving advice on how to survive in the aftermath of a relationship breakup with a narcissist or a psychopath. For example, websites like lovefraud.com has discussion forum posts from thousands of men and women who have fallen victims of exploitative, predatory partners. The Dark Triad has such a monumental influence on romantic relationships that it has become the

https://doi.org/10.1016/B978-0-12-814291-2.00004-8

focus of documentaries, films, self-help books, and internet sites, as well as a mushrooming of academic research.

The Dark Triad has been studied perhaps most extensively in the context of mating behavior. A wealth of research has investigated these traits in relation to different aspects of sex and relationships, including relationship preferences, promiscuity, tactics for attracting partners and repulsing rivals, relationship functioning (including aggression and infidelity), and so on. The key message from these studies is that the Dark Triad is associated with a preference for short-term, casual relationships, and higher likelihood of dysfunctional romantic relationships. These detached, promiscuous mating strategies could have a function in promoting a fast life history strategy. In this chapter, I will provide an overview of theories and empirical literature on the Dark Triad with regards to mating psychology and behaviors.

4.2 Preference for Types of Romantic Relationships and Partner Characteristics

When it comes to love and romance, individuals high in the Dark Triad continuum have distinctively different relationship preferences from those who exhibit lower levels of the traits. Socially aversive personalities often have short, emotionally shallow relationships, characterized by avoidance of commitment to single long-term partners. Interestingly, research has found that those high in psychopathy (Jonason, Lyons, & Bethell, 2014) and Machiavellianism (Brewer, Bennett, Davdison et al., 2018) have avoidant attachment styles, which entails feeling content without close social bonds. It is possible that avoidant attachment style evident in psychopathy and Machiavellianism is an adaptive mechanism enabling short-term relationships, which could be a feature of a fast life history strategy discussed in Chapter 1.

Studies on mating strategies and the Dark Triad have found other features that link the Dark Triad, especially psychopathy, to the pursuit of fast life history strategy. For instance, psychopathy is related to increased sex drive (Baughman, Jonason, Veselka, & Vernon, 2014), which could be a proximate facilitator of a fast strategy. In men, high sex drive, coupled with the willingness to have many partners with little commitment, could lead to multiple matings and potential conceptions. Indeed, research has found that the Dark Triad is connected to unrestricted sociosexual orientation, which entails an interest for multiple partners and sex without commitment (Jonason, Li, Webster, & Schmitt, 2009; Nascimento, Hanel, Monteiro, Gouveia, & Little, 2018). Some researchers have suggested that the Dark

Triad is adaptive for men in the pursuit of multiple sexual partners, claiming less adaptive significance of these traits for women (Jonason et al., 2009).

However, there is a pressing need for theories to accommodate the findings in women into evolutionary framework. The Dark Triad is linked to overall high sexual desire and preference for recreational sex in women too (Carter, Campbell, & Muncer, 2014; Jauk et al., 2016). Dark Triad women mate promiscuously, and specifically psychopathy and Machiavellianism are related to a fast life history cross-culturally, irrespective of biological sex (Jonason, Girgis, & Milne-Home, 2017). Women could gain multiple reproductive benefits from promiscuous mating, including "shopping" for good genes outside their partnership, acquiring resources, or finding a suitable long-term partner. It is obvious that high levels of the Dark Triad are not confided to men, but there is a need for incorporating theories for understanding women too.

Most studies that have proposed the Dark Triad as an adaptive fast life history strategy have used sex drive and number of matings as a proxy for reproductive success. There is less research investigating whether the Dark Triad is related to actual mating success in terms of increased number of offspring. Together with Greg Carter and Gayle Brewer, I explored the associations between the Dark Triad and existing children in an online sample of 314 participants (Carter, Lyons, & Brewer, 2018). We found that narcissistic men had more children, and psychopathy in both sexes had an association with fewer children. This is an interesting discovery, as it seems that the sex drive and multiple matings do not translate into higher number of children in psychopathic individuals. It is possible that the adaptiveness of multiple sexual partners (and possible conceptions) is offset by reduced fertility due to increased risk of sexually transmitted diseases. Narcissism has been suggested as an adaptive short-term mating strategy (Holtzman & Strube, 2011) and seems certainly to be beneficial for men in terms of increased number of offspring.

What kind of characteristics do Dark Triad individuals look for in a romantic partner, and do these characteristics differ between short- and long-term relationships? There have been a handful of studies on this topic. The key idea is that especially high Dark Triad men, who have a distinctively opportunistic, indiscriminating mating style, may be less demanding especially in casual relationships. Women should still exert some choice, as any relationship has a risk of pregnancy for women. Thus it would be expected that the Dark Triad is related to choosiness in mate selection in women, favoring traits that indicate resources, support, or good genes.

In a sample of women from Iran, Atari and Chegeni (2017) asked participants to rate the desired characteristics when choosing a mate. They found that narcissistic women were most choosy, demanding everything from prospective partners: status, resources, attractiveness, education, and intelligence. Machiavellianism was not related to any of the mate choice preferences, and psychopathy had a negative association with a preference for religiosity and kindness. Jonason, Valentine, Li, and Harbeson (2011) looked at importance of several mate characteristics in both long- and short-term contexts, and found that psychopathy related to reduced importance of kindness in both contexts. Narcissism associated with most demands in long-term relationships, where traits such as sociability and physical attractiveness were rated as important. In another study, Ináncsi, Láng, and Bereczkei (2016) investigated Machiavellianism and the important of several characteristics in an ideal mate. They found that Machiavellian men and women did not value warmth-trustworthiness or intimacy and loyalty. However, they did think that ideal partner's possession of status and resources is important. This reflects the long-term manipulative nature of high Machiavellian individuals, who could use the resources of the partner in increasing their own social standing.

4.3 Intra- and Intersexual Strategies

There are several features and behavioral tactics that individuals can use to enhance their success over other members of their own sex in acquiring partners. These fall within the umbrella of Sexual Selection theory, which can be further divided into intrasexual (i.e., within-sex) or intersexual (i.e., between-sex) strategies. It is common that in mammalian species with internal fertilization, males cannot be certain of their paternity, which negatively influences their investment in offspring that may not be genetically related to them. Males can increase their reproductive success, passing on their genes to the next generation, by acquiring multiple mating partners. Females, in turn, can always be sure that the children they give birth to are genetically related to them, and it makes sense to provide parental care in order to ensure the survival and future reproduction of their offspring. Therefore in many species with internal fertilization, females are more selective than males when choosing a mating partner. Female choice can be directed toward indicators of genetic quality in the male (which would be passed on to the offspring), and/or indicators of good resources or provision of parenting. In mammalian species, the common pattern is male-

male competition for sexual access to females, and female choice for good genes and/or provision.

However, in species such as humans where males do provide paternal care, competition for suitable male partners occurs between females too, and males can be choosy when selecting a long-term partner. Indeed, the boundaries between these different forces of selection are blurred, and inter- and intrasexual strategies are not mutually exclusive. For example, two young men engaged in a fight in front of young women may not only get access to the women (male-male competition), but the winner of the fight could be actively chosen as a partner by the women (female choice).

In humans, both male-male and female-female intrasexual competition are common and play an especially important role in individuals who have heightened short-term mating interests. Intrasexual strategies are those that are employed when individuals are competing among the members of their own sex for access to the opposite sex. These strategies can vary from subtle (e.g., spreading malicious gossip of the rival) to more visible (e.g., physical combat between the rivals). Overall, women are more likely than men to employ subtle strategies, including indirect aggression.

Intersexual selection usually takes the form on female choice and can lead to fancy displays such as the male paradise bird courting dance, and colorful features such as the tail of a peacock in males. It is possible that females choose these characteristics because they show something about the genetic quality of the male (i.e., the good genes hypothesis). In humans, the evolution of long-term pair-bonds has exerted intersexual evolutionary pressures on women too. For example, the use of epigamic displays such as makeup enhances the perceptions of youthfulness and fertility, which is important for male reproductive fitness in a long-term bond. If a male settles in a pair-bond with one female, it is crucial that the female is fertile and capable of reproduction. Epigamic displays enhancing youthfulness and fertility are utilized by women both in attracting a partner (intersexual selection) and competing with a rival (intrasexual selection). Another form of intersexual selection is not based on choice, but on conflict between the sexes. Sexual harassment and coercion are common in the animal kingdom, and it is usually perpetrated by males targeting female victims. Coercive strategies are common both within established relationship, and between acquaintances and strangers. In the following sections, I will give a brief overview of the current research on inter- and intrasexual strategies in relation to the Dark Triad, with a specific focus on courting behaviors.

4.3.1 Attractiveness

Possessing features that the opposite sex finds attractive confers obvious benefits in partner selection. For men, attractive features are those that indicate fertility and fidelity of the partner (e.g., youthfulness and estrogen-related traits). Women, in turn, may find features that indicate wealth and status attractive, due to the influence of resources in survival and success of the offspring. Research regarding the attractiveness of high Dark Triad individuals has contradicting findings and has focused largely on investigating women's choice for high Dark Triad features in men.

What seems to be typical of the Dark Triad (especially narcissism) is the relationship with superficial charm, which is often considered appealing after a short exposure (e.g., Holtzman & Strube, 2010). However, in the long term, the initial charm evaporates, resulting in a low desirability of narcissistic individuals as serious partners. The short-term appeal supports the idea that the Dark Triad is adaptive as a cheater strategy, geared toward immediate exploitation of resources, including mating partners.

In a meta-analysis, Holtzman and Strube (2010) found a small but consistent relationship between narcissism and ratings of attractiveness across a number of studies. It is possible that the association between physical attractiveness and narcissism is based on effective self-enhancement; increasing ones appeal by cosmetics, hairstyle, clothing, and fitness. Another possibility for initial attractiveness is overconfidence. Research has found that confident individuals are perceived as attractiveness in dating vignettes (Murphy et al., 2015), and overconfidence is one of the features typical of narcissism. Interestingly, findings on the attractiveness of the Dark Triad traits during initial encounters are somewhat conflicting, and the outcome seems to depend partially on the method that is used for research. Table 4.1 summarizes some of the research looking at all the Dark Triad traits together in terms of perceived attractiveness or desirability as a long- or short-term mate.

Much of the research on attractiveness has utilized vignettes, dating adverts, video-stimulus, or still photographs. There are less studies that have looked at real-life interactions between people, with a few notable exceptions. A study that investigated dynamics of German speed-daters found that those who scored high on narcissism were rated as more desirable as long- and short-term partners (Jauk et al., 2016). Interestingly, narcissism was also associated with extraversion and physical attractiveness. It is possible that women in this study liked narcissistic men because these men are also

Table 4.1 Attractiveness of DT

Study	*N* (Men/Women)	Method	Participant Context	Narc	Psy	Mach	DT
Brewer, Carter, et al. (2018)	0/96	Facial morphs	Alcohol administration, ST	–	–	–	n/a
Brewer, Carter, et al. (2018)	0/356	Facial morphs	Sensation seeking, LT, ST	LT–ST –	LT–ST –	LT–ST –	n/a
Lyons et al. (2015)	0/1758	Facial morphs	LT, ST	LT–ST –	LT–ST –	LT–ST –	n/a
Marcinkowska et al. (2016)	0/2370	Facial morphs	N of children ST, LT	LT–ST–	LT–ST –	LT–ST –	n/a
Lyons and Blanchard (2016)	0/564	Facial morphs	Assortative mating, LT, ST	LT–ST–	LT–ST –	LT–ST –	n/a
Lyons and Simeonov (2016)	0/365	Facial morphs	Resource scarcity, LT, ST	LT–ST –	LT–ST –	LT–ST –	n/a
Jonason, Lyons, and Blanchard (2015)	177/159	Vignettes	LT, ST	ST+ (W)LT –	ST+LT –	ST+LT –	n/a
Carter et al. (2014)	0/129	Vignettes	n/a	n/a	n/a	n/a	+
Jauk et al. (2016)	44/46	Speed dating	n/a	ST+LT+	ST+(M)	none	

Narc = Narcissism, Psy = Psychopathy, Mach = Machiavellianism, PP = Primary Psychopathy, SP = Secondary Psychopathy DT = Composite Dark Triad, attractiveness, LT = Long-Term relationship, ST = Short-Term relationship, M = men's preference, W = women's preference, – = negative preference, + = positive preference, n/a = the trait was not investigated, none = no relationship.
The results are not taking into account the context of the study, but reports and overall preferences when other variables are excluded.

extraverted, and that male speed-daters preferred narcissistic women because these women were also physically attractive. Thus there is a possibility that in short-term encounters, it is not narcissism that is preferred, but other aspects that relate to it. Another interesting experiment looked at how the mating success of men varying in the Dark Triad traits could be influenced by weather conditions, namely, whether it was a dark/cloudy or a bright/sunny day. In this field experiment, men were approaching women on the street during different weather conditions while being observed by researchers. The experiment found that men high in Machiavellianism profited from being shrouded in the veil of darkness, having more success in obtaining women's phone numbers in cloudy weather (Rauthmann, Kappes, & Lanzinger, 2014). These studies are few examples investigating how Dark Triad traits influence attraction and mating success in more ecologically valid settings.

Other aspect that influences attractiveness of potential partners is similarity (also known as "assortative mating" or "likes attract" hypotheses). Research has shown that established couples who are more similar in their personality traits also report more marital satisfaction (e.g., Russell & Wells, 1991). It would be expected that initial attraction is related to similarity in personality in courting situations, including a preference for a partner with similar levels of the Dark Triad (Kardum, Hudek-knezevic, Schmitt, & Covic, 2017). We investigated the role of similarity in a vignette study (Jonason, Lyons, & Blanchard, 2015). In this research, we created vignettes, manipulating the characteristics of the person so that they appeared to be either high or low in each of the three traits. We asked participants to rate the attractiveness of the vignettes as short-term mates, asking about how physically attractive and desirable as a one-night stand the vignettes were viewed. In addition to this, we also asked about how desirable the people depicted in the vignettes were as long-term partners, someone who the participant may want to marry or have children with. Fig. 4.1 shows how women rated the men's dating vignettes in different relationship contexts, and Table 4.2 contains example vignettes, and the preference of both sexes for the high and low vignettes.

When the participant's own Dark Triad scores were not taken into account, the high psychopathy and Machiavellian vignettes were rated as more desirable one-night stands by both sexes. However, the low adverts were viewed as more attractive, and they were also preferred as long-term partners, and the same patterns were found for both men and women. In summary, both men and women think that high Dark Triad partners are less

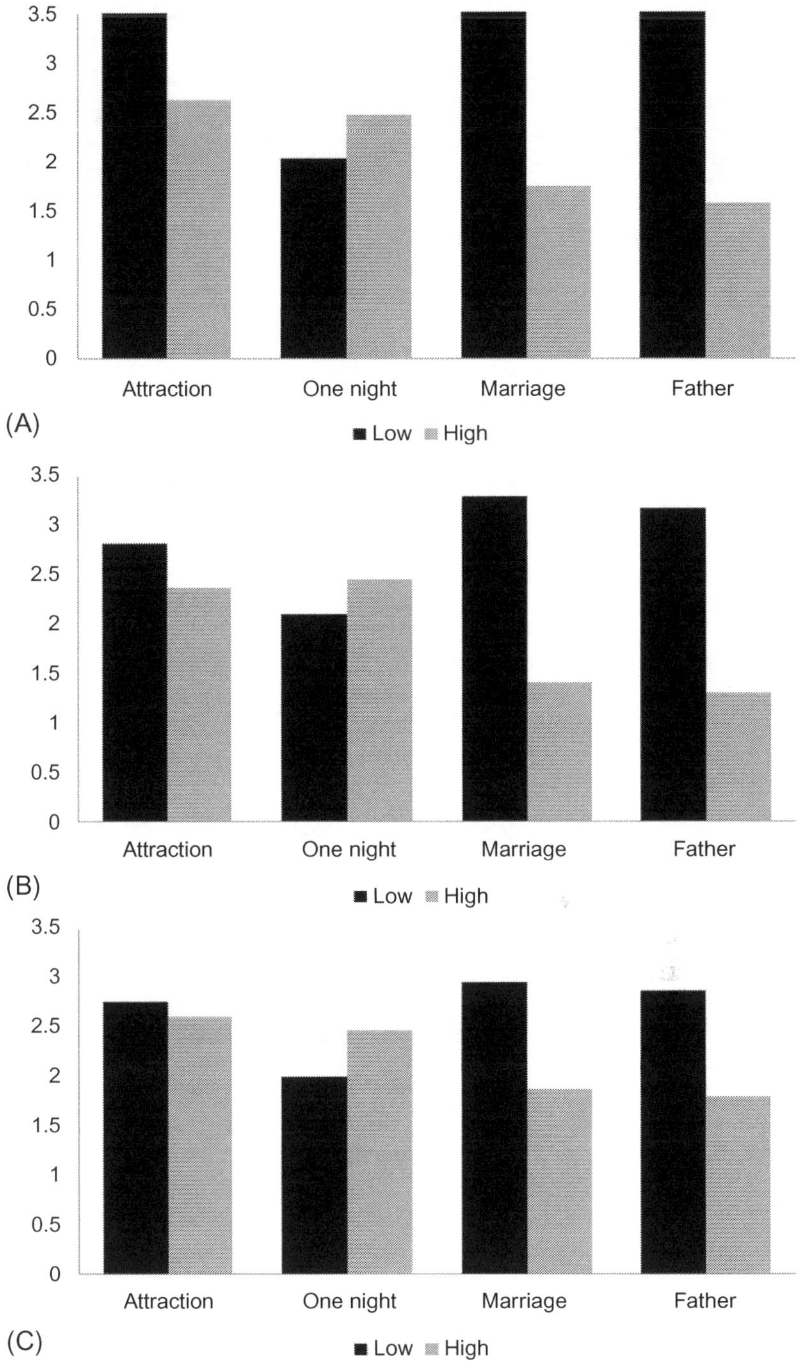

Fig. 4.1 Women's preference for high and low Dark Triad men's dating vignettes. (A) Mean ratings for high and low Machiavellian males. (B) Mean ratings for high and low psychopathy males. (C) Mean ratings for high and low narcissistic males. *(Figures reproduced from data presented in Jonason, Lyons, and Blanchard (2015))*

Table 4.2 Summary of short- and long-term preferences for Dark Triad vignettes

Example Vignette	Men's Short-Term Preference	Men's Long-Term Preference	Women's Short-Term Preference	Women's Long-Term Preference
Low psychopathy Someone who plays it safe and plans for the future. S/he feels it is very important to delay gratification today to get what s/he wants and needs in the future. S/he enjoys stability over all things.	Low more attractive	Low more desirable as a wife	Low more desirable as a husband	Low more desirable as a husband
High psychopathy Impulsive, a sensation-seeker, and someone who lives in the "now". S/he enjoys risky activities where s/he can get a rush like driving fast, drinking alcohol, and partying. S/he abhors monotony and changes jobs often.	High more desirable as one-night stand	Low more desirable as a mother of children	Low more desirable as a father of children	Low more desirable as a father of children
Low Machiavellian A person who is a team player. S/he enjoys being a small cog in a large machine, and claims s/he always speaks the truth. S/he would never say something he doesn't believe just to get ahead of the crowd.	Low more attractive	Low more desirable as a wife	Low more desirable as a wife	Low more desirable as a husband
High Machiavellian A person who is not afraid to offend a few people on his way. S/he speaks his/her mind but also says s/he's happy to	High more desirable as one-night stand	Low more desirable as a mother of children	Low more desirable as a mother of children	Low more desirable as a father of children

conceal some truths if beneficial in the long run. S/he is someone who could talk his/her way out of any situation by using charm and flattery.				
Low narcissistic A person who is not interested in new advertisements or fashions. S/he thinks s/he is no better or worse than other people, and that s/he would prefer to blend in with the crowd rather than stand out. S/he is essentially a modest person.	No differences in attractiveness	Low more desirable as a wife	No differences in attractiveness	Low more desirable as a husband
High narcissistic A person who is very assertive and rarely depends on others to get things done. S/he likes to be complemented and likes to look at him/herself in the mirror. S/he likes starting new fashions rather than simply following them.	No differences in desirability as one-night stand	Low more desirable as a mother of children	No differences in desirability as one-night stand	Low more desirable as a father of children

Reproduced from Jonason, Lyons, and Blanchard (2015)

attractive and less suitable for marriage or parenting than low Dark Triad partners are. However, high Dark Triad partners may be more desirable as one-night stands, possibly because they may be more exciting than those with lower levels of the traits.

We also asked our participants to complete questionnaires on the Dark Triad to get an index of their own personality characteristics. We found that both men and women at the higher end of the psychopathy spectrum had assortative preferences for high psychopathy partners both in long- and short-term relationships. High Machiavellian women preferred high Machiavellian men as marriage partners, and high narcissistic men disliked narcissistic women as potential long-term partners. The results suggest strong positive assortment for psychopathy, but less so for the other two traits. The lack of assortative preferences for narcissism and Machiavellianism could be due to the methods we used, as mate choice is dependent on a number of factors, and reading descriptions of potential mates may not be ecologically valid. A study that investigated couples in a relationship suggested that there, indeed, was initial positive assortment for all of the Dark Triad traits, which is likely to have been present since the start of the relationship (Kardum et al., 2017). Thus it is highly probable that likes do attract for the Dark Triad traits.

When investigating attractiveness of the Dark Triad, some of our studies have used still photographs of men's faces, computer manipulated to exhibit either low or high levels of narcissism, Machiavellianism, and psychopathy. In these studies, we have used prototype facial morphs created by Nick Holtzman (2011). In his initial study, Holtzman invited participants to his laboratory and asked them to fill in questionnaires on the Dark Triad. The participants also had their facial photographs taken for further research. He then merged the faces of those who obtained the highest and the lowest scores together to form a baseline form. Using the Psychomorph software, Urszula Marcinkowska, a colleague from Jagiellonian University in Krakow, imposed the prototype morphs onto faces of Latvian men who participated in a study by Rantala et al. (2012).

It is not quite clear what the differences between the high and low morphed faces are. We have asked people to rate them on dominance, masculinity, aggression, dangerousness, and happiness. The high morphs are perceived as more dominant, masculine, aggressive, and dangerous. The low morphs are perceived as less happy. However, the high morphs do not equate with masculinity in a straightforward manner, as in one study, women who preferred the masculinized facial morphs of a male face did not necessarily like the high

Dark Triad version of the same face (Lyons, Marcinkowska, Helle, & McGrath, 2015). Thus there is something more than masculinity that distinguishes the high morphed faces from their low counterparts.

We have now showed these faces to thousands of women in several different studies, and have found that without an exception, the high Dark Triad morphs are aversive as potential partners (Lyons et al., 2015). The high faces are also rated as more aggressive, dominant (Lyons & Blanchard, 2016), and dangerous (Brewer, Carter, Lyons, & Green, 2018) than the low faces, suggesting that the cranio-morphological features of these faces are communicating something about the aversive nature of the traits.

We have run several experiments, trying to find out if there are circumstances when women may find the Dark Triad male faces attractive. For instance, in a study conducted by my several undergraduate project students, we gave women alcohol, placebo, or lemonade, and asked them to choose between a high and a low Dark Triad face. We found that even when under the influence of alcohol, women disliked the high faces, and rated them as dangerous (Brewer, Carter, et al., 2018). In another experiment, we manipulated women's perceptions of poverty and wealth, expecting that high faces would be preferred in poorer conditions, possibly as a mechanism for increasing status. We found that despite the experimental manipulation, women still had an overall dislike for the high faces (Lyons & Simeonov, 2016).

Despite the evident aversion toward high Dark Triad men's faces, it is possible that preference for narcissism confers reproductive advantage to women. There are some characteristics of the women themselves that influence their preference for narcissistic faces. For instance, in one study, we found that those women who had unrestricted sociosexual orientation (i.e., preference for noncommitted sexual relationships) and did not use oral contraceptives had a preference for narcissistic faces (Marcinkowska, Helle, & Lyons, 2015). Women who have short-term mating interests are supposedly seeking for partners for genetic benefits, and it is possible that this is somehow communicated in the narcissistic men's face. This is supported by the findings that those women who have more children also prefer narcissistic faces (Marcinkowska, Lyons, & Helle, 2016). These findings support the proposition that narcissism is an adaptation for short-term mating and dominance, especially beneficial for men (Holtzman & Donnellan, 2015). However, Machiavellianism and psychopathy seem to be less popular in both short- and long-term partners, and it is possible that the self-reported mating success is based either on exaggeration or coercion of unwilling partners.

The facial morphing studies are interested in whether there is something in the cranio-facial features of the Dark Triad that influences attractiveness. However, there are other roads to sexual appeal than the bare facial structure. One strategy that is commonly used in competing and attracting mates is enhancement of one's appearance. It is difficult to disentangle the importance of the sexual selection forces here, as individuals may try to outcompete each other in attractiveness (intrasexual selection), but the enhancement of appearance could also be something that is preferred by potential partners (intersexual selection). According to the late Anne Campbell, enhancement of appearance is also called "epigamic" displays, or "epigamic selection," which is the "... within sex competition to display a particular attribute that is preferentially valued in a mate by the opposite sex" (Campbell, 1995, p. 103). There is some evidence that especially narcissism is important in terms of epigamic displays.

For example, Simine Vazire, Naumann, Rentfrow, and Gosling (2008) studied the manifestations of narcissism in a sample of 160 university students. The students were invited to a laboratory session, where the researchers took photographs of them. They also completed a battery of personality measures, including the Narcissistic Personality Inventory, and they were asked to recruit a friend to assess their personality too. In addition, undergraduate research assistants assessed the participants narcissism based only on their photographs. The researchers found a significant positive correlation between the assessment of narcissism based on the photograph of the participant, and the self and other-rated narcissism scores. In short, the results imply that it is possible to detect narcissism by just looking at a photograph of an unknown individual at zero acquaintance. The cues that were associated with accurate identification of narcissism indicated that individuals high in this trait invest more time in preparing epigamic displays. In both sexes, narcissism was connected to an appearance that takes a lot of time and resources to prepare: neatness, and expensive and stylish clothing. Narcissistic men were less likely to wear glasses, and narcissistic women had more feminine looks, used more makeup, paraded plucked eyebrows, and showed more cleavage. In another study, one of the aspects that influenced the link between narcissism and popularity at first sight if narcissistic was the neatness of clothing (Back, Schmuckle, & Egloff, 2010). These studies suggest that adornment plays an important role in creating positive first impressions, leading to (at least) short-term mating success. Enhancement of appearance could both be attractive to the opposite sex (i.e., intersexual competition), as well as deter potential competitors (i.e., intrasexual selection).

Not many studies have investigated epigamic displays and the three Dark Triad traits together. In one such study, participants were rating the adorned and unadorned photographs of targets with varied level of the Dark Triad (Holtzman & Strube, 2013). The results showed that the Dark Triad composite was a good predictor of effective adornment. When the shared variance between the three traits was controlled for, psychopathy (rather than narcissism) emerged as a significant predictor of adornment. Both narcissism and psychopathy are associated with short-term mating goals, and it makes sense that individuals high in these traits know how to enhance their mating appeal by epigamic displays. However, the lack of research on effective adornment and mating success makes it hard to decide what the relative importance of each Dark Triad trait is, and, indeed, whether individual's sex plays a role in this relationship.

4.3.2 Coercion

Sexual coercion is a form of intersexual strategy, based on a conflict between the sexes rather than on mutualistic interactions. Sexually coercive strategies are common and can vary from subtle (e.g., verbal manipulation) to more extreme (e.g., physical coercion). Sexual harassment and coercion are common both in relationships, as well as among acquainted people, and complete strangers. Coercive sexual strategies are most prevalent in men who have short-term mating interests (Yost & Zurbriggen, 2006), suggesting that harassment could be a successful tool for achieving promiscuous mating goals. However, sexual coercion is also perpetrated by women, and the Dark Triad is especially interesting in understanding who the coercive women are, and what strategies they employ.

Traditionally, research on the Dark Triad and sexual coercion has focused on psychopathy and narcissism in incarcerated sexual offenders (e.g., Porter et al., 2000). However, in order to understand how personality promotes exploitive sexual styles, it is important to investigate how people conduct themselves in their everyday lives. Emerging research evidence shows that normal variation in the dark traits does have an important influence on the likelihood of perpetration of sexual harassment of varying degrees. It is possible that the low empathy factor of the Dark Triad constellation is one of the driving proximate forces behind exploitive sexual strategies (Willis, Birthrong, King, Nelson-Gray, & Latzman, 2017).

The study of sexual coercion is tricky. The sensitive nature of the topic influences the willingness of people to admit that they have perpetrated coercion of any kind. One of the questionnaire measures that has been used to investigate this topic is the Postrefusal Sexual Persistence Scale (Struckman-Johnson, Struckman-Johnson, & Anderson, 2003). The idea here is that a tactic is deemed as coercive after the victim has indicated that she or he is not willing to have a sexual contact with the perpetrator, but the perpetrator still carries on pursuing sex. The scale has questions about whether the respondents have used a particular tactic after the partner has already indicated that they are not complying with the sexual advances. The scale has four subscales for strategies varying in severity. The less severe strategies include "sexual arousal," which entails things like persistently kissing or touching the partner, or taking ones clothes off in front of the partner. "Emotional manipulation and deception" subscale has items on verbal or psychological pressure, such as questioning the partners sexuality, threatening to break up with them, or blackmail them. These strategies are aimed at wearing down any resistance by playing on the receivers needs and deceiving them into sex. "Exploitation of the intoxicated" is a more exploitative tactic, which entails taking advantage of someone who already is intoxicated, or purposefully getting someone drunk in order to have sex with them. The most severe tactic is "physical force and harm," which included physical restrain, blocking the exit, hitting, tying the person up, or threatening with a weapon.

There are a few studies that have investigated individual Dark Triad traits with regards to harassment in community or student samples. Unfortunately, studies on all of the three traits with regards to tactics of different severity are lacking. With regards to psychopathy, primary psychopathy promotes sexually coercive strategies, ranging from emotional manipulation to physical force and threats in both men and women (Muñoz, Khan, & Cordwell, 2011). In addition, in women, primary psychopathy predicts nonviolent coercion tactics, such as emotional manipulation (Khan, Brewer, Kim, & Centifanti, 2017). Table 4.3 presents the prevalence of different coercive tactics and how they relate to the Dark Triad.

Narcissism seems to promote harassment and coercion via entitlement. According to the "narcissistic reactance theory" explaining sexual coercion and rape, when narcissistic individuals are refused sex, they react by using aggression and force (Baumeister, Catanese, & Wallace, 2002). The influence of narcissism on sexual coercion can also depend on the sex of the perpetrator and the aspect of narcissism. For example, my PhD student Victoria Blinkhorn found that men who possess leadership/authority aspects of narcissism are more likely to employ sexually coercive strategies, whereas for

Table 4.3 Sexual Coercion Tactics and the Dark Triad (% data from Struckman-Johnson et al. (2003))

Tactic	% of Male Perpetrating	% Women Perpetrating	Dark Triad Findings	Reference
Sexual arousal (e.g., kissing, touching, taking off clothes)	40.4	25.5	Narcissism positive predictor in both sexes	Blinkhorn et al. (2015)
			Primary psychopathy positive predictor in both sexes	Muñoz et al. (2011)
Emotional manipulation and deception (e.g., threatening to leave, questioning sexuality, blackmailing)	32.4	15.2	Narcissism positive predictor in both sexes	Blinkhorn et al. (2015)
			Primary psychopathy positive predictor in both sexes	Muñoz et al. (2011)
			Primary psychopathy stronger predictor in women than in men	Khan et al. (2017)
Exploitation of the intoxicated (e.g., getting a person deliberately drunk, or exploiting a drunken person)	13.1	5.2	Narcissism positive predictor in both sexes	Blinkhorn et al. (2015)
			Primary psychopathy positive predictor in both sexes	Muñoz et al. (2011)
Physical force and harm (e.g., restraint, tying up, hitting, threatening with violence)	43.2	26.5	Narcissism positive predictor in both sexes	Blinkhorn et al. (2015)
			Primary psychopathy in women stronger predictor than in men	Muñoz et al. (2011)

women, the entitlement/exploitativeness facet plays a more important role in coercion (Blinkhorn, Lyons, & Almond, 2015). This is an interesting finding, especially in the light of the high profile sexual abuse cases by powerful men such as the Hollywood film producer Harvey Weinstein. Leadership/Authority facet of narcissism is related to social success and power, and it may predispose some men to feel that they are entitled to have sex with anyone they like, by using any means they see appropriate.

A few studies have suggested that the common core (i.e., callousness, lack of empathy) shared by the Dark Triad traits explains sexual harassment and coercion better than the individual traits in isolation from each other. For example, Jonason, Girgis, and Milne-Home (2017) found that psychopathy alone, as well as the common core shared by all the three traits were good predictors of possessing rape-enabling attitudes. Similarly, other studies have found that the common core is also responsible for proclivity and sexual coercion in both sexes (Figueredo, Gladden, Sisco, Patch, & Jones, 2015; Zeigler-Hill, Besser, Morag, & Campbell, 2016). Overall, it seems that the Dark Triad constellation relates to predatory sexual strategies, based on exploitative short-term mating. Thus rather than having sex with consenting partners, those at the higher end of the continuum are more likely to achieve their mating goals via coercion and manipulation.

4.3.3 Direct and Indirect Aggression

Generally speaking, intrasexual selection has been equated with direct male-male combat for accessing resources (which females can find attractive) or gaining mating opportunities. For instance, the "young male syndrome" idea posits that dangerous, competitive acts (sometimes leading in homicide) can be best understood from the perspective of male intrasexual selection (Wilson & Daly, 1985). One idea is that males are violent because it is adaptive in mate competition. Individuals high in Dark Triad traits should put more effort into acquiring mates, and it would be expected that they would utilize more aggressive competitive strategies.

A study by Westhead and Egan (2015) aimed to disentangle the relationship between the Dark Triad, mating effort, and violence in an online questionnaire study. The study was building on previous research that has suggested that both mating effort and the Dark Triad have independent relationships with violence. The interesting question is whether the relationship between personality and violence occurs because of increased mating effort associated with the Dark Triad. The authors found that both mating effort and the Dark Triad were independently related to increased violence. However, violence was not a result of increased mating effort associated with the Dark Triad. When the shared variance between the traits was controlled for in regression analysis, psychopathy was the only Dark Triad trait that was associated with increased violence. These findings indicate that the Dark Triad individuals are not necessarily using more aggressive intrasexual competition strategies when competing for mates.

Indirect aggression is perhaps a slightly less (physically) costly form of competition. Rather than engaging in a direct, potentially dangerous physical confrontation, more subtle intrasexual strategies include trying to derogate competitors so that they would look undesirable in the eyes of the opposite sex. It has to be noted that although there has been a reasonable amount of research on the Dark Triad and indirect aggression, most of it has not been directly in the context of mating competition.

One way of investigating intrasexual competitiveness in humans is to look at how threatening the members of the same sex are perceived in the mating context, and the likelihood and willingness to engage in competition in order to gain access to partners. One widely used questionnaire is the Buunk and Fisher (2009) Intra-Sexual Competition scale, which asks about the attitudes about confronting others when competing for partners (e.g., "I can't stand it when I meet another man who is more attractive than I am" and "I always want to beat other men"). Using this scale, Gayle Brewer and Loren Abell (2015b) investigated how Machiavellianism influences competitive behaviors in long-term, committed relationships. They found that those who score higher on the Machiavellianism instruments were also, irrespective of their sex, more likely to endorse competitive attitudes toward same-sex individuals.

Studies that have included all the three traits and a variety of competitive strategies have found that the three traits differ slightly with regards to the use on intrasexual tactics. Goncalves and Campbell (2014) asked their participants what their likelihood of using intrasexually competitive strategies ranging from outshining the rival (e.g., in sports context) to derogating the rival (e.g., questioning their fidelity in front of the potential mate). They found that in both men and women, narcissism was associated with a willingness to outshine their competitor, psychopathy with spreading damaging rumors about the rival, and Machiavellianism with making rude comments about the rival. The findings suggest that Machiavellian and psychopathic intrasexual tactics are directed toward indirect attack on the competitor, whereas narcissistic individuals are more concerned about being better than their competitors.

In another study, Semenyna and Honey (2015) investigated an aspect of intrasexual competition, striving for dominance and ruthless self-advancement, which are often directly related to willingness to overpower same-sex competitors. Although the authors did find that both are more typical to high Dark Triad individuals, they did not directly investigate whether dominance and self-advancement were directed to members of the same sex. It is possible that these behaviors are more typical to high Dark Triad individuals because they could be beneficial in competition for potential partners.

Finally, bullying (indirect and direct) can be a form of intrasexual competition, taking that the target is someone who the bully is in competition with in attracting mates. A study by Holly Baughman, Dearing, Giammarco, and Vernon (2012) investigated the relationship with the Dark Triad and bullying behavior in an internet sample. They found that all the three traits had a positive association with direct, indirect, physical, and verbal bullying. Although the authors did not investigate in greater detail what the context of the bullying was, it is possible that the proclivity of those high on the Dark Triad traits to bully others is adaptive in the context of intrasexual competition. Greg Carter and colleagues (Carter, Montanaro, Linney, & Campbell, 2015) looked at intrasexual competition in a women-only sample, and found that all the three traits had significant positive associations with competition (including derogating and manipulating competitors, as well as competing with appearance in order to get male attention). The authors suggested that it may be difficult to make a distinction between intra- and intersexual selection, as some aspects (e.g., enhancing appearance) may be desirable to opposite partners, and deter the same-sex competitors. This is why enhancement of appearance can be considered part of both mate choice and mate competition.

4.4 Established Relationships

Courtship with a high Dark Triad individual can proceed quickly into a serious relationship, where the other party is open for abuse, exploitation, and cheating. High Dark Triad individuals are oppressive, domineering, and abusive, with a potential for high levels of psychological damage to the partner. This harm is apparent in online groups (e.g., https://narcissist.supportgroups.com/; approaching 43,000 members in 2018) that have been established in order to provide peer support for those who have survived a relationship with a high Dark Triad individual. However, empirical literature does not always support the "victim" hypothesis, but has suggested that there is at least some level of assortative mating for these traits. Research on the Dark Triad in long-term romantic relationship has investigated different aspects of relationship functioning, such as quality of the bond, jealousy, infidelity, and intimate partner violence (IPV).

4.4.1 Relationship Quality

Most of the literature has focused on relatively new romantic partners, investigating how the Dark Triad influences satisfaction and commitment early on in the relationship. Smith et al. (2014) measured relationship commitment, satisfaction, and the Dark Triad in 45 heterosexual dating couples. They utilized an "actor-partner interdependence model" in exploring how an individual's Dark Triad score influence the commitment and satisfaction of the partner, as well as their own commitment and satisfaction. They found that those high in the composite Dark Triad were less committed and satisfied in their relationships. Looking at the individual traits, female partners of high Machiavellian men were more satisfied in their relationship, indicating that Machiavellian men may be able to bring happiness to their relationships. Women who had high psychopathy partners and who reported being satisfied with the relationship also reported high commitment to their partners. It seems that satisfaction is a key to commitment, and in some cases, high Dark Triad can result in more satisfaction and commitment. However, the overall picture from this study is that Dark Triad traits result in lower quality relationship, at least in young dating couples. In another similar study, Kardum, Hudek-Knezevic, Mehic, and Pilek (2018) studied the Dark Triad and relationship satisfaction in 100 young dating couples. When controlling for the partners and the actors Dark Triad traits in simultaneous regressions, psychopathy emerged as the most detrimental trait for relationship quality. This was located to high psychopathy men, rather than women. Overall, high psychopathy men were dissatisfied in their relationships and had unhappy partners too. The findings of these two studies point toward a higher importance of men's Dark Triad in relationship quality in heterosexual dating couples.

What could be the reason for the detrimental influence of men's psychopathy on romantic relationships? Goetz and Meyer (2018) suggested this could be due to mate value discrepancies (MVDs). There are two different MVDs that can be calculated for individuals in a relationship. First one is the partner-self MVD, which is the difference between a person's own value in relation to other potential mates and their partners value in relation to other potential mates. If the person is partnered with someone who has a much lower value to potential mates than the person him/herself, it can result in a dissatisfaction with the current relationship. The second one is the partner-potential partner MDV, which indicates the distance between the mate value of the current partner, and the mate value of other potential partners. If there are more alternative partners than the current one, the result can be a lower satisfaction in the relationship. In a sample of 211 undergraduate students who were in a relationship, Goetz and Meyer investigated whether low relationship satisfaction is related to high Dark Triad individual's propensity to have discrepancies in the mate value of themselves, other potential partners, and their current mate. They found that the composite Dark Triad, as well as Machiavellianism and psychopathy was associated with higher MVDs between current and potential partners, resulting in higher dissatisfaction in the current relationship. Thus one of the reasons for being dissatisfied in a relationship could be because of a high number of potential partners that match the ideal mate characteristics better than the current partner does. Perhaps high Machiavellian and psychopathic individuals are always in a lookout for better partners, perceiving others as more attractive, which could influence a higher propensity for infidelity and relationship dissolution.

There is less research looking at longitudinal influences of Dark Triad on relationship quality over a period of time. Most of the research and theories have focused on specifically narcissism. William Campbell (2005) proposed a "chocolate cake model" of relationship satisfaction, which can be applied especially for narcissism. In a similar way as a piece of chocolate cake can be initially sweet, rich, and indulging, those who start a relationship with a narcissist may be originally highly infatuated, rating the relationship quality as very high. However, when consumed in large quantities, narcissism (just like chocolate cake) can become overbearing over time, resulting in a low relationship satisfaction. Limited evidence suggests that the initial attractiveness of narcissistic partners can end in dissatisfaction over time. For instance, in a cross-sectional study, Lamkin, Campbell, and Miller (2015) found that the longer the relationship, the more dissatisfied the couples were if both of the partners scored high on the entitlement/exploitativeness facet of narcissism. Lavner, Lamkin, Miller, Campbell, and Karney (2016) studied a sample of newly wed couples over a period of first four years of marriage, investigating how narcissism predicts the trajectory of marital quality as years go by. Unlike the cross-sectional studies, this research found that it was the wives, rather than husband's narcissism that had a bigger influence on marital quality over time. Marital satisfaction declined more rapidly in relationships where the wives had higher total narcissism as well as entitlement/exploitativeness scores.

Because of the low satisfaction and low investment in relationships, it would be expected that high Dark Triad individuals (especially Machiavellian and psychopathic) are not feeling very distressed when the relationship breaks up. Moroz, Chen, Daljeet, and Campbell (2018) investigated the Dark Triad, and breakup distress in a sample of 264 University students in Canada. Unexpectedly, they found that participants who scored higher on Machiavellianism and psychopathy reported higher distress after breaking up. In regression analyses where the shared variance between the traits was controlled for, the authors found that those who were higher on Machiavellianism experienced higher levels of distress after a break up. It is clear that Machiavellianism does not automatically lead to lower quality attachments with romantic partners, and taking the results from studies I reviewed before, it can even have an association with increased relationship satisfaction. Machiavellianism relates to more long-term planning, and individuals high in this trait can have high investment in a partner, resulting in heightened distress if the relationship dissolves.

4.4.2 Romantic Jealousy

Romantic jealousy is a complicated negative emotion, which can be induced by an imagined or real threat to a valued relationship, in the presence of imagined or actual rival. Behaviors related to jealousy (whether making someone jealous or feeling jealous oneself) can be part of mate-retention tactics, aimed at keeping the partner in the relationship. According to evolutionary psychologist, romantic jealousy has an important adaptive function in monitoring the relationship for infidelity and cuckoldry. It has been suggested that the sexes differ in their jealousy experience due to basic differences in reproductive potential. There are individual differences in a person's proclivity to feel emotions, including romantic jealousy. Pfeiffer and Wong (1989) suggested that romantic jealousy consists of three different components: emotional (how individuals feel when jealous), cognitive (how individuals appraise jealousy-inducing situations), and behavioral (the actions of individuals when jealous). Cognitive and behavioral jealousy can lead to adverse consequences, such as interpersonal violence, which will be discussed later in this chapter.

Taking the shallowness of emotional experiences of those on the high end of the Dark Triad continuum, it would be expected that the lack of emotions is also transferred to lower jealousy and less mate guarding in romantic relationships. As demonstrated before, individuals high in the Dark Triad are not inclined to form long-term, serious relationships, and when they do, the relationships are often of lower quality. The motivation to pursue multiple short-term relationships may also relate to lower experiences of relationship jealousy. It seems pointless to be jealous about partners if there are no intentions for long-term relationships, potentially leading to having children. On the other hand, the callousness, manipulativeness, and the proclivity to bully others indicate that those at the higher end of the Dark Triad continuum may be more likely to use varied means in inducing jealousy in their partners.

A study by Massar, Winters, Lenz, and Jonason (2017) focused on primary and secondary psychopathy, and experiences of emotional, cognitive, and behavioral jealousy. In line with the callous interpersonal nature associated with primary psychopathy, this trait did not relate to the feeling of jealousy. Secondary psychopathy, which is associated with anxious, impulsive interpersonal style, was linked with higher experiences of emotional and suspicious (i.e., cognitive and behavioral) jealousy.

Chin, Atkinson, Raheb, Harris, and Vernon (2017) studied the three Dark Triad traits and jealousy in a sample of 453 student and community participants. All of the three traits had a positive relationship with behavioral jealousy, including a higher likelihood of quizzing a partner about their whereabouts. Cognitive jealousy, which is about consciously suspecting that a partner is seeing someone else, had a negative correlation with Machiavellianism, and no association with the other two traits. This is an interesting finding, as the overall suspicious, low-trusting nature of those high in Machiavellianism does not seem to translate to their romantic relationships. Finally, Machiavellianism and narcissism had a positive association with emotional jealousy, meaning that those higher in this trait reported more upset as a result of, for instance, seeing their partner flirting with another individual.

Barelds, Dijkstra, Groothof, and Pastoor (2017) explored reactive, anxious, and preventive jealousy, which pretty much correspond with emotional, cognitive, and behavioral jealousy, respectively. They found that irrespective of the sex or sexual orientation, Machiavellianism and narcissism had weak, positive correlations with anxious (i.e., cognitive) jealousy, having insecurities and paranoid thoughts about one's partner's infidelity. This is the opposite to the findings by Chin et al. (2017), who reported that those high on Machiavellianism were less likely to experience cognitive jealousy. The discrepancies between the findings could be attributed to the scales used in the study or the sample characteristics. In a similar manner as in Chin and colleagues, all Dark Triad traits had an association with preventive (i.e., behavioral) jealousy. This type of jealousy results in active behavior that prevents one's partner from getting in contact with third parties.

In summary, rather than presenting with a detached, uncaring relationship style, the Dark Triad individuals do feel jealous about potential infidelity of their partner. The two studies that have looked at all of the three traits demonstrate that those who are high on socially aversive traits engage in behavioral strategies indicating jealousy, such as checking their partners email and social media behavior, or preventing them from interacting with people they perceive as rivals. Jealousy-related feelings and strategies have a close connection with inducing jealousy in a partner, which can result in a vicious circle. If an individual thinks that their partner has a romantic interest in someone else, they may try to make their partner jealous by showing that they are desired by other people too. Yet, rather than stemming from one's own insecurity, individuals may have an interest in inducing jealousy for multiple other reasons as well.

Researchers have suggested five main reasons for why someone might want to make their partner jealous: Revenge, power/control, testing the relationship, security assurance, and self-esteem boost (see Tortoriello, Hart, Richardson, & Tullett, 2017). The motivations around revenge and power/control are malevolent and offensive, and have their roots in the need to "keep the partner in their place" by making clear the person has plenty of other alternatives available. The other three motivations are defensive and more benign in nature, stemming from insecurities of the person around themselves and their relationship. A few studies to date have investigated jealousy induction in socially antagonistic personalities.

Massar et al. (2017) focused on primary and secondary psychopathy, and motivations for inducing jealousy in a partner. They found that those high in primary psychopathy had the tendency to make their partners feel jealous, and the motivations behind jealousy induction were offensive. Cold, callous individuals were more likely to induce jealousy because they wanted to gain power over the partner or get a revenge over a perceived wrongdoing. However, secondary psychopathy had strikingly different motives, using defensive, rather than offensive strategies. Rather than attempting to gain power, those high in secondary psychopathy induced jealousy in their partners out if insecurity in the relationship, in order to gain higher self-esteem, or test the strength of the relationship.

Tortoriello et al. (2017) were interested in jealousy induction in narcissistic relationship partners. Narcissistic individuals may engage in behaviors such as flirting with others and talking about attractiveness of romantic rivals—actions that are designed for making their partner feel jealous. Grandiose narcissism (as measured by the NPI) related to jealousy induction due to the need to exert power, whereas vulnerable narcissism associated with more diverse motivations, both offensive and defensive in nature. The authors also analyzed the data using Machiavellianism and self-esteem as mediators, and found that grandiose narcissists' manipulative nature assists jealousy induction, whereas their high self-esteem suppresses it. For vulnerable narcissism, jealousy induction was explained by high manipulativeness and low self-esteem. It appears that grandiose narcissism relates to more instrumental relationship tactics and strives to keep their partners under control. Vulnerable narcissists seem to use more haphazard strategies, utilizing jealousy induction that aims both to test the relationship and control the partner.

Although small levels of jealousy could be beneficial in aiding behaviors that maintain the relationship, excessive jealousy can be harmful. Jealousy can spiral out of control, leading to aggression and violence. Mate guarding and IPV are examples of darker side of relationships. These mate retention strategies can stem from jealousy and have disastrous consequences.

4.4.3 Mate Guarding and IPV

Mate guarding is a common tactic used in relationships. It has been studied extensively in the evolutionary literature, as losing a partner to a competitor, or even worse, having a partner impregnated by a competitor can have detrimental consequences for the evolutionary fitness of an individual. Mate guarding strategies range from constantly checking on the partner to physically restricting their contact with potential romantic competitors. Mate guarding is closely linked to the emotion of jealousy, which, at extreme levels, can lead to behaviors that are detrimental to both parties, including interpersonal violence. Owing to the callous nature of those high in the Dark Triad, it is no surprise that these personality traits are an important factor in both physical and emotional abuse in relationships. IPV does not only comprise of physical acts such as hitting, slapping, and coercing the partner into having sex, but also emotional abuse, such as threatening with violence, controlling, deceiving, and manipulating the partner. Although there has been more research investigating the role of individual Dark Triad traits in perpetrating IPV, not many studies have looked at the three traits together in order to establish their relative importance.

Carton and Egan (2017) considered how the Dark Triad relates to both IPV perpetration and victimization in relationships. Surprisingly, none of the Dark Triad traits were associated with perpetration of physical abuse, but this aspect of IPV was explained better by one of the Big Five traits, low agreeableness. However, the Dark Triad did contribute to different aspects of emotional abuse. For instance, those who were higher in psychopathy were more likely to use dominance and intimidation toward their partner, as well as denigration (i.e., wrongly accusing them for things that they haven't done). Further, narcissism and psychopathy were associated with restrictive engulfment, the attempt to control the partner so that they become engulfed with the relationship, shunning out the external world. These findings are interesting and suggest that psychopathy is the most adverse of the traits in terms of partner abuse. However, the participants were women, and the findings cannot be generalized to the strategies that high Dark Triad men may use. Another study in a Japanese sample, including both sexes, had similar results (Kiire, 2017). When the shared variance between the traits was controlled for in regression analyses, only psychopathy was a significant predictor of different types of IPV (including physic, sexual, and verbal) in both sexes. Together, these studies indicate that when the shared variance between the Dark Triad traits is statistically controlled for, psychopathy is the most relevant trait in influencing IPV in romantic relationships.

4.4.4 Infidelity

One of the most important aspects of committed, monogamous partnerships in humans is partner fidelity. Infidelity is a common destroyer of relationships. In both men and women, fidelity is rated as highly important when choosing partners (e.g., Mogilski, Wade, & Welling, 2014). Nevertheless, evolutionary costs of infidelity are different for the two sexes. Evolutionarily speaking, infidelity can be costly to men if they end up bringing up offspring that is genetically related to them. For women, the costs are associated with the risk of the partner leaving the female in order to pursue other reproductive opportunities, withdrawing the support that could be crucial for bringing up the offspring. Infidelity has potentially high costs for the partner who is being cheated on too. They may be at risk of aggression and desertion from their partner, which could also be directed toward the couple's offspring (especially if the man suspects cuckoldry). Thus it is important to understand how personality impacts the likelihood and consequences of infidelity in committed relationships.

What is clear is that there are individuals who are drawn into infidelity, even when they are satisfied in their current relationships (Weeks, Gambescia, & Jenkins, 2004). This could reflect an increased reproductive drive associated with a fast life history strategy. Those who prioritize mating opportunities are more likely to pursue extra-pair sex while living happily in a committed relationship. Cheaters often have no intention to end their primary relationship. The patterns of infidelity can be quite different, from the spur of the moment encounters to more strategic, long-term extra-pair partners. Research has found interesting, sex-specific patterns with regards to the Dark Triad and infidelity, which depend on the individual trait.

In a large internet sample, Jones and Weiser (2014) investigated the Dark Triad and infidelity and relationship consequences of infidelity. They found that in men, psychopathy was a significant positive predictor of infidelity in current (or most recent) relationship, whereas in women, both Machiavellianism and psychopathy predicted infidelity. Only psychopathy (in both sexes) related to relationship dissolution after cheating. Interestingly, women who were more narcissistic were less likely to have cheated in their relationship. This was exactly the opposite finding to a study by Gayle Brewer and her colleagues (2015) who found that narcissism in women had an association with greater incidence of infidelity in relationships.

As well as investigating actual behaviors, research has also looked into the intentions to cheat in a relationship. In a female-only sample, recruited from a British University, Brewer et al. (2015) demonstrated that intentions to cheat in future relationships were associated positively with narcissism and psychopathy. Brewer and Abell (2015a, 2015b) replicated the same findings in a study that looked at Machiavellianism, showing that the trait had a positive relationship with intentions to cheat in the future. Alavi, Mei, and Mehrinezhad (2018) researched infidelity in a sample of participants from Malaysia. They found that participants who had intentions for future infidelity were more Machiavellian and psychopathic, but no relationships were found between infidelity intentions and narcissism.

The emerging picture suggests that infidelity is especially pertinent to men and women who are high on psychopathic traits. Psychopathy relates to both actual infidelity and intentions to cheat in the future. With regards to

Machiavellianism, some studies have found that cheating is more common in high-Mach women, and others have found that Machiavellianism drives infidelity in both sexes. Relationships between narcissism and infidelity have not been consistent from one study to another, with findings that go in opposite directions.

4.5 Conclusion

Research on mating, dating, and romantic relationships indicates that high Dark Triad individuals have an overall preference for short-term, uncommitted affairs. When in serious partnerships, they are more prone to cheat, and use violence and other strategies as means of controlling their partner. There is some evidence that narcissism is attractive at first sight, but in the longer run, narcissism can be an overbearing trait in a relationship partner (i.e., the "chocolate cake" model). It is likely that the initial attractiveness of narcissistic individuals relies on effective adornment, fancy clothing, extraverted behaviors, and self-confidence. This increases the initial allure of narcissistic individuals, which may result in successful short-term relationships. Attractiveness may not run that deep, as our facial morphing studies have shown that rather than preferred, Dark Triad faces of men are disliked by women. In several studies, testing thousands of women, we have shown that the cranio-morphological features of high Dark Triad faces are found quite aversive in both short- and long-term relationships. It is possible that the self-reported short-term mating success of high Dark Triad individuals is based on putting on an effective façade, or using coercive strategies.

Attractiveness of the Dark Triad may also depend on factors such as personality similarity. The few studies that have investigated assortative preferences for similar partners have found that there is, indeed, initial preferences for similarity. Further, couples in established relationships are alike in socially aversive traits, although the similarity may not always translate into well-functioning and happiness. In long-term relationships, socially aversive traits are toxic, and especially psychopathy and Machiavellianism relate to infidelity and IPV. Narcissism seems to be the most adaptive of the traits, especially for men, relating to increased offspring number, whereas psychopathy and Machiavellianism may be less adaptive, at least in the socioecological environments (i.e., WEIRD populations, Henrich, Heine, & Norenzayan, 2010) where most studies have taken place.

Further Reading

Barelds, D. P., Dijkstra, P., Groothof, H. A., & Pastoor, C. D. (2017). The dark triad and three types of jealousy: its' relations among heterosexuals and homosexuals involved in a romantic relationship. *Personality and Individual Differences*, *116*, 6–10.

Campbell, W. K. (2005). *When you love a man who loves himself: how to deal with a oneway relationship*. Chicago: Sourcebooks Casablanca.

Holtzman, N. S., & Strube, M. J. (2011). The intertwined evolution of narcissism and short-term mating: An emerging hypothesis. In *The handbook of narcissism and narcissistic personality disorder: theoretical approaches, empirical findings, and treatments* (pp. 210–220).

Lyons, M., & Blanchard, A. (2016). "I could see, in the depth of his eyes, my own beauty reflected": women's assortative preference for narcissistic, but not for Machiavellian or psychopathic male faces. *Personality and Individual Differences*, *97*, 40–44.

Moroz, S., Chen, S., Daljeet, K. N., & Campbell, L. (2018). The dark triad and break-up distress. *Personality and Individual Differences*, *132*, 52–59.

Struckman-Johnson, C., Struckman-Johnson, D., & Anderson, P. B. (2003). Tactics of sexual coercion: when men and women don't take no for an answer. *The Journal of Sex Research*, *40*, 76–86.

CHAPTER FIVE

Dark Triad and Friendships

Chapter Outline

5.1 Introduction

My best friend … I love her and we have been friends for years but she is very very hard work. Incredibly self involved and very disinterested in anything that's going on in my life - I have a 15 month old and she has seen him twice, never asks after him or about anything going on in my life. I can accept that because I know that she does care really, it's just that she can be very focussed on herself. There is a lot of 'drama' too - drunken phone calls at 2am telling me she's left her partner, I get all involved and then it blows over the next day an I am annoyed I have wasted time and energy supporting her when she doesn't even seem bothered herself. It can be very draining and I have commented to DH that I get very little out of the friendship really, despite how much I give. The reason we are still friends is that I care about her, she is very funny and we have a lot of history together. She wasn't always like 'this' and I miss who she used to be I guess. I try not to get heavily involved now, which I did in the past, because I felt like I was overinvesting myself and I found it very stressful. It also put a strain on my relationship at one point. (crayfish; Wed 05-Oct-16; 12:13:29; https://www.mumsnet.com/Talk/relationships/).

The writing above is from a popular UK parenting website, Mumsnet. Trawling through countless heartfelt posts complaining about troubled friendships, it is glaringly obvious that as well as being a source of solace

The Dark Triad of Personality
https://doi.org/10.1016/B978-0-12-814291-2.00005-X

and support, friendships can be mentally and physically draining. In some friendships, the other party is volatile, manipulative, and uncaring, exerting a major negative influence on the quality of the friendship. Manipulation and coldness are central features of the Dark Triad and are likely to be tactics that are used in influencing friendship dynamics. The focus of this chapter is on reviewing research findings on the Dark Triad and different aspects of friendships.

Friendships are long-term affiliative, nonsexual social bonds that have a fundamental importance for well-being and survival not just in humans, but in other species too. Friendships have been researched widely in primates, and they seem to have a strong contribution to reproductive fitness (Seyfarth & Cheney, 2012). In primates such as chimpanzees and baboons, friendships are manifested by preferential grooming, coalitional support, childcare, and close spatial proximity. In humans, the dynamics and complexity of friendships have taken another dimension. We maintain social bonds with a large number of fellow humans who we call our friends, where the relationships are often embedded in larger social networks which often cross geographical boundaries. With the invention of modern technology (e.g., internet and social media), it is possible to keep in touch with people who we would otherwise see only on very rare occasions.

Close, nonsexual bonds are common within same-sex individuals, but also occur between the sexes. The male-female friendship bonds may have very different motivations to female-female or male-male relationships. It is common for opposite-sex friendships to have hidden, underlying romantic or sexual motivations (e.g., Lemay Jr & Wolf, 2016). In this chapter, I will focus the discussions around same-sex friendships in order not to confuse potential mating motivations with the willingness to form social bonds for nonmating purposes.

Friendships are characterized at least by some levels of altruism between the friends. Friends provide emotional, physical, and sometimes resource-related support to each other, which means that there is also room for cheating. Evolutionarily speaking, affiliative, nonsexual bonds with unrelated people could be based on the rules of reciprocal altruism (Trivers, 1971). In reciprocal relationships, the fitness costs that come from helping a friend could be mitigated by the fitness benefits from the help received from the same friend. If counting of the favors between friends happen, it is probably more of a subconscious process. Although in one study, we found that the expectation of reciprocity is stronger from a friend than from a relative (Rotkirch, Lyons, David-Barrett, & Jokela, 2014); people do not normally consciously engage in bookkeeping about the help given and the help received.

To illustrate the point, I might volunteer financial aid to a struggling friend, help out in looking after their children, and try to protect them from an abusive ex-partner. All of these actions are costly in terms of my time, resources, and a potential risk to my safety and well-being. The altruism toward a valued friend could be detrimental to my own reproductive fitness, resulting in reduced number of offspring for me, who is acting as the altruist. I may engage in excessive helping of a friend who I consider as being needy, without the expectation that this help is repayed in the future. The lack of bookkeeping in reciprocal relationships leaves a space open for exploitation. Deceitfulness is a key feature of those high on the Dark Triad, which could also translate into a cheater strategy in friendships. It is possible that high Dark Triad individuals are those who are responsible for negative aspects of friendships, sponging their friends support without paying the cost of helping. Of course, if over the course of time I feel exploited by my friend, I may take actions in order to end, or at least "phase out" the friendship.

Friendship may not always have visible benefits, but could bring countless, important unseen rewards. In the words of Flora (2016), "good friends improve immunity, spark creativity, drop our blood pressure, ward off dementia among the elderly, and even decrease our chances of dying at any given time. If you feel you can't live without your friends, you're not being melodramatic" (https://aeon.co/essays/when-a-friendship-turns-sour-more-than-feelings-get-hurt). However, this is only in the case where the friendship is perceived as rewarding. "Bad friends" can have the opposite effect, exerting a negative influence to both perceived and actual health.

It is clear that not all friendships are equal, and occasionally one of the parties takes advantage of the other. Sometimes friendships are toxic, where one of the friends in a social network exploits or bullies others. Individuals do not have the same social standing in their dyadic friendships or within a wider friendship group. Sometimes one friend puts more importance in the relationship than the other, who might not value the friendship as much. Think about your own friends, and how important they are to you. Now, how many of them do you think rates you as important as you rate them? We often overestimate our own importance in the face of other friends. Further, some people are popular members of a wider social network group, basking in the admiration from others, whereas others are relegated to playing the second (or third or fourth) fiddle. Investigations into the influence of socially toxic personalities in friendship dynamics are still in its infancy, but taking the antagonistic nature of the Dark Triad, it would not be expected that high levels of these traits lead to popularity in (at least adults) social networks. It is clear that personality is fundamentally important in who becomes friends with whom, how close and deep the friendship is, and the position that an individual has in a wider friendship network. Indeed, friendship research can take two different approaches—the investigation of how individuals function within a dyadic friendship or their popularity in a wider network of friends.

Most friendship research in humans has focused on children and adolescents, with larger gaps in the literature on adult friendships. Relevant to the Dark Triad research, many studies have investigated Machiavellianism, antisocial behaviors, and bullying in friendship networks of children of different ages. Only a few studies have looked at the Dark Triad traits together, and most of the research has focused on aggression, bullying, and popularity in the school setting.

As a whole, the Dark Triad is characterized by interpersonal antagonism, leading to difficulties in social relationships. This may influence the quality and longevity of friendships, as well as the kind of tactics that people employ when dealing with their friends. In this chapter, I will focus on research that has explored the Dark Triad (either together, or as a constellation) in same-sex friendships, looking at things like similarity between the friends, reasons for entering a friendship, tactics used in friendships, quality of the social bonds, and individual popularity. In the recent years, there has been a mushrooming of research on friendships in social media. This chapter will concentrate on off-line relationships, and the internet friendships will be considered in Chapter 7.

5.2 Friendship Goals

There is much diversity in the incentives for individuals in entering and staying in a social relationship with others. Friendship motivations vary from the need to form close, mutually supportive bonds with others (i.e., communal needs) to the manipulative use of friends as a means for achieving individual goals (i.e., agentic needs). The selfish, agentic interpersonal style of people who are high on all the three dark traits implies that they may also use friends as a tool for attaining own personal goals. These types of friendship motivations are also more likely to lead to quicker friendship dissolution, as in the long run, people either get fed up being exploited, or those who exploit might find better victims to satisfy their needs.

Friends can be useful in the "mating market," providing help (deliberately or without an intent) in attracting and acquiring partners. Physical attractiveness is important in this regard. Social psychology experiments have demonstrated that when a person is in a group with attractive people, they receive higher ratings of attractiveness than they would if they were alone (van Osch, Blanken, Meijs, & van Wolferen, 2015). This is also called the "cheerleader effect," after the character Barney Stinson in TV series "How I met your mother." It has been suggested that our brains somehow average out the attractiveness of individuals in a group of people, which increases the lure of the less attractive group member (Walker & Vul, 2014). Attractiveness seems to rub off on others, and surrounding oneself with good-looking friends might be a good tactic for receiving the attention of potential partners. The cheerleader effect should be more pronounced in those who have heightened interests in mating. Research reviewed in the previous chapter suggests that the Dark Triad traits relate to increased short-term mating motivations, which makes the Dark Triad traits a great candidate for choosing friends who are physically attractive.

A study that investigated the Dark Triad and the reasons for making friends found that these traits do, indeed, relate to using friends as agentic tools (Jonason & Schmitt, 2012). For example, narcissistic women preferred same-sex friends who were attractive, which could boost and validate the ego of a narcissist (i.e., having "trophy friends"), as well as increase the attractiveness of the high narcissistic female in the eyes of potential suitors. High Machiavellian women, in turn, preferred friends who were high in social status. This indicates that Machiavellian women use their friends in climbing up the social ladder. Men who were high in psychopathy chose same-sex friends who could be useful in facilitating mating efforts, which makes sense in the light of short-term mating interests of individuals high in this trait. It is clear that rather than seeking friends who would be suitable for close, mutually supportive friendships, the Dark Triad individuals prefer those who they can use as instruments to satisfy their mating and status-related needs.

Narcissism is probably the most sociable of the three traits. Narcissistic individuals thrive from the buzz of social relationships. They seek for admiration from others and wish to be in the center of attention all the time. They are oriented toward social rewards, such as having fun with their friends. According to Foster, Misra, and Reidy (2009), narcissistic friendships are characterized by approach, rather than avoidance motivations. Approach orientation aims to maximize positive social outcomes, whereas avoidance orientation is related to avoiding negative interactions. One example of approach orientation is a friend giving a compliment to another friend, whereas avoidance orientation is when a friend avoids criticizing another friend in order to avoid conflict. In a study on narcissism, overall approach orientation, and friendship approach orientation, Foster et al. (2009) found that although narcissism was related to friendship approach goal (e.g., wanting to have fun with friends or wanting to establish deeper relationship), it did not have an association with an avoidance goal (e.g., not wanting to hurt a friend in order to avoid conflict). Further, the study found that overall approach orientation score fully mediated the relationship between narcissism and friendship approach goals. To put more simply, those who were narcissistic were more approach oriented in all aspects of their lives, with a "go-get" attitude that makes them more motivated to pursue a goal. This attitude explains why individuals are motivated to seek for entertaining friendships, which could dissolve if the friendship goals are not achieved. Because of the lack of avoidance motivation, it is possible that highly narcissistic individuals experience termination of friendships more easily. They are less motivated to avoid insulting their friends, and if the friendship goals are not met, they might be more likely to seek for opportunities elsewhere.

The coldness and detachment associated with trait psychopathy suggest that their friendship motivations are drastically different from narcissistic friendship goals. There are also likely to be large differences between different aspects of psychopathy (i.e., between the affective-interpersonal and lifestyle-antisocial facets). Psychopathy is related to lower value of long-term affiliative bonds with others, and thriving on negative social rewards, such as those gained from being cruel toward their friends (Foulkes, McCrory, Neumann, & Viding, 2014). The affective-interpersonal (or primary psychopathy/Factor 1 psychopathy; see Chapter 1) aspects of psychopathy is especially important in not caring about close friendships with others. A study by Foulkes, Seara-Cardoso, Neumann, Rogers, and Viding (2014) looked at different components of psychopathy and relationship goals. They found that those who were higher on the cold, callous aspects of psychopathy were more concerned about one's own image and gaining dominance over others, rather than about having warm, affiliative long-term friendships (Foulkes, McCrory, et al., 2014). The interpersonal-affective facet also had a relationship with feelings of liking, and desiring to be similar to a vignette character who displayed traits of coldness and dominance.

The relatively sparse research on the Dark Triad and motivations to seek for friendships suggest that narcissism relates to approach-motivations (e.g., having fun) and mating interests (e.g., having attractive friends in order to attract the opposite sex), Machiavellianism is associated with having friends that could help to climb up the social ladder, and psychopathy links with using friends as a tool for gaining sexual partners, as well as for dominating others for own gains.

5.3 Friendship Selection—Similarity or Exploitation?

One interesting question in friendship research is the initial stages of selecting friends and influence of similarity in personality. Are individuals who become friends similar to each other? Or is it possible that high Dark Triad individuals are attracted to social partners who can give them something, for example, selecting friends who are popular, good looking, and sociable? Or do they choose to socialize with others who are easy to exploit and manipulate? Although research has shown that especially narcissists are attractive as friends as first sight, the arrogance and grandiosity makes the attractiveness fade quickly as the time goes by. Still, Dark Triad individuals are not completely without friends, so there must be some characteristics that make people tolerate each other more. Perhaps similarity is a key to tolerance in friendships, leading to long-term bonds with others.

Indeed, research at a cellular level has found that friendship networks are more likely to share the same variants of a dopamine receptor gene DRD2 (Fowler, Settle, & Christakis, 2011). Different variants of this gene have been found to be related to psychopathy, as well as behaviors such as sensation seeking, risk-taking, and drug abuse. It is plausible that birds of feather flock together when it comes to forming friendship networks, and this similarity should be observable for the Dark Triad traits as well.

In the previous chapter, I explored aspects of assortative mating (also called homophily, or likes attract hypothesis) between romantic partners. Along with increasing cohesion between romantic couples, similarity can increase the functioning and closeness of people in nonromantic friendships. Likeness between friends is apparent not only in humans, but also in chimpanzees. A study that looked at personality and friendships in chimpanzees (measured by the amount of time individuals were choosing to sit together) found that furry friends were more likely to be more similar in their levels of sociability and boldness (Massen & Koski, 2014). Similarities in personality traits could make individuals more tolerant toward each other, increasing the likelihood of contact with the person.

There are not many studies on the Dark Triad and personality similarity in dyadic friendships, nor within wider friendship groups. In one study investigating dyadic similarity in Dark Triad scores between pairs of friends, Maaß, Lämmle, Bensch, and Ziegler (2016) used a sample of German sports students (who had been friends for at least two years) as participants. They found that pairs of friends were similar in all of the Dark Triad traits. This shows that in long-term friendships, people who remain together are likely to have similar levels of socially aversive personality traits. Especially for narcissism, the higher the similarity, the more similar the friends were in the Big Five of personality too. It is possible that in order for the friendships to work between those who are high in aversive personality traits, they need to be similar in other aspects of personality as well (e.g., extraversion, agreeableness, etc.).

Although there is a dearth of research on similarity in the Dark Triad traits in long-term friendships, there is some evidence for preference for self-similar traits during initial interactions when people are getting acquainted with each other. Research has found that in initial interactions, people who are high in narcissism are more tolerant of those who possess similar traits to them. However, those who are not high in narcissism initially dislike those who are narcissistic (Burton et al., 2017). Perhaps narcissists also have a long-term preference for friendships with similar people to themselves. Those who are high on narcissism get a kick out of social relationships that are characterized by shallow intimacy and the need to have fun. Perhaps nonnarcissistic individuals do not accept shallow friendships as easily and are more likely to prefer to socialize with those who are not high on narcissism.

Similarity for preference for friend's personality can also happen at different levels of the trait. This was the topic of investigation of Ilmarinen, Lönnqvist, and Paunonen (2016), who looked at manipulation and egotism in a sample of male military cadets in Finland. They asked the cadets to fill in personality measures and to rate their platoon friends on a series of personality factors, as well as indicate the likeability of the friend. Unbeknown to the participants, their platoon mates engaged in the same rating process. The authors analyzed the dyadic ratings between the cadets and found that low levels of manipulativeness and egotism were preferred, but only at the low levels of these traits. In short, homophily for dark personality traits does exist, but only for honesty and selflessness. These findings are echoed in a study that focused on freshmen at a University in Netherlands, investigating the role of the Big Five in this process. The results indicate that agreeableness (a trait that all the Dark Triad traits have a negative relationship with) related to selection of similar kind of friends, but only in students who were high on agreeableness themselves (Selfhout et al., 2010). Together, these studies indicate that kindness, cooperativeness, and friendliness are preferred by individuals who fit these criteria themselves. Those who are more selfish (i.e., have darker personalities) do not care about whether their friends are kind or unkind. This assortative preference for low Dark Triad traits at the lower levels of the constellation has interesting implications for pertaining questions about the evolution of altruism. Perhaps altruism is, indeed, a viable evolutionary strategy if altruists are preferentially grouping together and helping each other.

Although few studies have looked at similarity in friends in adulthood with regards to all the three Dark Triad traits together, a large body of research has found that in children and adolescents, antisocial characteristics (e.g., delinquency, bullying) are similar in friendship networks. For example, psychopathy in adolescents is correlated with deviant behavior in their peers, lower quality of friendships, as well as a higher likelihood of offending with their friends (Muñoz, Kerr, & Bsic, 2008). However, it is also possible that people become similar to the company they keep. A longitudinal study that looked at psychopathy, peer delinquency, and quality of social bonds in offending adolescents found that those who had higher quality friendships had lower psychopathy scores in the long run, and those who had friends with higher levels of antisocial behavior had higher psychopathic traits (Backman, Laajasalo, Jokela, & Aronen, 2018). The results indicate that although initially individuals may have matching traits and behaviors with their friends (e.g., psychopathy and delinquency), if the friendship bond quality is good, it can result in a reduction of psychopathy over the time. Nonetheless, we have a scant knowledge at the moment on the developmental pathways from the characteristics of childhood friends to the company we keep in adulthood.

Overall, these studies indicate that birds of "dark" feather do not necessarily, at least intentionally, flock together. Although those who have dark personality features may not rate similar characteristics as aversive as other people do, they do report having a higher than average liking for similar traits in friends either. It looks like the active preference for similarity is more likely at the lower levels of the traits. This means that people are more drawn into potential friends who are kind, honest, and caring if they themselves are presenting with these features.

5.4 Popularity

Popularity is an important aspect of a fundamental human need—belongingness to a social group. Popular individuals are those who people would preferentially like to associate with and/or who are liked by others. These are not mutually exclusive, as sometimes popular individuals (e.g., the school ground Machiavellian bully) are necessarily not popular because people like them, but because they have charisma that draw others into them. Indeed, theories on popularity (based on children's social networks in school) have identified two types of popular peers—"populistic" (popular, but not necessarily liked by others) and "prosocial popular" (popular, and well liked and accepted by others; De Bruyn & Cillessen, 2006). Most studies on popularity have focused on children, leaving a shortage of research on adults. Considering the averse, antisocial characteristics of the Dark Triad, it would be expected that if these individuals are popular at all, the popularity is based on being populistic rather than prosocial.

Studying popularity in social groups can be tricky, as not only is it measured by internal factors (e.g., personality, age, skills, status of individuals), but also by external influences that are related to the group dynamics. For instance, a person within a social group could be disliked just because another group member finds them annoying. Most studies on adults have investigated popularity at a dyadic level, not taking the complexities of social networks into account.

The picture that is emerging with regards to Machiavellianism and popularity in children indicates that high-Mach kids are both popular (Abell et al., 2015; Hawley, 2003) and unpopular (Abell et al., 2015). Patricia Hawley, featured in Box 5.1, has suggested that Machiavellian children possess both positive and negative characteristics, having ability to switch tactics between being prosocial to being aggressive.

Abell et al. (2015) observed school playground interactions in children between the ages of 9 and 11. The observations indicated that high-Mach boys used a constellation of aggressive and prosocial strategies in their interactions with others. On the one hand, they showed prosocial behavior by accepting other children to join their playgroups. On the other hand, they also exhibited elevated levels of direct (i.e., physical), as well as indirect (i.e., ostracism) aggression toward others. High-Mach boys also appeared to be popular, and they were accepted to join other groups at higher frequencies. A different picture emerged for Machiavellian girls, who had a more aloof,

BOX 5.1 Professor Patricia Hawley

Pat Hawley, a Professor of Educational Psychology and Leadership at the Texas Tech University, has been instrumental in advancing evolutionary theories and research on the development of social relationships in children and adults. Resource Control Theory (RCT) is one of her central theories, explaining aggressive and prosocial strategies from evolutionary perspective. According to RCT, friendships are adaptive in terms of allowing increased access to resources by forming long-term cooperative alliances. However, there is also another route to controlling resources—coercion and aggression. Professor Hawley's research has been important for understanding adverse friendship behaviors as adaptive, rather than as abnormal and pathological.

According to Professor Hawley's research, individuals can be categorized into groups depending on the propensity to employ combinations of these two strategies when socializing with others. Some individuals are skillful in using both coercive and prosocial friendship tactics. These individuals are named "bistrategic controllers." Children (and adults) who have mastered the use of both coercive and prosocial tactics in their social relationships are acutely aware of social conventions and morality, but they lack an internalized conscience. They may exhibit low levels of guilt after moral transgressions. In many ways, bistrategic controllers display features of Machiavellianism and primary psychopathy, moving adeptly in their social environments by using manipulation and flattery. Mastering both prosocial and coercive tactics relates to social competence, and material and social success.

> *In one study, Hawley (2003) collected data from over 1700 German adolescents, asking them about the frequency of using prosocial (e.g., "I influence others by doing something in return") to coercive (e.g., "I usually force others to do what I want") strategies. In addition, she measured their self-reported social skills, and also asked for peer and teacher nominations for the use of strategies, popularity, social skills, and so on. Children who were bistrategic controllers (i.e., more Machiavellian) were rated as aggressive by their peers, but not by their teachers, implying the ability to hide coercive strategies from authority figures. They were well-adjusted, socially skilled, popular figures in their peer groups.*
>
> *Here Machiavellianism refers to an apparently effective approach that entails the (perhaps) careful balancing of "getting along" and "getting ahead." These children admit that they are aggressive (the most aggressive), claim to be hostile, and confess that they cheat in school. Peers also cast them in a similar light and report them to be the most aggressive children in the schoolyard. Yet they are also seen as effective, socially central, and are reasonably well liked (Hawley, 2003, p. 239).*

Continued

BOX 5.1 Professor Patricia Hawley—cont'd

Recommended Reading

Hawley, P. H. (2014). The duality of human nature: coercion and prosociality in youths' hierarchy ascension and social success. *Current Directions in Psychological Science, 23*, 433–438.

and less popular standing in their playground groups. They were less likely to accept or reject other peers who wanted to join their group. They were also less likely to be accepted by others when they were initiating contact with a new group. This sex difference is interesting, suggesting that it is the Machiavellian boys rather than girls who reach a popular status in their peer groups. As mentioned earlier, we don't really know what the influence of Machiavellianism is on popularity in adult friendship networks, something that should be on the radar for future research.

There has been a fair amount of interest in narcissism and popularity, especially in young adults. Narcissism is a trait that can influence, from the very first interactions with new friends, the likeability and status than an individual attains in a friendship groups. Carlson and DesJardins (2015) described three different patterns of status (i.e., how much prominence, influence, and respect someone gets in the eyes of others) and popularity (i.e., how much an individual is liked by others): Maintenance pattern,

Waning pattern, and Null pattern. According to Maintenance pattern, narcissists should be able to gain status and popularity among friends, and also maintain these over the course of time. The Waning pattern predicts that although narcissists may initially be able to gain status and popularity, their façade of charm wanes over time, resulting in lesser liking and respect by their friends. Narcissistic individuals work toward putting on a show that grabs attention of others, often by using clever jokes, neat clothing, and showing seemingly superior social skills by using pleasant movements and facial expressions (Back, Schmuckle, & Egloff, 2010). In the short term, others are often attracted to the showmanship exhibited by narcissistic individuals. However, the adverse patterns of egotism and selfishness may lead to dislike in long-term relationships. Finally, the Null pattern predicts that narcissism is nothing special when making and maintaining friends, and is unrelated to both popularity and status. The Null pattern could be a result of positive (e.g., extraversion, attractiveness) and negative (e.g., hostility, grandiosity) features of narcissism canceling each other out. There is some experimental evidence that narcissism is associated with both negative and positive pathways to popularity, suggesting that whatever happens during initial acquaintance, narcissists are controversial in eyes of others—they are either disliked or liked (see Küfner, Nestler, & Back, 2013). Those who see narcissists as assertive may like them, and those who view them as hostile will dislike them. These two patterns could lead to, statistically speaking, results that are characterized by null findings.

There is some work on all of the Dark Triad traits during initial encounters when individuals are getting familiar with each other. In a laboratory study, John Rauthmann (2012) organized undergraduate students into dyads, where each dyad had to work on the "NASA-game," sorting out items in order of importance for getting from moon back to the base station. After the collaborative exercise, participants were asked to rate the properties of the interaction, and fill in personality measures for themselves, and for their interaction partner. People high in narcissism did not make particularly positive nor negative impressions on their new acquaintances. This would support the Null pattern of popularity, although it is not clear from the results whether the null pattern is a result of liking and disliking canceling each other out, or whether narcissism leads to neutral ratings in collaborative interactions. However, the results for Machiavellianism and psychopathy were distinctively different from narcissism. Both of these traits were related to initial dislike and negative first impressions. Something in the behavior of high Machiavellian and psychopathic individuals leads to low popularity and disliking in circumstances that would be ideal for making new friends.

Whether narcissism is related to initial popularity or neutral liking, the socially attractive veneer of narcissists does not seem to last for long, and some studies on this topic support the Waning pattern. Anna Czarna and colleagues have investigated the popularity of narcissistic individuals over time, as well as popularity at one snapshot in time. Their studies have analyzed personality and popularity in larger peer networks using social network analyses. In one study, they asked Polish university students in study groups to nominate peers who they like and do not like. They also measured the student's grandiose and vulnerable narcissism. The idea behind this research was that not only may some individuals be low in popularity (i.e., indifferent to other people), but they may also be actively disliked by others. As vulnerable narcissism relates to lower self-esteem, and probably lower visibility in social networks, they expected that vulnerable narcissism leads to invisibility in the social network, resulting in less nominations for being a likeable peer. The social show put on by individuals high in grandiose narcissism may prove to be irritating to others in the long run, resulting in more nominations for being a disliked person.

The findings of Czarna, Dufner, and Clifton (2014) indicate that indeed, vulnerable narcissism is associated with less popularity in terms of being liked by fewer group members. The antagonistic, more introverted nature of vulnerable narcissism was also reflected in liking fewer individuals in the network themselves. Grandiose narcissism was associated with increased number of nominations for a disliked individual, indicating that they were actively detested by others in their study group. Interestingly, both types of narcissism had also a central role in their network for disliking, and being disliked by other group members who had no dislike for each other. In short, narcissistic individuals had a central standing in their networks for being disliked by others. These results support the Waning pattern in that narcissistic popularity does not last for long and is not conductive to being popular in established friendship networks.

In another study, Czarna, Leifeld, Śmieja, Dufner, and Salovey (2016) studied the influence of narcissism and emotional intelligence among university students at the beginning of the formation of a new social network (i.e., at zero acquaintance), and again, after three months of acquaintance. They were interested in investigating not only narcissism, but also emotional intelligence in influencing popularity in a friendship group over time. They found that both narcissism and emotional intelligence were important predictors of popularity. Narcissistic individuals received more nominations from their peers at the initial encounter, and less nominations after a three-month period of acquaintance. Narcissism seems to be a trait that is initially attractive, but over time, their popularity decreased, probably because of the socially aversive aspects of narcissism. Emotional intelligence, in turn, is an important part of popularity in the long term. Those who had higher emotional intelligence increased in popularity over the three-month period, which indicates that the ability to understand and regulate the emotions of others as well as one's own emotions could be an important determinant of popularity.

It is useful to remember that popularity is also a dyadic process, and who likes whom also depends on the personality of both of the parties. Although individuals who are high on the Dark Triad traits may not be that popular within their networks, they may still be tolerated, and even liked by those who possess high levels of the traits themselves. For instance, Lamkin, Maples-Keller, and Miller (2018) found that although on average, people rated high Dark Triad traits (mainly, antagonism) as dislikeable, those who were high on the trait themselves did not dislike them as much. The findings echo that of Burton et al. (2017), who found that individuals who are high on narcissism do not dislike this trait as much as people who are lower in narcissism. Thus those who are at the high end of the Dark Triad of personality may tolerate the same traits better in friends.

The Big Five trait agreeableness has received some interest in terms of popularity during first encounters, as well as popularity in long-term friendships. Agreeableness is relevant to the Dark Triad research, as disagreeable people are also those who score high on the dark personalities. The warmth and kindness of agreeable individuals may not immediately attract others during first encounters, but in the long run, agreeable individuals receive more nominations in friendship network studies, and also have large, stable networks because other people prefer their company (Harris & Vazire, 2016). In terms of forming successful long-term relationships, core features of the Dark Triad (i.e., disagreeableness) seem to be a hinder.

5.5 Tactics in Friendships

People employ different tactics in making new friends and in maintaining existing friendships. The tactics can vary from benign (e.g., using self-disclosure, flattery, or gifts in order to influence the other person) to aversive (e.g., bullying, harassing, and gossiping in order to benefit from the other). One tactic that is relevant in getting closer to others is self-disclosure, revealing something personal about oneself. Disclosing something of a personal nature can be a great way of drawing people together and creating an atmosphere of closeness and intimacy. Self-disclosure can be deep, revealing the fears, hopes, and significant events in one's past. It can also be more trivial, including personal information about food, music, and media preferences. Although self-disclosure has a positive impact in established friendships, it can also be used as a manipulative tool for gaining the trust of a new acquaintance, leaving them open for being manipulated by someone who they haven't had an opportunity to get to know properly.

Self-disclosure has the potential for being a manipulative tool for gaining access to initial acquaintances and deepening the relationship faster because those who engage in intimate self-disclosure are liked more by others. However, people are sensitive to the right amount of disclosure at different stages of a friendship. At initial stages, trivial disclosure seems more appropriate, and the more personal level is achieved later as the friendship deepens. When someone is disclosing too much and too soon, it can make them look suspicious and alienate people.

The research on self-disclosure in initial and established friendships has focused mainly on Machiavellianism, probably due to the scheming, political interpersonal tactics associated with this trait. In earlier studies, researchers were interested in the influence of Machiavellianism in self-disclosure between strangers in laboratory experiments. Interestingly, several studies found that women (but not men) who were high on Machiavellianism were more willing to self-disclose personal information to strangers (Brown & Guy, 1983; Domelsmith & Dietch, 1978; O'connor & Simms, 1990). The interpretations of the findings were that high-Mach women may use self-disclosure as a tactic to gain control over others. Intimacy and self-disclosure are more typical in female relationships, and it may evoke more suspicions among men if a new acquaintance is revealing too much personal information. Self-disclosure could be a more beneficial strategy for Machiavellian women in getting close to new friends than it is for Machiavellian men.

Unfortunately, there is a lack of research on the relationship between the Dark Triad and self-disclosure as a strategy for gaining new friends and maintaining established friendships. It is possible that all the three dark traits influence the amount of self-disclosure at early stages of the friendship. It could be used as a manipulative strategy in order to get close to others and/or gain more friends. However, in the long run, self-disclosure may play a lesser part in the friendships. The friendship styles of Dark Triad individuals are less intimate and more instrumental, and disclosing important information of oneself is not expected, unless it is an instrumental tool for gaining the sympathy of a friend in order to get something from them. Self-disclosure is an important aspect in establishing and maintaining friendships, and would benefit from more attention in future studies on aversive personality and friendship tactics.

There are also other, more negative tactics that individuals use when dealing with their friends. Relational (or indirect) aggression is a common, aversive friendship tactic, used in dyadic relationships as well as in wider social networks. It involves social manipulation by means of threats, ostracism, and gossip, and the aim is often to damage the status or reputation of a friend. Relational aggression is different from direct aggression in that it is much more subtle, highly psychologically damaging to the victims, and can be difficult to detect. In the common language, friends who use relational aggression are called "frenemies" (friends + enemies), and people classify their relationships with these kind of friends as ambivalent (neither positive nor negative, but a mixture of both). Based on the characteristics of high Dark Triad individuals, they make good candidates for frenemy friends, those who are toxic but still categorized as being friends.

The reasons for resorting to relational aggression in friendship are varied and depend on the personality of the friends and the dynamics of the relationship. Research has found that the triggers for relational aggression vary from being provoked to aggress to actively seeking to aggress without any external triggers. Reactive aggression is a hostile, defensive response to a perceived threat from a friend, which is caused by actual or perceived provocation. For example, an individual who engages in reactive aggression may block a friend from their social network site if they think that the friend is guilty of doing something that puts the aggressor in bad light.

Proactive aggression is more deliberate and planned, and does not require provocation. An individual who engages in proactive aggression is using it as a tool for gaining something at the friend's cost, for example, increased status or power within the social networks. As an example, a popular high school girl might perceive a friend as a threat to their status and use their social power in shunning the friend by barring them from access to the friendship group. This type of aggression is commonly depicted in films and TV series popular with adolescents and young adults (e.g., Coyne & Archer, 2004). Relational aggression and its different forms has been studied widely in the friendship networks of adolescents and children, but less so in adult populations.

Only few studies have investigated relational aggression together with all the three Dark Triad traits, using adults as participants. In one such study, Knight, Dahlen, Bullock-Yowell, and Madson (2018) examined both proactive and reactive aggression in college students, looking at the influence of the Big Five as well as Machiavellianism, psychopathy, and both vulnerable and grandiose narcissism. Relational aggression was measured with questions tapping into reactive and proactive aggression. Interestingly, the authors found that those who were high on grandiose narcissism were less likely to employ any kind of strategies of relational aggression toward their friends. Grandiose narcissists are more secure in their relationships with others and do not have the need to exert negative influence on their friends. People who were high on vulnerable narcissism and psychopathy, in turn, were more likely to use both proactive and reactive aggression in friendships. Narcissistic vulnerability seems to be an important factor in socially toxic strategies in friendships and could be motivated by a hostility stemming from low self-esteem and insecurity about one's position in the social network. Relational aggression in friendships of those who are high in psychopathy is likely to occur for different reasons, possibly just out of meanness and strive to control and dominate others.

Another study investigated the role of primary and secondary psychopathy in promoting relational aggression in university students and their friends (Czar, Dahlen, Bullock, & Nicholson, 2011). The tactics that they asked their participants included things like spreading rumors about their friend. The authors found that both the cold, callous, and the risk-taking, impulsive facets of psychopathy were associated with increased use of relational aggression. These findings strengthen the idea that "frenemies" in close social bonds are those who are high on psychopathy and its subcomponents.

Emotional manipulation is another commonly used toxic strategy in friendships, part of indirect, mostly proactive relational aggression. Emotionally manipulative individuals try to induce their friends to feel guilty by making them feel like "bad" friends. They may also evoke the green-eyed monster by making their friends jealous. Jealousy induction can take many forms, for example, spending time with other people and making sure that the friend knows about it (something that is made easy by the inception of the internet and the social media sites), or excessively praising other people. Emotionally manipulative people are happy to make their friends embarrassed or ashamed, and put them down in front of other people. However, emotional manipulation also includes tactics of flattery and complements, and they can be used as a cheap strategy to get the friend to do something for the manipulating individual. Emotionally manipulative individuals can do significant amount of harm in a network of friends, as they have the ability to play people against each other.

Emotional manipulation in friendships has mainly been studied using self-reported questionnaire measures (e.g., Austin, Farrelly, Black, & Moore, 2007). A scale created by Elizabeth Austin and colleagues is asking people to rate how much they endorse questions such as "I can pay someone compliments to get in their 'good books,'" or "I can make someone feel anxious so that they will act in a particular way." In their initial validation study, the authors found that Machiavellian participants were more likely to agree with the questions about emotional manipulation, but also had lower levels of emotional intelligence (i.e., the ability to understand and manage the feelings of others and the self). This indicates that either understanding others is not necessary for successful emotional manipulation, or Machiavellian individuals are not very successful in their attempts to employ emotional manipulation.

Another study had similar findings with regards to Machiavellianism, but not for psychopathy and narcissism. Nagler, Reiter, Furtner, and Rauthmann (2014) explored the Dark Triad in relation to emotional manipulation and "socioemotional intelligence," which they divided into six subcomponents including controlling and expressing own emotions, understanding other's feelings, and being able to engage other's socially. The authors found that although Machiavellianism did relate to higher proclivity to use emotional manipulation, Machiavellian individuals were poor in their socioemotional skills. Perhaps Machiavellian individuals are just "shooting in the darkness," and using manipulation as a default without understanding what the outcomes of this behavior might be in influencing the dynamics of the friendship. However, the results also showed that narcissism and psychopathy were quite different from Machiavellianism. Both traits had an association with increased use of emotional manipulation, but only narcissism related to higher levels of self-reported socioemotional intelligence. In a moderation analysis, Nagler et al. found that narcissism and psychopathy both moderated the relationship between emotional intelligence and emotional manipulation (Nagler et al., 2014). In other words, narcissism and psychopathy could be examples of "dark intelligence." This finding suggests that emotional intelligence is useful in emotional manipulation, especially when it is put in practice by those who are high on narcissism and psychopathy.

Although emotional manipulation is a skill that would be expected to be beneficial especially in friendships, not many studies have explicitly investigated this with regards to all of the Dark Triad traits. However, several studies have explored the relationship between Machiavellianism and emotional manipulation in women's friendships. In one of their studies, Abell, Brewer, Qualter, and Austin (2016) employed an online sample of women, who were asked to answer questions about emotional manipulation in relation to their best friend, focusing on being both a victim and a perpetrator of manipulation. Interestingly, and also coinciding with the suspicious nature associated with Machiavellianism, the authors found that High-Mach women perceived their friends as being emotionally manipulative toward them. There are a few possible explanations for this finding. Referring back to the study of Maaß et al. (2016) with regards to the similarity between friends, it is conceivable that Machiavellian women have best friends who are Machiavellian as well, and thus will use more manipulation toward their friends. The other explanation is that Machiavellian individuals are suspicious toward others even when there is no need for the suspicion, which could lead to flawed perceptions of having friends who are emotionally manipulative.

Abell and colleagues were also interested in whether Machiavellian women are more likely to use different emotional manipulation tactics themselves, and how good they thought they are at doing this. Indeed, Machiavellian individuals reported being skilled at using emotional manipulation toward their friend, including making them feel ashamed, embarrassed, and guilty. They also deployed strategies such as sulking and trying to make their friend feel jealous. These types of tormenting friendship behaviors are likely to lead to low quality bonds between the individuals, ultimately resulting in a dissolution of the friendship.

Competition between the friends is another potentially detrimental tactic in friendships. There are individual differences in competition, where some individuals have a constant need to outshine their friend, trying to prove one's superiority over the other. The competition can happen in any domains of life, including education, work, relationships, money, exercise, and parenting. Competition between friends is common, and as with other friendship research, has been studied more widely in children and adolescents, and less so in adults.

Looking at posts from "mumsnet" reveal that competition between women is common and could stem from insecurity, coupled with manipulativeness. For instance,

> *... I have a 'friend' lets call her X. Live locally and kids go to the same school so see each other a lot. I won't list the specific comments as it will out me but suffice to say she is one of those people who consistently makes digs at me about the size of my house, money, weight, competitive about children etc. She is also invasively nosey. Knocks on my door without invitation (I hate that) and generally asks lots of questions about money etc (I avoid replying) whilst boasting how she doesn't need to budget etc. An example of her invasiveness is her and her husband going to see a house they knew we had looked at it just to check it out! Not that they were looking to live there. WTF! She is now going through a phase of slagging someone else off we know. I am pretty sure it's because this person has something she wants (she's lost a lot of weight). However, in a time of need X can be incredibly generous and is the first to offer to help ... (Samnella; Sat 09-Mar-13; 07:40:28; https://www.mumsnet.com/Talk/am_i_being_unreasonable/1703580-to-ask-how-to-deal-with-A-frenemy).*

The "frenemy" depicted in the post shows fierce competitiveness in all domains of life, including looks, finances, and achievements of children. She appears both Machiavellian and insecure. The lack of subtleness of her tactics could be a reflection of the low emotional intelligence related to Machiavellianism, which could lead to competition and emotional manipulation that is not necessarily successful. Hundreds of similar posts in mumsnet are asking for advice on how to break up a relationship like this, which speaks for the short-lived friendships with those who are manipulative and competitive.

Empirical research on the Dark Triad and friendship competition is sparse. There are some studies on the Dark Triad and competition in the workplace, romantic relationships, and sports. For example, research on workplace attitudes has found that Machiavellianism and psychopathy (but not narcissism) relate to perceptions of competition in the office (Jonason, Wee, & Li, 2015). Greg Carter, Montanaro, Linney, and Campbell (2015) found that in a women-only sample, all of the Dark Triad traits were significant positive correlates of overall competitiveness, as well as competition for romantic partners. However, narcissism was the strongest predictor of the three traits. It is possible that competition in friendships is different from overall competitiveness, or more general intrasexual competitiveness. Competition with friends could relate to jealousy stemming from social comparison and low self-esteem. Especially grandiose narcissism is immune to self-doubts like these and would be expected to have a lesser influence on the need to compete with a friend.

In one study, together with Gayle Brewer and Loren Abell, we investigated how Machiavellianism influences competition with friends, and how both competition and Machiavellianism impact on a positive friendship behavior, the intent to self-disclose personal information about oneself (Brewer, Abell, & Lyons, 2014). We found that the participants who were higher in Machiavellianism endorsed more items such as "I don't like my friend to achieve more than I do" and "I like to compete with my friend." Interestingly, in female participants, both Machiavellianism and competitiveness were negative predictors of the future intention to disclose personal information, as well as the depth of the disclosure. In short, Machiavellian individuals are more competitive with their friends, and Machiavellianism and competition together can result in a less intimate relationship. So far, research has not investigated how psychopathy and narcissism relate to competition and intimacy in friendships, which is something that should be taken into consideration in future research. Further, the subtleties of competition between women have been largely ignored (see Carter et al., 2015; Singleton & Vacca, 2007), and the sparsity of research on the Dark Triad and competition in women could stem from the misconception that socially aversive traits are more adaptive for men than for women, and that competition plays a minor part in enhancing women's reproductive success. This is obviously not the case, and hopefully future theories and research will fill the vacuum in the literature.

There are times when the opinions of friends differ, resulting in interpersonal conflict. Conflicts are an essential part of communication between friends, and disagreements do not necessarily need to be unpleasant and confrontational in nature. Indeed, the way that conflicts are often resolved is that one party persuades the other to agree to see things their way. Jonason and Webster (2010) studied the Dark Triad in relation to different tactics that people use when trying to persuade a friend into an agreement. Table 5.1 outlines the results from the study, including the types of tactics used, and their relationship to the Dark Triad traits. The tactics themselves vary from positive (e.g., using charm, bribing with money, promising reciprocal returns, or emphasizing pleasure) to negative (coercing, playing hardball, giving the friend a silent treatment).

Overall, participants who scored high on trait psychopathy used fewer persuasion strategies. Psychopathy had, indeed, a negative correlation with using positive strategies, such as pleasure induction (convincing the friend that they will get pleasurable benefits out of agreeing with the persuader).

Machiavellianism had a relationship with a multitude of persuasion strategies, both positive and negative. Those at the higher end of Machiavellianism scale tended to coerce their friends, play hardball, or give them the silent

Table 5.1 Social Influence Tactics for the Dark Triad of Personality in Same-Sex Friends

Tactic	Narcissism	Machiavellianism	Psychopathy
Coercion (trying to force the friend)	Positive	Positive	Neutral
Responsibility invocation (trying to evoke feelings of duty)	Positive	Neutral	Neutral
Hardball	Neutral	Positive	Neutral
Charm	Neutral	Neutral	Neutral
Silent treatment	Neutral	Positive	Neutral
Regression	Neutral	Neutral	Neutral
Reciprocity	Positive	Positive	Neutral
Pleasure induction	Neutral	Positive	Negative
Debasement	Neutral	Neutral	Neutral
Reason	Positive	Neutral	Neutral
Social comparison	Positive	Neutral	Neutral
Monetary reward	Positive	Neutral	Neutral
Seduction	Positive	Neutral	Neutral

Adapted from Jonason and Webster (2010), who simultaneously regressed the Dark Triad traits against the different strategies. "Neutral" indicates a nonsignificant beta value for the trait (even if in some cases, the values approached significance), "positive" indicates a significant positive beta value, and "negative" a significant negative beta value.

treatment until the friend would conform. On a positive note, they were also more likely to lure their friends by promising to reciprocate, using money to bribe them, and emphasizing the pleasurable aspects of reaching an agreement. Narcissism was also related to a range of tactics, including playing on responsibility and reasoning, but also using coercion.

5.6 Friendship Quality

The quality of social relationships varies widely between individuals. Friendship bonds differ from warm and mutually supportive to shallow and superficial. Maintaining satisfying, close relationships with friends is crucial for mental and physical well-being, and can have a positive contribution to overall quality of life. The interesting question is that who are the people who can establish and maintain satisfying relationships with their friends? Many individuals struggle with friendships, and not all get happiness from having friends. In comparison to satisfaction in romantic relationship or in the workplace, friendship satisfaction had not received much attention in psychology research (e.g., Wilson, Harris, & Vazire, 2015).

Because the Dark Triad is associated with agentic, selfish interpersonal styles and shallow emotions, it would be expected that the friendships of people high in these traits are also of lower quality. Christian, Sellbom, and Wilkinson (2018) made an important distinction between the presence of a bond between others (i.e., whether it exists or not) and the quality of the bond (i.e., what the bond is like). The authors made an analogy between friendships and cars, stating that "… one would not conflate the quality of their motor vehicle with possessing or owning a motor vehicle. A poor quality vehicle could still be used for the purposes of transport, but would not be considered that same as entirely lacking a vehicle" (Christian et al., 2018, p. 4). The Dark Triad individuals are likely to make "poor quality vehicle" friends, not providing the same level of support as a good quality friend would.

Most research on friendship quality has concentrated on Machiavellianism, and mainly on how individuals high in Machiavellianism perceive their social bonds with others. We know much less about the perceptions of friendship quality from the friend's perspective—how do friends of Machiavellian (and narcissistic and psychopathic) individuals view their relationship with a manipulative friend? It is possible that from the friend's perspective, the quality of the bond with someone who is high on the Dark Triad shallow and the friendships can be short-lived in nature. Friendship quality and dissolution in adults is an underinvestigated domain of research, with many potential links to the Dark Triad.

In one of my earlier studies, we investigated the influence of Machiavellianism on the perceived importance and quality of friendships (Lyons & Aitken, 2010). Irrespective of the biological sex and age of the participants, Machiavellianism was a negative correlate of self-reported importance of having good quality friendships with others. The emotionally cool and detached interpersonal style of high-Mach individual translates into emotional detachment in their social relationships too. This could be partially due to the belief that others are untrustworthy, which could make high Machiavellian individuals to like their friends less. One of the factors influencing the detached friendship style of High-Machs could be the experiences with their parents as a child. Parenting provides a template for children to work on when establishing relationships as adults, including friends as well as romantic partners. In as study with Loren Abell and Gayle Brewer (Abell, Lyons, & Brewer, 2014), we investigated how Machiavellianism relates to the quality of friendships in adulthood, and whether this could be understood via the parenting experiences individuals had when they are children. We found that those who recalled their mothers as cold and uncaring, and their fathers as controlling and overprotecting also had higher

Machiavellianism scores, and reported having lower quality friendships. Thus Machiavellianism does have a relationship with poor quality friendships, and this could be born out of childhood experiences with parents.

Carrying on with the same theme, Abell et al. (2016) investigated Machiavellianism and friendship functioning with the best friend in several domains, including companionship, help, intimacy, and emotional security. They found that women who scored high on the Machiavellianism measure reported lower friendship functioning in all of the measured domains. Finally, Brewer, Abell, and Lyons (2013) investigated friendship quality in terms of how attached people feel toward their friends, finding that Machiavellianism related to lower quality friendships. Together, the results of these studies indicate that the cool, detached interpersonal style of high Machiavellian individuals also relate to lesser quality friendships.

Envy against a friend is a common factor in friendships, exerting a great influence on the quality of the bond between friends. Those who are envious of their friend, whether it is about looks, achievements, or money, may also gloat in the feeling of "schadenfreude," feeling pleased about any misfortunes that the friend encounters. Abell and Brewer (2017) studied the influence of Machiavellianism, envy, and competition on schadenfreude in women's friendships. The study participants read vignettes depicting three different types of misfortunes—academic (bad grade), looks (bad haircut), and relationships (relationship break-up), and rated their feelings (e.g., amusement, satisfaction, and pleasure) toward the friend. The authors found that Machiavellian women were pleased when their friend had a misfortune in terms of a relationship breakup or getting a bad haircut. As well as Machiavellianism, those who had high levels of competition and envy toward their friend also had higher levels of satisfaction when a friend experiences a misfortune.

Finally, Christian et al. (2018) investigated the four-factor model of psychopathy in relation to attachment bond toward friends, and number of individuals in an individuals close support network in an online sample of community participants. Only the callousness facet of psychopathy had a negative relationship with attachment toward friends, indicating that high levels of callousness have a negative influence on the quality of friendship bonds. With regards to number of individuals that people nominated for their close friendship network, antisocial aspects of psychopathy were negatively correlated with the number of close friends. The study suggests that quality and quantity of friends are influenced by different factors of psychopathy—those who are callous have lower quality friendships, and those who are antisocial have fewer friends.

5.7 Conclusion

Despite the relative sparsity of studies into the influence of the Dark Triad on friendship behaviors, strategies, and motivations, an interesting picture is emerging from the existing research. High Dark Triad individuals seem to be more instrumental in their motivations to select and maintain friendships, preferring friends who can satisfy their needs in the arena of mating and climbing up the social ladder. All of the traits relate to shallow friendships, and probably (although this is yet to be investigated) a lack of reciprocity in the help received from friends. Narcissism is the "lightest" of the dark traits, characterized by approach orientation toward friendships, prioritizing social contacts and having fun. Especially those who are high in Machiavellianism are likely to make good "frenemies," friends who are jealous, competitive, and potentially toxic. Psychopathy relates to a lack of social influence tactics in friendships, which could relate to the detached nature of the trait. Psychopathic individuals seem to be loners who are not bothered with friendships and have no need to try to influence their friends either. Research into friendships and the Dark Triad is still in its infancy, and there are many more questions to be answered here through empirical studies. Friendship literature has an unleashed potential for helping to advance our understanding of similarities and differences in the evolutionary adaptiveness of the three socially aversive traits.

Further Reading

Jonason, P. K., & Schmitt, D. P. (2012). What have you done for me lately? Friendship-selection in the shadow of the dark triad traits. *Evolutionary Psychology*, *10*(3).

Kennedy-Moore, E. (2014). Frenemies. *Psychology Today*, Retrieved from: https://www.psychologytoday.com/gb/blog/growing-friendships/201404/frenemies. Accessed June 2018.

Maaß, U., Lämmle, L., Bensch, D., & Ziegler, M. (2016). Narcissists of a feather flock together: Narcissism and the similarity of friends. *Personality and Social Psychology Bulletin*, *42*, 366–384.

CHAPTER SIX

The Dark Triad in the Workplace

Chapter Outline

6.1 Introduction to Dark Triad in the Workplace

Most of us have encountered someone in the workplace who could be described as "a conniving cheat, an arrogant braggart, or a callous hedonist" (LeBreton, Shiverdecker, & Grimaldi, 2018, p. 388). With these three portrayals, LeBreton and colleagues succinctly described the key features of Machiavellianism, narcissism, and psychopathy, evoking a somewhat accurate image of Dark Triad characters that loom at large in workplaces. The Dark Triad has received considerable interest in the fields of occupational, business, and organizational psychology. It is perhaps of no surprise, as cold, callous manipulation can have drastic implications not only for individual well-being at work, but also for the overall workplace functioning, sometimes affecting whole societies and global economies. Indeed, some have suggested that the global financial meltdown in 2008 was caused by immoral, greedy psychopaths employed in high positions in financial corporations (Boddy, 2011). Due to their attraction to power and status (Lee et al., 2013), high Dark Triad individuals are expected to be drawn to occupational

The Dark Triad of Personality
https://doi.org/10.1016/B978-0-12-814291-2.00006-1

fields where they can achieve these goals. Further, the Dark Triad is related to materialism, consumerism, and placing more importance on money than on humanistic values (Lee et al., 2013), which could lead to greed and selfishness in their professional lives. Workplace behaviors of those high in the Dark Triad are often geared toward maximizing their own incomes at the cost of the well-being of others.

The Dark Triad is not only associated with the fields of study and work that individuals are attracted to, but it also has an influence on behavior at work as an employee. People at the higher end of the continuum may exhibit counterproductive work behaviors (CWBs), such as stealing from work, being late or absent, or bullying coworkers. These behaviors can be detrimental to work colleagues, teamwork dynamics, as well as to the workplace as a whole. On the other hand, depending on the context, Dark Triad traits might be beneficial as well. For example, in insecure circumstances where potential gains are large, it may good to take risks, which is something that high Dark Triad individuals are more likely to do. Smith, Hill, Wallace, Recendes, and Judge (2018) warned against dichotomizing employees into "dark" and "bright," and equating dark with detrimental, and bright with beneficial. The interaction between workplace environment and the Dark Triad is complicated. There are likely to be multiple factors, such as workplace politics, work autonomy, and opportunities for career advancement, all of which can act as moderators between personality and different consequences in the workplace. Despite the media and popular science fascination with the Dark Triad in the context of employment, there is surprisingly little empirical research on aversive personality traits in the place of work (Smith & Lilienfeld, 2013). Many of the existing studies focus on people's attitudes to work, rather than on their behavior in the actual workplace. Although much has been written about "psychopathic bosses" in books such as "Snakes in suits" (Babiak & Hare, 2006), the empirical literature is lacking behind the theories and generic ideas surrounding the topic. This chapter is an attempt to bring together the existing empirical and theoretical literature in order to provide an overview of the Dark Triad in the workplace, considering both attitudes and behaviors, from both employee and management perspectives.

6.2 Are the Dark Triad Traits Associated with Career Choice?

According to the Attraction, Selection, Attrition (ASA) model posited by Schneider (1987), people are drawn to different companies and fields of work depending on how close match they provide with the individuals' personality, values, and interests. Not only do employees seek for workplaces that suit their personalities, but companies also actively look for workforce that match culture of the organization. For instance, in some extreme cases, companies are advertising for workforce with psychopathic tendencies ("Psychopathic New Business Media Sales Superstar £50k-110k", https://jobs.theguardian.com/job/6404273/psychopathic-new-business-media-sales-executive-superstar-50k-110k/). Some of the characteristics of high psychopathy (such as callousness, superficial charm, greed for money) have been perceived as positive in occupations that require persuading others. The ASA model predicts that those whose personalities are more likely to match with the workplace culture and ideologies are more motivated to stay in their job and less likely to be fired or made redundant. Over time, this should lead to homogeneous workforce within a company. Dutton (2012) compiled a list of top ten occupations that high psychopathy individuals should be attracted to. On the top of the list were CEOs, lawyers, journalists, and salespeople. These occupations may offer a good fit with the company values and the employee personality, providing support for the ASA model.

Since the Dark Triad is related to heightened interest in money and power, we would expect that students who study subjects that give them an opportunity to earn lucrative salaries and gain status (e.g., business and law) score higher on the Dark Triad than students in disciplines where money and power are lesser motivators (e.g., humanities and social sciences). Earlier studies, using the Big Five framework, found that in fields where competitiveness and ruthlessness could be beneficial for achieving success (e.g., business, economics, and law), students are lower in trait agreeableness than those in "softer" disciplines (e.g., arts and humanities; Vedel, 2016). As discussed in Chapter 1, the Dark Triad is associated with specifically low agreeableness, which would suggest that students in disciplines such as business score higher than students in other fields.

This idea was investigated in a study by Vedel and Thomsen (2017). They looked at the Dark Triad traits among newly enrolled students majoring in different disciplines: psychology, law, business, and economics. They found that in comparison to business and economics students, psychology students obtained lower scores on the Dark Triad scales. This study was especially interesting because it was conducted on new students who are unlikely to have been affected by the nature of the discipline that they study. Another study, conducted by Krick et al. (2016), compared the Dark Triad scores of beginner and advanced business and management students, with the idea that if the discipline makes individuals more manipulative, the scores should be higher in students who have studied longer. The authors found that more advanced students were not higher on the Dark Triad than novice students. They also found that business and management students scored higher on the Dark Triad traits than those enrolled on humanities and social sciences degrees. The results of both Vedel and Thomsen (2017) and Krick et al. (2016) suggest that people who operate in the business world don't necessarily become more ruthless and manipulative because of the nature of their discipline, but that those who already possess these traits are drawn into fields where Dark Triad traits could be of advantage.

Psychopathy and its subcomponents are of specific interest in the field of occupational choice. The idea of successful psychopathy (reviewed in Chapter 1) lends support to a prediction that students in fields of study that promise financial success score high on the cold, callous, and unemotional facets of primary psychopathy. This was the focus of a study of Wilson and McCarthy (2011), who looked at the two-factor structure of psychopathy in students in different disciplines. They expected to find that those majoring in commerce score higher on primary psychopathy than students majoring in arts, science, or law. In a sample of over 900 university undergraduates, they found that those who were enrolled on a commercial degree did, indeed, obtain higher scores on primary psychopathy than students in other degrees. As expected, there were no differences between disciplines in secondary psychopathy, characterized by impulsive, risk-taking behaviors. It is possible that people who are motivated by greed can consolidate their career goals by studying a topic that can open doors into the corporate word, aiding in climbing up the social ladder. The authors proposed that primary psychopathy features, such as lack of empathy and guilt, greedy risk-taking, and superficial charm of financial leaders could have had a major contribution to the global economic crisis in 2008.

In a more recent study, Litten, Roberts, Ladyshewsky, Castell, and Kane (2018) investigated empathy and psychopathy in business and psychology students in different cohorts across several years of study. As expected, psychology students had higher empathy and lower psychopathy scores than business students. Empathy levels did not change in either discipline from first to third year of study. The findings suggest that although those who are higher in empathy may initially choose to study psychology, the degree itself does not make students more empathetic as the years of study progress. The same applies in business students, who were initially lower in empathy, and had similar scores across the different years of study. However, psychopathy scores were significantly lower in third year cohort of psychology students. This could imply that those who are initially low in psychopathy may self-select to study psychology, and that the nature of the discipline influences students so that they become even less psychopathic when they progress in their degree. This was not the case for business students, who scored initially higher in psychopathy and had similar scores in different years. The study provided some evidence for the ASA model, as psychology as a profession is more geared toward helping others, whereas business is more about making money. However, the limitations (such as a relatively small sample size and cross-sectional nature of the study) warrant some cautions with interpreting the results. This study (like most research on the Dark Triad) would benefit from replication with larger samples and longitudinally following students from one year of study to another.

Research in organizational psychology has shown that not just students, but also those who are in employment in different fields could self-select to those fields according to their personality traits. For example, people who work in the corporate business world are often ruthless and manipulative, exhibiting traits of primary psychopathy (Babiak & Hare, 2006). The idea of a "successful" psychopathy has become popular in the recent years (Smith, Watts, & Lilienfeld, 2014), although writing about the topic has been more prevalent in popular science and media than in actual academic research (Smith & Lilienfeld, 2013).

In his book "The wisdom of psychopaths," Kevin Dutton, a psychologists based at Oxford University, lists a number of occupations that are likely to attract people who are high on psychopathy. Among the top five are CEOs, lawyers, people who work in media and sales, and surgeons. These occupations are characterized by getting ahead by manipulation, boldness, and low empathy, and individuals who are high in psychopathy may excel, and get enjoyment out of these jobs. The top occupations that attract high psychopathy individuals are also well paid, and the performance is sometimes related to financial rewards. In some of the top list of occupations for high psychopathy, individuals are required to work with a cool head, without overt empathy. For example, in order to perform a surgery, medical practitioners should focus on the complicated job, rather than worry about the patient. Dutton also listed the occupations that are least likely to attract high psychopathy individuals. Not surprisingly, those occupations consisted of roles that provide help and care for others (e.g., nurse, care-aid, therapist, doctor). However, there currently are not many studies exploring psychopathy (or indeed, the Dark Triad) and attraction to different occupations.

Studies that have considered the relationship between the Dark Triad and broad career interests have found that all the traits are related to unique career aspirations. For example, Peter Jonason and colleagues (Jonason, Lyons, Baughman, & Vernon, 2014; Jonason, Wee, Li, & Jackson, 2014) investigated the interests for different types of occupational interests using John Holland's career typology of realistic, investigative, artistic, social, enterprising, and conventional (RIASEC model). They found that psychopathy had a positive relationship with a preference for realistic and enterprising careers. Machiavellianism was negatively correlated with preference for artistic, social, and enterprising careers. Narcissism, in turn, had a positive relationship with a preference for artistic, social, and enterprise careers. In a more recent study, Kowalski, Vernon, and Schermer (2017) found that narcissism, again, was associated with artistic, social, and business interests. Machiavellianism had a negative correlation with social careers, and psychopathy a positive correlation with interest in physical sciences and engineering, jobs that are adventurous, and some aspects of business world, including sales and finance. Psychopathy also had a negative relationship with socially focused careers. These results support the idea that many people who are drawn into artistic careers (such as performing arts) have a narcissistic need for admiration, and careers such as acting can lead to admirations by masses of people (Dufner et al., 2015b; Box 6.1).

BOX 6.1 Narcissism in the entertainment industry.

"There is only one thing in life worse than being talked about, and that is not being talked about" (Oscar Wilde). This famous quote from the writer Oscar Wilde is epitome of narcissism—the burning desire to be the center of attention and the object of admiration by others. The occupation that would fulfill this goal is in the entertainment industry, especially performing arts—acting, music, and dance. "I like to be the centre of attention," and "I wish someday someone would write my biography" sound like statements from any budding celebrity. In fact, these are items from the Narcissistic Personality Inventory, indicating excessive exhibitionism and grandiosity, typical to many of those in the limelight of celebrity worlds.

A few academic studies have investigated narcissism in celebrities. Young and Pinsky (2006) studied narcissism in 200 celebrities (actors, comedians, musicians, and reality television personalities) who took part in a radio show "Loveline3," hosted by Dr. Drew Pinsky. The radio show invites the listeners to phone in with their relationship problems, and the celebrities offer advice to them, together with their host. They found that female celebrities were much more narcissistic than male celebrities,

BOX 6.1 Narcissism in the entertainment industry.—cont'd

especially in exhibitionism, superiority, and vanity. This may be an indication that women who have a celebrity status are more occupied with their appearance than male celebrities are. When looking at different types of celebrities, the authors found that reality TV stars had the highest scores on narcissism, followed by comedians, actors, and finally, musicians, who had the lowest narcissism scores. Celebrities in this sample were much more narcissistic than MBA students or the general population. Years in the entertainment business were not related to narcissism, which suggests that people who get into this area of work are initially driven by narcissistic goals, rather than turning narcissistic as a result of the limelight.

Dufner et al. (2015b) studied narcissism in acting students and improvisational theater actors in Germany, Austria, and Switzerland. They found that acting students and professional actors were higher than the control groups on narcissistic admiration. Narcissistic admiration is an interpersonal style driven by the need to get attention and admiration from others, and behaving in ways that maximize the likelihood of getting attention that feeds the grandiose self-views. In the world of acting, receiving the applause from the audience works as a positive motivation for acting as a career choice, at least for those who are high in narcissistic admiration.

"I am a Gods vessel. But my greatest pain in life is that I will never be able to see myself perform live"; "I feel like I'm too busy writing history to read it"; "I am Warhol. I am the No 1 most impactful artist of our generation. I am Shakespeare in the flesh". These quotes from the rap artist Kanye West provide a full embodiment of narcissistic grandiosity and the need for admiration. The scant academic studies hint at the importance of narcissism as the driving force behind wanting to have a career in the world of entertainment, a world that promises the fulfillment of one of the narcissistic goals, the need to be admired by crowds of people.

REFERENCES

Dufner, M., Egloff, B., Hausmann, C. M., Wendland, L. M., Neyer, F. J., & Back, M. D. (2015b). Narcissistic tendencies among actors: craving for admiration, but not at the cost of others. *Social Psychological and Personality Science, 6*(4), 447–454.

Young, S. M., & Pinsky, D. (2006). Narcissism and celebrity. *Journal of Research in Personality, 40*(5), 463–471.

6.3 The Dark Triad in Job Interviews

The potential detrimental influence of dark personalities begins early in the employment, often during the recruitment process. Individuals who convincingly lie about their achievements and qualifications in job applications and during the interview are more likely to be appointed for the posts they are applying for. This could result in employment of candidates who are actually not best for the job. Even more, it can result in employing candidates who will potentially carry on with deceitful tactics after they have been hired.

Due to incessant self-promotion, superficial charm, and positive impression management tactics, it is possible that those on the high end of the continuum are more likely to be successful in job interviews. According to Paulhus, Westlake, Calvez, and Harms (2013), self-promotion is an effective job interview tactic aiming at impressing an audience. It can be further divided into self-praise (i.e., bragging about one's specific talents) and self-enhancement (i.e., unwarranted exaggeration about one's talents). Both of these tactics are used widely by high narcissistic individuals. In laboratory experiments, narcissism has been related to positive first impressions (Back, Schmuckle, and Egloff, 2010), which could lead to a higher likelihood of success in acquiring a post after an interview. The other two traits, Machiavellianism and psychopathy, are largely perceived in a negative light at zero acquaintance (Rauthmann, 2012) and could even be a hinder in job interview settings. Despite the relevance of the Dark Triad in job interview situations, there is not much research looking at these traits in actual or simulated job interview settings.

Paulhus et al. (2013) conducted experiments using simulated job interviews, where the interviewees were filmed while completing a task on "Impress the interviewer with your competence in the field of psychology." The participants were divided into two groups—low and high accountability. In the low accountability condition, they were told that the interviewer was a second-year English student with little knowledge of psychology. In the high accountability condition, participants were informed that the interviewer was a psychology graduate who is an expert in the field. Some of the questions were specifically designed to elicit overenhancement, exaggeration of one's knowledge. For example, the participants were asked questions about psychology topics that in actuality do not exist. Those who self-enhance are more likely to try to blag their way through the questions and answer confidently.

The videos were counted for instances of overenhancement, for example, phrases like "yeah, I know that one." The results suggested that when narcissists are in the high accountability condition (i.e., being interviewed by an expert), they use more self-enhancement. However, the reverse was true for nonnarcissists, who were more likely to self-enhance in the low accountability condition. It is possible that when narcissists are faced with a situation where they have an opportunity to impress an expert, they are more willing to employ every possible self-promotion tactic, even those ones that involve blatant lying. Narcissistic self-promoters were given higher ratings for suitability for the job, especially if they were of European (rather than Asian) inheritance. The self-promotion in job interviews could explain why narcissism is common in high-powered occupations, as individuals who confidently exaggerate and pretend to know everything are more likely to be given the job after the interview.

In addition to self-promotion, another route to success in job interviews is a strategy characterized ingratiation (making oneself likeable) and image protection (hiding undesirable characteristics). In a study on Machiavellianism and job interviews, Hogue, Levashina, and Hang (2013) asked their undergraduate participants to answer questions on the likelihood of behaving in certain ways in a future job interview, such as pretending to agree with the interviewer while secretly disagreeing with them (i.e., ingratiation), and failing to mention that they would need additional training in order to be able to do the job (i.e., image protection). They found that both men and women who are high on Machiavellianism were more likely to use diverse tactics of self-enhancement, image protection, and manipulating the interviewer to like them more. In real-life interview situations, providing these tactics is performed in a believable manner, they can result in a success in obtaining the job.

Roulin and Bourdage (2017) followed a group of business students who were interviewed in local organizations for a 3-month placement opportunity. They found that students who were less experienced, low in honesty-humility, and high on all of the Dark Triad traits were more likely to engage in deceptive impression management tactics, including protecting their image via hiding any weaknesses. High Dark Triad scores (especially psychopathy) were also related to dynamic change in the impression management in successive interviews, adapting and increasing their strategies (such as exaggeration of achievements) from one interview to another. All together, these studies implicate that faking in interviews is typical to high Dark Triad applicants. They use diverse strategies, including compliments, hiding information, and exaggerating and lying about past achievements. Disingenuous behavior during the applicant selection process has the potential to lead to successful employment. This may put the companies in risk of having employees who engage in misbehavior, causing financial and reputational damage.

6.4 The Dark Triad and Leadership

Leadership is of major importance in the organizational context. Leaders vary from transformational, inspirational motivators to destructive, incompetent bullies. Leadership has significant consequences for the performance and well-being of individuals, teams, and the whole organizations. Indeed, the influence of leadership can be analyzed at three different levels: one-to-one interactions, team dynamics, and organizational functioning.

Personality impacts leadership styles and has received much research attention in organizational psychology. With regards to leadership and the Dark Triad, there has been a lot of interest investigating psychopathy in businesses. There are fewer studies on narcissism, Machiavellianism, or the whole trio of the dark traits together. Table 6.1 presents a constellation of studies on different leadership outcomes with regards to the Dark Triad.

The idea of the "psychopath boss" has become popular in the media since the publication of "Snakes in suits" by Babiak and Hare (2006). In the book, featuring real-life case studies, the authors give advice on how to identify, and deal with corporate psychopaths. Despite tremendous popularity of the concept of psychopathic corporate climbers, there has been surprisingly little empirical investigations into the Dark Triad and leadership in organizations, probably because of the sensitive nature of the research. Regardless of the lack of empirical literature, corporate workers are readily labeling their coworkers and leaders as psychopaths (Caponecchia, Sun, & Wyatt, 2012), probably as a result of extensive media attention, popular science literature, and web resources aimed at helping to identify workplace psychopaths.

There is some evidence to suggest that psychopathy is represented at disproportionately high numbers at the upper echelons of organizations (Babiak, Neumann, & Hare, 2010; Boddy, Ladyshewsky, & Galvin, 2010). For instance, Babiak et al. (2010) investigated psychopathy in over 200 corporate professionals, using the Psychopathy Checklist-revised (PCL-R). They found that those at the higher end of the scale were more likely to hold managerial/supervisory positions. Another study found that number of psychopathic individuals was excessively high especially in the higher levels of management (Boddy et al., 2010). Thus not only is psychopathy related to working in the corporate world, but it can also affect an individual's position in the organization. Features such as dominance, charisma, and fearlessness could have an association with at least short-term success in a leadership position.

Table 6.1 The Dark Triad and Leadership Outcomes

Study	Sample	Dark Triad Construct	Findings
Volmer, Koch, and Göritz (2016)	811 employees, Germany	N, P, M	Leader N = higher salary and more promotions. Leader M = lower career satisfaction and emotional wellbeing
Tokarev, Phillips, Hughes, and Irwing (2017)	508 employees, US	N, P	Leader N and P = more bullying, higher depression
Wisse and Sleebos (2016)	225 supervisors, 740 subordinates in Holland	N, P, M	Leader M = abusive supervision when supervisors think they have power
Braun (2017)	Meta-analysis of 45 studies	N	Charismatic, bold and daring, start new initiatives, preferred in uncertain conditions. Trigger negative emotions in followers, hinder collaboration, damage company image.
Mathieu et al. (2014)	612 managers and employees, Canada	P	Higher psychological distress and lower job satisfaction when manager is perceived as psychopathic
ten Brinke, Kish, and Keltner (2018)	101 hedge fund managers	N, P, M	Manager P = worse investors Manager N = decreased risk-adjusted returns
Blickle, Schütte, and Genau (2018)	154 managers, 154 superiors, 258 subordinates, Germany	P	Lower superior-rated job performance when good future work prospects and mistreatment of subordinates

Continued

Table 6.1 The Dark Triad and Leadership Outcomes—cont'd

Study	Sample	Dark Triad Construct	Findings
Babiak et al. (2010)	203 professionals in management development program, US	P	Higher performance ratings of charisma/ presentation style, lower ratings of responsibility/ performance
Zhang, Ou, Tsui, and Wang (2017)	206 CEOs, 63 CEOs, 518 top managers, and 645 middle managers, China	N	CEO N related organizational innovation but only in those who were humble in front of their subordinates

N = narcissism, P = psychopathy, M = Machiavellianism.

What kind of leaders do high Dark Triad individuals make? Are superiors who shout, bully, and undermine the work of employees likely to be high on the psychopathy spectrum? Interestingly, there are not many studies looking at leadership style and psychopathy in the actual place of work. Westerlaken and Woods (2013) investigated psychopathy and leadership styles in undergraduate students with management experience (although the students were not necessarily currently employed in companies). The researchers found that those high in psychopathy had laissez-faire leadership styles, which means that they preferred leading with a passive, hands-off style, delegating much of the tasks to the subordinates. Another study that researched employee perception of leadership style and psychopathy in their supervisors had similar findings—those who rated their boss as a psychopath also thought that their leadership style was passive (Mathieu, Neumann, Babiak, & Hare, 2015). Perhaps high psychopathy bosses are more interesting in advancing their own careers at the cost of taking care of the employees or the company. They may be inclined to lead with minimum effort in order to free up more time for selfish career enhancement.

Employees who think that they have a psychopathic supervisor suffer from multiple detrimental outcomes. A study found that individuals who rated their boss as being high in psychopathy also thought about leaving their job, had less work satisfaction, reduced work motivation, and more neglectful attitudes toward performing well in their job (Mathieu & Babiak, 2015). Interestingly, in this study, perceptions of supervisor psychopathy had a more negative influence than their leadership style. Thus irrespective of what kind of leader and individual is, if they are high in psychopathy, the outcomes are negative for the employees. In a similar study on employee perceptions of psychopathy, Clive Boddy (2014) analyzed data from a sample of over 300 individuals working in corporations in the United Kingdom. He found several interesting associations between perceived psychopathy of the manager, and employee well-being and behaviors. First, those who thought that their boss is a psychopath reported conflict and bullying in the workplace. Also, employees who perceived their superior as psychopathic reported feeling more anxious, angry, bored, and depressed. This suggests that psychopathic bosses have a negative impact on the emotional well-being of the employees. Finally, those who reported the presence of a psychopath boss also had less motivation to perform well in their job, indicated by less effort, more absences, and even sabotaging the work or work equipment. Being a recipient of an unfair treatment in the workplace lowers work motivation, which can result in behaviors that are counterproductive. Thus psychopathic bosses can also lead to CWBs by their employees.

However, not all aspects of "dark" leadership have detrimental outcomes. In terms of boldness and decision making, high Dark Triad traits can also lead to leadership that can be successful not necessarily for individuals, but for the companies as a whole. Thus when leadership success is measured in terms of profits and losses, rather than at an individual employee level, the Dark Triad traits may not always be harmful in a leader. For example, bold risk-taking could translate into success in an ultimate political leadership role, that of a president of a country. Lilienfeld et al. (2012) analyzed the expert ratings of the personality of 42 US presidents, and concluded that fearless dominance aspect of psychopathy had a positive association with crisis management, initiating new projects, and having the image of being a world leader. Similar results were found for narcissism in US presidents, suggesting that especially grandiose narcissism had a positive relationship with persuasiveness, crisis management, and winning popular votes, as well as exhibiting a host of unethical behaviors (Watts et al., 2013). Thus during turbulent times, the ruthlessness connected to some of the Dark Triad traits may be beneficial in dealing with crisis situations. According to Lilienfeld et al. (2012), psychopathic traits associated with boldness in social and physical situations could contribute to the success in achieving a leadership position. The same boldness could be beneficial when drastic leadership decisions are needed.

6.5 The Dark Triad, Career Satisfaction and Success

Sometimes toxic employees are able to climb up the ladder in the workplace, achieving power, promotions, success, and pay rise through confident manipulation of colleagues and superiors. Climbing the corporate ladder is facilitated by colleagues who fail to see the calculating tactics of their coworker, and supervisors who are blind to the selfish scheming of their subordinate. If the manipulative workplace tactics are, indeed, successful, those at the higher end of the dark continuum should have an accumulation of success in terms of salaries, promotions, and power. Success can also mean good performance in the work role, which could be related to a number of interacting factors including personality and the type of work individual is doing. However, success can also be measured by the gratification that an individual gets from their job, which is not necessarily related to material benefits from the work. In the following section, I will be reviewing research on the Dark Triad and work success in terms of material benefits, work performance, and subjective satisfaction that individuals get from their work.

Although much of the research has focused on the negative side of the Dark Triad in the workplace, these traits can also lead to excellent job performance, depending on the context. For instance, the shallow affect associated with Machiavellianism and primary psychopathy may be beneficial in situations that require cool-headed, rational decision making. A surgeon performing a demanding brain surgery would not necessarily be able to perform the task calmly and efficiently if they had strong levels of affective empathy toward the client. Furthermore, impulsivity typical to secondary psychopathy could be required in occupations where there is a need for fast, risky actions, for example, a fire personnel rescuing someone from a burning house. The emerging picture suggests that the Dark Triad is a double-edged sword in the workplace, with a mixture of positive and negative behaviors and outcomes.

The studies that have looked at the Dark Triad and success in terms of work performance have mixed findings. For instance, Babiak et al. (2010) were interested in how psychopathy relates to performance ratings in several companies in the United States. One of the researchers conducted interviews with supervisors and their subordinates, making assessment of psychopathy with the aid of PCL-R. Coworkers also evaluated a subsection of the participants on different aspects of work, such as communication skills, leadership skills, and creativity/innovation. The researchers found that all of the four aspects of psychopathy assessment (interpersonal, affective, lifestyle, and antisocial) had a negative relationship with ratings of performance, as assessed by the performance management records. This indicates that psychopathy does not lead to work success in terms of enhanced performance, but quite the opposite. However, coworker ratings of work performance presented a mixture of favorable and unfavorable perceptions. Coworker ratings of communication skills, strategic thinking, and creativity had a positive correlation with researcher-rated psychopathy scores, and this was the case for all of the psychopathy subcomponents. In addition, coworker ratings of being a team player, having good management skills, or having high overall accomplishments had negative ratings with researcher-rated psychopathy scores.

Overall, the findings of Babiak and colleagues indicate that psychopathic individuals are good at managing impressions, leading to positive views about creativity and strategic thinking. They may also be able to use persuasive communication strategies in order to get their points across to others. On the other hand, work colleagues note that high psychopathy colleagues are not good team players or leaders, and their actual work performance is poor. The impression management skills may allow high psychopathy individuals to rise to the top, while being poor or incompetent in the work that they have been employed to do.

Generating, promoting, and implementing new ideas is an important part of work success in some occupations. Wisse, Barelds, and Rietzschel (2015) investigated 306 supervisor-employee pairs in order to find out whether the Dark Triad traits in employees were associated with their supervisor's ratings of innovativeness, and how the supervisor's own Dark Triad scores influenced their perceptions. They found that supervisors rated high Machiavellian employees as less innovative and narcissistic employees as more innovative. Machiavellian individuals are not approach oriented or sociable than narcissistic individuals, who might be more comfortable in communicating and promoting their ideas. Interestingly, only those supervisors who were low in narcissism thought that the narcissistic employees are more creative. One of the explanations offered by the authors was that narcissistic supervisors could see through the façade of other narcissists and not fall for the illusion of creativity they are trying to create. This ties in with other work that has found that narcissistic individuals think that they are creative, but in fact, they are not (Jonason, Abboud, Tomé, Dummett, and Hazer, 2017). It is likely that none of the Dark Triad traits are related to work success in terms of true innovativeness.

However, Machiavellianism and work performance could be situational, and in certain circumstances, Machiavellian individuals may be motivated to work in a manner that makes them more successful. For example, Smith and Webster (2017) found that when high Machiavellian individuals were socially undermined in the workplace, it activated their political skills, leading to better supervisor ratings. Indeed, political skills are related to a good understanding of social situations in the workplace and the ability to form strategic networks in ones' own advantage. In terms of career advancement, political skills could be a strategic way for high Machiavellian individuals to get ahead at work.

Other research has conceptualized "dark" personalities in terms of low honesty-humility, one of the HEXACO traits that is closely related to the Dark Triad traits (see also Chapter 1). Individuals who are low in honesty-humility are egotistic, exploitativeness, and untrustworthy. Templer (2018) explored the role of low honesty-humility in the workplace with regards to supervisor ratings of task performance, political skills, and success in facilitating team work. They found that employees who were low in honesty-humility and also had high self-rated political skills were given supervisor ratings on task performance and team facilitation, but only by those supervisors who also thought that the employee was politically skilled. Performance is important for advancing one's career, and the results go some way to explaining why dark personalities are sometimes successful in their careers.

Career success can also be measured in terms of subjective satisfaction with one's career path. A few studies have investigated components of the Dark Triad in terms of objective (i.e., salaries, promotions) and subjective (i.e., feeling content about one's work) work success. Eisenbarth, Hart, and Sedikides (2018) were interested in the three-factor model of psychopathy (i.e., self-centered impulsivity, fearless dominance, and coldheartedness), and how it may influence subjective satisfaction with one's career paths (i.e., promotions, salaries) as well as objective material success (annual salaries, professional standing, and a number of promotions). The idea of "successful psychopathy" lends room for predictions that coldheartedness and fearless dominance would be relevant in terms of a higher material success. They found some support for fearless dominance, which did have a positive relationship with both satisfaction and material success. It is, indeed, possible that aspects of psychopathy, such as fearlessness, translate into workplace behaviors that pave a way to more subjective and objective success.

Another study investigated the relationship between the Dark Triad and success in promotions and pay rise, as well as subjective satisfaction with one's job (Spurk, Keller, & Hirschi, 2016). The researchers collected data from of almost 800 early career employees in a private section in Germany. They found that narcissism had a positive relationship with higher pay, Machiavellianism related to higher subjective job satisfaction and leadership position, and psychopathy had an association with lower job satisfaction, salaries, and leadership position (Spurk et al., 2016). These results would suggest that narcissism and Machiavellianism have an association with favorable, and psychopathy has a relationship with unfavorable occupational outcomes. However, this research used the 12-item Dirty Dozen measure, which cannot distinguish between different components of psychopathy or narcissism. It is still conceivable that aspects of psychopathy relate to career success, but the findings of each study are reliant on the measures that the researchers are using.

Jonason, Koehn, Okan, and O'Connor (2018) investigated yearly earnings in a sample general population of just over 500 individuals in Australia. In a similar way to German employers, narcissism was positively related to the annual salary of the participants. However, contrasting the findings of Spurk and colleagues, psychopathy in the Australian sample had a small, positive correlation with salaries, mainly in the female participants. Again, these differences could be a function of the instruments that the researchers used in their studies. Jonason and colleagues used the 27-item short dark triad questionnaire, which has a better convergent validity with longer instruments. Across different studies, narcissism seems to be consistently related to higher success in terms of higher earnings. The overconfidence and assertiveness of narcissistic individuals could be an asset when discussing promotions and starting salaries, resulting in higher pay.

Ullrich, Farrington, and Coid (2008) conducted interviews with a sample of 304 British men from inner city London when they were at the age of 48. During the interview schedule, participants answered questions regarding their childhood, relationships, health-related issues, housing conditions, aggressive and violent behavior, and substance abuse. The interviewee completed a screening version of the psychopathy checklist in order to evaluate levels of psychopathy on the basis of the behavior and answers during the interview. They found no evidence of psychopathy and career success in terms of income and social status. On the contrary, both Factor 1 (i.e., affective deficiency) and Factor 2 (i.e., impulsive/lifestyle and antisocial) psychopathy were negatively related to status and wealth. Thus at least in this sample of participants, psychopathy exerted a negative influence on success.

Finally, the Dark Triad has a relationship with entrepreneurial activities. Starting up new ventures can be risky and requires certain levels of boldness and assertiveness. Indeed, studies that have investigated entrepreneurial interests in students have found that narcissism, especially, related to intentions to start a business (Hmieleski & Lerner, 2016). A study that looked at primary (i.e., callous/unemotional predisposition) and secondary (i.e., risk taking/impulsivity) psychopathy in young professionals found a moderate positive correlation between primary psychopathy and entrepreneurial tendencies (Akhtar, Ahmetoglu, & Chamorro-Premuzi, 2013), although no association was found with actual self-reported activities. The authors suggested that primary psychopathic traits of glibness, coldness, and fearlessness could be beneficial when exploring new opportunities. Further, the researchers found that primary psychopathy was negatively correlated with one aspect of entrepreneurial activity—that of social entrepreneurship, benefiting communities.

The motivations for entrepreneurship can vary from productive motives (i.e., value creating: willingness to engage in meaningful work, employ others, deliver services that benefit society) to unproductive motives (i.e., value appropriating: desire to increase ones' own income). Hmieleski and Lerner (2016) found that psychopathy had an association with unproductive motives, and narcissism with productive motives, albeit with small effect sizes.

6.6 The Dark Triad and CWBs

"Directors feel 'betrayed' after employee steals almost £78,000 from Waterlooville company's funds and spends it on new clothes and holiday" (Salked, 2018). "Fast-food worker spits in customer dinner, then says I want to go home"(Buck, 2018), "Disgruntled employee spends three years destroying work computers with Cillit Bang" (The Telegraph, 03/02/2013).

These newspaper headlines tell not-so-uncommon stories about an employee who steal, sabotage, and destroy. Some employees who get promoted to positions where they deal with the company finances abuse their power by stealing from the company. Others resort to sabotaging the company property as a silent protest against the lack of promotions or destroy the company's image by behaving in an inappropriate manner. These are just few examples of many types of CWBs that employees engage in, causing direct harm to their company. CWBs are workplace behaviors that can be directed to individual coworkers (e.g., bullying, harassment, sabotage of other's work) or to the company (e.g., stealing, deliberately working in an inefficient manner, sabotaging company property, or damaging the company reputation). The motivations for CWBs as varied as the acts themselves, ranging from revenge and laziness to greed for money.

The relationship between the Dark Triad and CWB is complicated and depends largely on the trait in question, organizational context, and the motivations driving the individual (O'Boyle, Forsyth, Banks, & McDaniel, 2012). Dark personality does not always equate to detrimental workplace conduct. In the right circumstances, individuals high in the Dark Triad can even be helpful toward their colleagues, work in a productive manner, and have the company interests in their hearts. There are many possible moderators and mediators between personality and CWB, and the current research has only scratched the surface in understanding how dark personalities function in the workplace.

One of the theories that have been used as a basis for understanding CWBs is the Social Exchange Theory. According to this idea, behavior of the employees in the workplace is contingent on the perceived benefits that the workplace gives to them. The benefits could be, for example, financial remuneration, social or emotional support, or gaining status and power. If the perceived benefits are high, it is expected that individuals will be happy to support the workplace, refraining from activities that are detrimental to the employer. If the perceived benefits are low (e.g., low salary, no appreciation, little opportunities for promotion), it is expected that individuals are more likely to engage in CWBs.

According to the person-situation approach, the way that an individual responds to their environment depends on their personality, and the responses may vary from one situation to another. Thus those high in the Dark Triad could work in a conscientious, reliable manner if they perceive that there are personal gains in being a "good" employer. A study that looked at the Dark Triad, CWBs, and perceived organizational support found that although overall the Dark Triad had an association with a higher frequency of CWBs, those who were higher in psychopathy and narcissism had lower incidences of CWBs if they perceived their workplace environment as supportive (Palmer, Komarraju, Carter, & Karau, 2017). Another study investigated Machiavellianism, competitiveness over resources, and undermining coworkers in the workplace (Castille, Kuyumcu, & Bennett, 2017). The researchers found that individuals high in Machiavellianism undermined their coworkers more only in work environments with high levels of competitiveness. Machiavellian individuals are skilled, political workplace maneuvers who may be able to gauge the surrounding atmosphere for cues of competition. When competition is high, they may attempt to gain more success by engaging CWBs that are directed toward undermining others.

In a sample of 161 target-coworker triads, Blickle and Schütte (2017) examined psychopathy features of self-centered impulsivity and fearlessness with regards to CWBs and variables such as educational levels and power to influence others in the organization. The targets filled in measures on psychopathy, and two of their coworkers provided an assessment of the target's work performance, social influence, and CWBs. They found that self-centered impulsivity of the employee was positively related to coworker ratings of CWBs. High levels of fearless dominance (also branded as an aspect of successful psychopathy) were related to higher incidence of CWBs in employees who had low educational level and low interpersonal influence. However, fearless dominance was unrelated to CWBs at higher levels of influence and education. These findings speak for the importance of situational and other individual differences factors in influencing the likelihood of an employee engaging in CWBs.

6.6.1 Types of CWBs

Research has identified several CWBs. Robinson and Bennett (1995) classified CWBs according to how minor or serious they are, and whether they are directed toward individuals or toward the organizations. These could be classified into (i) personal aggression (e.g., sexual harassment, verbal, or physical abuse), (ii) political deviance (e.g., favoritism, gossip, blaming others, unproductive competitiveness), (iii) production deviance (e.g., leaving early, wasting resources, taking excessive breaks), and (iv) property deviance (e.g., sabotage, lying, thieving). Several empirical investigations and meta-analyses of existing research have found that the Dark Triad is, indeed, associated with many different types of CWBs. Generally speaking, those who score high on the Dark Triad (especially psychopathy and Machiavellianism) are more likely to be absent from work, purposefully damage or steal equipment or property in work, hurt or bully others, or persistently do their work incorrectly or in a lazy manner (Jonason and O'Connor, 2017; Jonason, Slomski, and Partyka, 2012; Palmer et al., 2017).

6.6.2 The Dark Triad and CWB Motivations

The motivations behind CWBs are varied, ranging from thrill-seeking and status enhancement to laziness and seeking revenge. Vengeance is a powerful motivator of CWBs. Research in organizational psychology has shown that when individuals think that they have been treated wrongly by their supervisors or the organization, they are willing to "get even" by revenge (e.g., Jones, 2009). Revenge can take different forms varying in severity, from putting less effort into work than would be expected to deliberate sabotage of equipment or work achievements. Depending on the context, these behaviors are directed toward the immediate supervisor, work colleagues, or the organization itself. It is possible that those who are high on the Dark Triad traits are more provoked by perceived injustice than other individuals. There is some research to support this, for example, Giammarco and Vernon (2014) found that those high in psychopathy and Machiavellianism (but not narcissism) were more vengeful than those high in these traits. Although this suggests that the Dark Triad is, indeed, related to overall vengefulness, this still remains to be studied within the organizational context.

Another powerful motivation behind CWBs is the maximization of self-gain. The key characteristic of the Dark Triad is seated in selfishness, the attempt to gain benefits for oneself without caring about others. This selfishness could translate into motivations to gain status, power, and resources, which could be more achievable with the aid of CWBs. Research, mainly outside of the work environment, has shown that individuals in at the high end of the spectrum (especially psychopathy and Machiavellianism) are more likely to lie (Jonason, Lyons, et al., 2014; Jonason, Wee, et al., 2014) and steal (Lyons & Jonason, 2015), both of which have the potential to lead to temporary increase in status and resources. Thus it would be expected that strive to gain status in the work environment relates to CWBs in those who are higher in the Machiavellian and psychopathy continuum.

6.6.3 Bullying in the Workplace

Bullying in the workplace is a serious problem that contributes negatively to organizational productivity as well as to poor mental and physical health of the victims. At an individual level, being the victim of bullying has been related to poor physical health, sleep problems, and suicidal ideation. Victimization is also associated with a variety of mental health problems, including anxiety and depression (Einarsen & Nielsen, 2015). In some more serious cases, bullying can lead to more severe forms of mental distress, such as psychosis or posttraumatic stress disorder (Nolfe, Petrella, Blasi, Zontini, & Nolfe, 2007). At an organizational level, absenteeism associated with bullying can lead to lowered productivity and higher turnover of employees.

Although the consequences of bullying have been relatively well researched, there has been less studies on looking at the individual characteristics of those who engage in bullying.

The Dark Triad is a promising candidate for a personality characteristic relevant to workplace bullying. Those high in narcissism have fragile egos and could react to perceived ego threats by interpersonal aggression. The manipulative and cunning strategic interpersonal orientation related to Machiavellianism could have an association with bullying in the form of ostracism or gossip, which could serve to improve the individuals standing in the organization. A few studies from outside out the organizational contexts have, indeed, demonstrated that the Dark Triad does relate to increased frequency of bullying. A questionnaire study by Holly Baughman, Dearing, Giammarco, and Vernon (2012) found that out of the three Dark Triad traits, psychopathy was the strongest positive correlate of bullying, followed by Machiavellianism. This was the case for both direct (i.e., physical) and indirect, (i.e., verbal) bullying. In this study, narcissism had significant association with bullying too, but to a much lesser magnitude, and mainly in the form of indirect bullying rather than direct aggression. The relationship between bullying and the Dark Triad extends to the world of the internet, too. Studies have found that although all the three traits were related to increased bullying, the association is mainly driven by the unique features of psychopathy (Goodboy & Martin, 2015; Pabian, De Backer, & Vandebosch, 2015). If the findings from these samples can be extended to the corporate world, it would be expected that out of the three traits, especially psychopathy is associated with bullying in the place of work as well.

The relationship between bullying and victimization is far from being clear-cut. Workplace bullies are sometimes victims, and victims often turn into bullies, especially in the case of verbal abuse and undermining of work (Lee & Brotheridge, 2006). The reciprocal relationship between being a perpetrator and a target would suggest that those who are involved in workplace aggression share similar personality traits. This is, indeed, what a study by Linton and Power (2013) discovered. In their university student sample, both those who were frequently victims and those who were perpetrators had Dark Triad characteristics. However, as the results of this study may be difficult to generalize to the whole population, as the participants consisted of University students with a relatively low-paid entry-level jobs. Another study, focusing on Machiavellianism in employees in Poland, found that those who were bullies and bully-victims had higher scores on Machiavellianism than those who were only victims, or had no involvement in bullying (Pilch and Turska, 2015). It is possible that those who are high on the Dark Triad traits are provocative victims: hostile, aggressive, annoying, and vindictive. These features may provoke bullying from others who have the same traits and also incite the victims to start bullying in return.

6.7 Organizational Citizenship Behaviors

Broadly speaking, organizational citizenship behaviors (OCBs) are pro-social actions that are not a compulsory part of the job. OCBs are performed by the individual employees as a result of their own personal choice, rather than out of pressure from the employer. Examples of OCBs include the willingness to guide a new employee, pro-social sharing of information in order to make the work of others easier, and attending meetings and seminars that are not necessary. Although OCBs are not officially recorded by the employer, they have a large contribution to the functioning of organizations. There are large individual differences between employers who do and employers who do not participate in OCBs. Individuals who engage in OCBs are pro-social, willing to help their coworkers, and conduct themselves in a manner that benefits the organizational culture. In many ways, the pro-sociality embodied in OCBs are the opposite of the selfish Dark Triad behavioral tendencies.

Not many studies have focused on OCBs and the Dark Triad. In a study that investigated the three traits simultaneously, Szabó, Czibor, Restás, and Bereczkei (2018) studied OCBs in a sample of 256 Hungarian working adults. Thy categorized OCBs into those that are directed toward individual work colleagues (e.g., "I go out of my way to help new colleagues") and those that are beneficial to the organization (e.g., "I give advance notice when I'm unable to come to work"). They also measured self-rated in-role behaviors (e.g., "I meet formal performance requirements for the job" in order to evaluate how the dark traits relate to performance in their actual jobs. As control, they also assessed the participants' job satisfaction, the extent that people identify with the organization, and the Big Six personality traits. In cross-correlational analyses, they showed that all of the Dark Triad traits were associated with less OCBs directed toward the organization, and Machiavellianism and psychopathy were negatively related to OCBs directed toward individuals. However, a different picture appeared when the control variables were added as predictors in regression analyses. Psychopathy emerged as the only dark trait that had a negative relationship with both individual and organizational OCBs, as well as in-role behaviors. This suggests that high psychopathy individuals are employees who are unwilling to voluntarily help others and the organization as a whole. Furthermore, high psychopathy individuals are reluctant to perform the tasks that have been assigned to them as part of their role. In turn, the relationship with OCBs and Machiavellianism told a very different story. When the shared variance between the two other Dark Triad traits and the control variables was taken into account, those who were high on Machiavellianism reported performing OCBs toward the organizational at higher frequencies. This speaks for the strategic nature of high Machiavellian individuals, who may see extra role tasks that are viewed positively by their superiors as a way to advance their careers.

6.8 Conclusion

Research into the Dark Triad traits in organizations is still in its infancy. Emerging evidence suggests that people who have socially aversive personality traits self-select to careers and occupations that allow them to use ruthless tactics in gaining power and money. At the job interview stage, high Dark Triad individuals, especially those high in narcissism, may use tactics of strategies of self-promotion and self-enhancement in charming the employers into hiring them. When in employment, high Dark Triad traits relate to CWBs, including stealing, bullying, and sabotage of work property. When Dark Triad individuals are promoted into a leadership role, their followers report being more stressed, with intentions to find a new job. However, the success of the Dark Triad depends on the organizational context and other characteristics of the individual. There certainly is a need for more research looking at moderating factors between the Dark Triad and workplace outcomes. Overall, the exploitative cheater strategy embodied by socially antagonistic personalities translates into selfish behavior in the workplace context as well as in other aspects of life.

Further Reading

Babiak, P., Neumann, C. S., & Hare, R. D. (2010). Corporate psychopathy: talking the walk. *Behavioral Sciences & the Law*, *28*, 174–193.

Braun, S. (2017). Leader narcissism and outcomes in organizations: a review at multiple levels of analysis and implications for future research. *Frontiers in Psychology*, *8*, 773.

Eisenbarth, H., Hart, C. M., & Sedikides, C. (2018). Do psychopathic traits predict professional success? *Journal of Economic Psychology*, *64*, 130–139.

Volmer, J., Koch, I. K., & Göritz, A. S. (2016). The bright and dark sides of leaders' dark triad traits: effects on subordinates' career success and well-being. *Personality and Individual Differences*, *101*, 413–418.

CHAPTER SEVEN

The Dark Triad and Internet Behavior

Chapter Outline

7.1 Introduction

In the past few decades, the cyberspace has become a rich source of information for psychology research. Over 3.2 billion people access the internet on a daily bases, using it for a range of social, personal, and business purposes (International Telecommunication Union, 2015). Due to the anonymity and/or physical invisibility of the online environment, people may behave in a less inhibited way they would behave in real-life off-line interactions with others. For example, how many of those men who have sent an unsolicited picture of their penis to a woman they have talked to on a dating website would reveal their genitals in a real-life dating situation? Sending "dickpicks" is a common, low-cost, and low-risk behavior when it happens in an online environment (Waling & Pym, 2017). Off-line, however, this could be classed as an indecent exposure, which is a criminal offense.

The Dark Triad of Personality
https://doi.org/10.1016/B978-0-12-814291-2.00007-3

The anonymity of the internet sometimes intensifies aversive behavioral tendencies, partially because they often go unpunished. This could be down to two kinds of disinhibition effects occurring on the internet—benign disinhibition (disclosing emotions, fears, and wishes, exhibiting acts of kindness and generosity), and toxic disinhibition (expressing anger, hatred, threat and criticism, accessing violent and pornographic information that one would not access in off-line environment; Suler, 2004). The short-term mating orientation, coupled with the disinhibited, toxic nature, makes the Dark Triad a great candidate for studies focusing on online behaviors. It would be expected that the anonymity and detachment provided by the internet works in amplifying the aversive nature of the Dark Triad traits.

With regards to the different types of online behaviors, the Dark Triad has received most attention in the realm of social networking platforms. Social media sites (e.g., Facebook, Twitter, Instagram) are those that allow users to actively generate, modify, and share personal information with other users, resulting in online communities. These sites have expanded in the past few decades. It is estimated that as much as a third of the world's population are actively using social media (Statista, 2017). The reasons for why people use these sites are varied, and range from maintaining relationships and socializing to killing time and playing games (Ryan, Chester, Reece, & Xenos, 2014). In some cases, social media consumption has addictive qualities, where the user spends so much time online that it detracts them from other activities.

As well as being potentially addictive, online environment entices people to use deception and exaggeration when presenting information about oneself. On an interesting note, although the Dark Triad relates to fibbing in the off-line world, it may be that everybody is a liar when it comes to self-presentation in the online world. Drouin, Miller, Wehle, and Hernandez (2016) asked people about online deception in different venues (online dating, chat rooms, social media, and sexual websites), and found that rather than the Dark Triad, the strongest predictor of lying online was the perception that everybody else is lying too. It seems that the online social norms are accepting lying, expecting this from people, which leads to deception irrespective of the levels of the Dark Triad traits.

In this chapter, I will bring together the burgeoning research on the Dark Triad and internet behaviors. Research on the Dark Triad in the internet environment spans from self-presentation (i.e., how people want the outside world to see them), cyber-aggression (i.e., trolling, stalking, threatening, and bullying others) to sexual and criminal behavior (i.e., accessing pornography). The research on internet and the Dark Triad is growing rapidly, and by the time that you are reading this, it is likely that tens of new publications on the topic have already come out. There are many surprising gaps in the literature (e.g., Dark Triad and internet dating), which hopefully will be addressed in the near future by the growing number of new researchers and research programs in this area.

7.2 Intensity and Problematic Internet Use

The rapid explosion in use of the internet, especially social media, has not escaped the interest of clinical psychologist. Although internet addiction is not officially recognized as a mental disorder in the diagnostic manuals, the latest version of the DSM-5 has a section for diagnosing Internet Use Gaming Disorder. The interest in problematic social media use has led to the development of measuring tools aimed at assessing the levels of disruption in life caused by a constant need to use social media. One of the questionnaires, the Social Media Disorder scale (van den Eijnden, Lemmens, & Valkenburg, 2016) has nine items with yes/no answers. The questions ask about whether social media use leads to neglecting other activities, conflict with others, using social media for escaping negative feelings, lying to others about the use of social media, and so on. Those who have become overly concerned about social media have an uncontrolled desire to check their social networking sites and experience anxiety when not being able to use them. Studies have found that addictive use of social media is associated with many forms of mental distress, including anxiety and depression. The causal links are not clear in this case. We don't really know whether social media leads to mental distress, or whether those who experience mental distress are more likely to get addicted to social media.

Personality is one probable factor influencing the likelihood of problematic use of social media. Higher Dark Triad scores (especially narcissism and psychopathy) have already been linked to addictions such as substance abuse behaviors (Stenason & Vernon, 2016) and disordered gambling (Trombly & Zeigler-Hill, 2017). It is possible that the need for instant gratification, typical to high Dark Triad individuals, influences susceptibility to high intensity, potentially problematic internet use. So far, there are not many studies that have investigated addiction-type online behaviors in high Dark Triad individuals. In one relevant study, Kircaburun, Demetrovics, and Tosuntaş (2018) explored relationship between the Dark Triad and addictive social media use in a sample of University students in Turkey, using the

Social Media Disorder scale. Based on the scores obtained in the disorder scale, they categorized participants into two different groups—those who are, and those who are not in a risk group for a social media addiction. They found that the group of participants that were classified as having a disorder also scored higher on all the Dark Triad traits than the group that were determined not to have a disorder. In more complicated path analyses, Machiavellianism and narcissism (but not psychopathy) were related to problematic use of social media. One of the possible explanations given by the authors was loneliness. Previous research has found that all the Dark Triad traits relate to feeling lone (Zhang, Zou, Wang, & Finy, 2015), and that social media addiction also contributes to loneliness (van den Eijnden et al., 2016). It is possible that individuals high on narcissism and Machiavellianism care more about human contacts than high psychopathy individuals, but their manipulativeness, self-centeredness, and lack of empathy lead to low quality relationships, leaving the individual feeling lonely. The internet could create a temporary feeling of having human contact, which could lead to using the social media as a substitute to real-life contacts.

Intensity of internet use does not automatically mean that a person has problems with it. As well as reporting addiction-like social media use, studies have found that those who score high on the Dark Triad (especially narcissism) spend more time on social media sites (Fox & Rooney, 2015), and rather than causing harm, it could have a positive influence on the individual. Narcissists may get their much-needed attention in the social media, which could lead to increased mental well-being. Indeed, those who have more adaptive aspects of narcissism use social media more than people who are insecure narcissists. For example, a meta-analysis on a sample of over 13,000 users found that grandiose (but not vulnerable) narcissism related to increased time spent on social media, frequency of tweets or status updates, number of friends or followers, and frequency of posting selfies (McCain & Campbell, 2016). An even more recent meta-analysis had similar findings, suggesting that grandiose narcissism is relevant in using social media for self-presentation and gathering friends and "likes" (Gnambs & Appel, 2018). It is interesting that both meta-analyses found that grandiose narcissism is related to social media activity. Grandiosity is associated with healthy self-esteem, confidence, and happiness, whereas narcissistic vulnerability is related to a fragile sense of self and susceptibility to mental distress. Grandiose narcissists could use social media as an extension (rather than a substitute) to their off-line social networks.

One pertaining question is the causal relationship between social media intensity and narcissism. Is it possible that spending more time on platforms such as Facebook actually increases how narcissistic people are? In the end of the day, much of the activities on social media are about the self-promoting by posting materials that make the person look desirable. Walters and Horton (2015) studied the directional relationship between grandiose narcissism and Facebook use in male US college students, using a four-day diary study. The participants were asked to record several times their Facebook use intensity, as well as fill in a measure on grandiose narcissism. Analyses of the data suggested that although grandiose narcissism related to higher intensity of using Facebook, the use did not influence how narcissistic the men were. The authors suggested that "… it seems appropriate to close the door on the notion that Facebook use promotes narcissism. The data simply do not support such a conclusion" (Walters & Horton, 2015, p. 329). However, another study by Halpern, Valenzuela, and Katz (2016) found that taking and sharing selfies increased the selfie-takers narcissism over time, suggesting that social networking sites may have a contribution to increase in self-centeredness.

Social media provides an unrivaled venue for self-presentation and impression management. Indeed, the evidence overwhelmingly points at the importance of social media in facilitating narcissistic goals of self-promotion and ego boosting. Although there may be links with addictive, pathological social media use and the Dark Triad of personality, there are likely to be other factors that moderate the relationship. Further, those who are high on grandiose aspects of narcissism are likely to benefit from higher activity on social media, experiencing gratification from attention from followers.

7.3 Cyber-Aggression

Cyber-aggression is a common form of noxious behavior on the internet, which often results in drastic, negative consequences to the victim. Grigg (2010) defined cyber-aggression as "intentional harm delivered by the use of electronic means to a person or a group of people irrespective of their age, who perceive(s) such acts as offensive, derogatory, harmful or unwanted." (p. 152). Cyber-aggression can be as harmful to the victim as off-line bullying, resulting in significant mental distress, and in some unfortunate cases, culminating in suicide. Understanding the causes and consequences of cyber-aggression is crucial in preventing future bullying and providing help to the victims.

Indeed, cyber-aggression in different forms has become so prevalent that it has pretty much changed the nature of the internet (Stein, 2016).

Although many would think that the perpetrators have some special characteristics that make them more likely to aggress against others, experimental research has suggested that in the right circumstances anyone can become a bully (Cheng, Danescu-Niculescu-Mizil, Leskovec, & Bernstein, 2017). The dynamics of cyber-aggression are multifaceted and subtle, and the online environment can result in creation of social rules characterized by nastiness. This can lead to behaviors that would not be observed as readily in real-life settings. While everyone has the ability to use the online environment to anonymously aggress against others, personality is still a strong predictor of a diverse array of aversive internet behaviors. Because of the aggressive, dominating, and bullying tendencies of those who are high on the Dark Triad, these traits are greatly relevant in understanding the personality of online bullies.

Trolling, bullying, and stalking are different types of acts of cyber-aggression, all of which could have different underlying motivations. Trolling is distinctive from cyberbullying in that trolling involves meaningless aggravation and harassment of the victims, where the perpetrator often does not personally know the individual who they are tormenting. Cyberbullying, in turn, is often directed toward individuals who the bully already knows, and the perpetration is not meaningless, but the victims are targeted for very specific reasons. Cyberstalking is repeated, unwanted contact and monitoring which can be perpetrated by both strangers, and people who are known to the victim. Cyberstalking commonly takes place in romantic relationships, where the partners or ex-partners can be under obsessive surveillance of the stalker. All of the three forms of cyber-aggression have potential to be hostile and violent in nature, causing psychological damage to the victim. In Table 7.1, you can see a brief description of these three acts, as well as a summary of studies where the shared variance between the Dark Triad or the Dark Tetrad traits has been statistically controlled for.

7.3.1 Trolling

Trolling on the internet involves leaving threatening, derogatory, and frequently anonymous comments on the victim's social media pages. The comments often violate social and moral conventions, and include attacks toward race, gender, sexuality, political orientation, religion, and so forth. The comments sometimes mock dead people and their families, or consist of threats of violence toward the victim or their families.

Table 7.1 Types of Cyber-Aggression and Relevance to the Dark Triad/Tetrad

Act	Description	Motivation	Relevance to Dark Triad and Dark Tetrad
Bullying	Repeated, deliberate, intentional harassment and intimidation. The perpetrator often knows the victim	Change the behavior/mood of the victim in order to benefit the perpetrator (e.g., increase social status of perpetrator)	High psychopathy children (Pabian et al., 2015) High psychopathy adults (Gibb & Devereux, 2014; Goodboy & Martin, 2015) High sadist adults (Van Geel et al., 2017)
Stalking	Repeated, unwanted contact with, and monitoring of the victim. The perpetrator may, or may not know the victim	Reverse, correct, or revenge a rejection or seek for a new relationship	All Dark Tetrad traits = cyberstalking intimate partners (Smoker & March, 2017)
Trolling	Meaningless aggravation and harassment of victims in order to evoke a response. Starting quarrels or upset by posting inflammatory comments, Perpetrator often does not personally know the victim	Enjoyment in provoking a response Doing it for "lolz" (laughs)	High psychopathy = anonymous trolling (Seigfried-Spellar & Lankford, 2018) High sadism and psychopathy = identity as a troll, high Machiavellianism = enjoyment in trolling (Buckels et al., 2014) High psychopathy = condoning trolling of popular people (Lopes & Yu, 2017) High psychopathy and sadism = trolling in order to exert power over others (Craker & March, 2016) Trolls are likely to be men, high in psychopathy and sadism, and lack affective empathy (Sest & March, 2017)

For example, a feminist blogger had to close down her social media pages temporarily because of threats to rape her young daughter (see Stein, 2016, for more examples). Sadly, examples like these are not rare, and there are cases where trolling has led to prison sentences. With regards to the motivations behind trolling, it does not seem to serve any other purpose but to cause fear and disgust, and provoke a reaction from the victim, which the troll can then enjoy.

With regards to the identity of the internet trolls, the Dark Triad and the Dark Tetrad are of specific interest due their associations with the willingness to exert negative influence on others (Craker & March, 2016). Sadism facet of the Dark Tetrad is particularly important, as those high on this trait get a kick out of inflicting pain on others for their own enjoyment. This is also a key characteristic of trolling behavior—tormenting others for no other reason but "lolzs" (i.e., laughs). There are a few studies looking at the role of aversive personality traits and engagement in online trolling, and the results are perhaps not that surprising—out of the tetrad of traits, sadism is the strongest predictor of inflicting harm on others for no other reason but the enjoyment in the activity.

Erin Buckels, Trapnell, and Paulhus (2014) compiled a questionnaire on Global Assessment of Internet Trolling (GAIT), which they tested with regards to the Dark Tetrad in two large online sample on over 1000 participants. GAIT questions include people's identity as an internet troll and the levels of enjoyment that trolls gain from meaningless harassment of others in the online environment. The authors found that especially sadism related to a stronger identity as a troll, and this could be due to the pleasure that sadistic individuals get from hurting others. To a lesser extent, Machiavellianism also emerged as significant positive predictor of enjoyment in trolling, and psychopathy related to a stronger identity as a troll. The results indicate that narcissism play a lesser role in trolling, perhaps because narcissistic individuals are too busy focusing on themselves to start harassing others for fun.

Other studies have looked at the reasons for why high Dark Triad individuals might engage in trolling. A study by Lopes and Yu (2017) used fake Facebook profiles that were manipulated to be high or low in popularity. The profiles were accompanied by comments indicating trolling. As an example, when the status update talked about getting a good grade in an exam, the trolling comment below was asking which lecturer the profile owner slept with in order to get the grade. The participants had to rate their level of agreement with the nasty comments. The results showed that those high on psychopathy agreed more with the trolling comments, especially if the targets had popular profiles. It is possible that because high psychopathy individuals are more likely to engage in trolling, they also "preach what they practice," and accept trolling perpetrated by others. It is also interesting that the acceptance of trolling was directed toward people with popular profiles, which indicates that high psychopathy individuals could be influenced by motives related to jealousy and competition.

There may be other motives that influence trolling in those high on psychopathy and sadism, such as the wish to exert negative power and influence over others, also named as "negative social potency." Craker and March (2016) investigated the Dark Tetrad and negative social potency, and found that psychopathy and sadism were significant predictors of trolling on Facebook, and this could happen because of the drive to have power over others. It is possible that narcissists are too self-interested, and Machiavellians too calculating to engage in trolling for negative social rewards.

Why are internet trolls more sadistic and psychopathic then? Could there be other traits that relate to these two aspects of the Dark Tetrad, explaining their similarity when it comes to trolling? Sest and March (2017) expanded the research on internet trolls to look at another relevant aspect in nasty behaviors—empathy. They were interested in different aspects of empathy, affective (i.e., the ability to feel what others feel) and cognitive (i.e., the ability to understand other's emotions and what is causing them, without feeling the emotion itself). They found that trolls were more likely to be men, have higher levels of psychopathy and sadism, and lower levels of affective empathy. It is possible that what makes trolling possible from the perpetrator point of view is the inability to put oneself in the shoes of others, and try to imagine how the victims might feel. Interestingly, higher levels of cognitive empathy predicted more internet trolling, but only in the participants who had high scores on psychopathy. These findings suggest that having the ability to understand and predict how others may feel can be a tool for online bullying, especially in individuals who already are callous (i.e., high psychopathy) in nature.

Social media sites like Facebook are normally not completely anonymous, and the users often have at least some kind of an idea of the identity of the people commenting on their statuses. Perhaps more intimidating are applications ("apps") that permit a complete anonymity among the users. Under the veil of anonymity, users can act freely without thinking of the consequences, which could fuel those who already have inclination for nastiness to behave in an even more disinhibited manner. One such anonymous (now closed) social media phone app was Yik Yak. This app allowed people who were in geographical proximity to each other to post anonymous messages. Yik Yak was banned from many educational institutions in the United States due to racism and out of control bullying, leading to arrests of some of the trolls. Seigfried-Spellar and Lankford (2018) studied the Dark Triad and trolling in Yik Yak. In a similar way as in earlier studies, psychopathy (but not narcissism or Machiavellianism) had a positive association trolling on this anonymous online app. The emerging picture suggests that despite of the nature of the social media app, psychopathic and sadistic users are more likely to inflict nastiness on their fellow users.

Other types of online apps providing a stomping ground for internet trolls are dating applications. Online dating apps are increasingly popular for seeking for serious relationships as well as casual sex. Location-based real time dating apps such as Tinder are created with the principle that people can connect to each other based on geographical proximity in real time. Dating apps like these have become a primetime venue for hostile sexism, where trolling often starts when the troll is rejected by a potential date. Indeed, this is such a common behavior that many online daters, especially women, have been subjected to trolling as a response to rejection. As a counterresponse, there are numerous online campaigns (e.g., #byefelipe on Instagram), exposing men who have turned nasty when ignored or rejected. March, Grieve, Marrington, and Jonason (2017) examined self-reported trolling in location-based real time dating apps, including dysfunctional impulsivity and the Dark Tetrad as the predictor variables. The authors found that psychopathy, sadism, and dysfunctional (i.e., uncontrolled) impulsivity predicted dating app trolling. More specifically, dysfunctional impulsivity related to trolling in those who were medium or high in trait psychopathy. It seems that individuals who have more difficulties in impulse control are be more likely to write derogative comments on a whim, but only if they already are higher on psychopathy.

The picture that is developing from studies that have explored the Dark Tetrad and internet trolling points at sadism and psychopathy as the main factors in this behavior. Although it is not clear what the motivations for trolling are, it is possible that sadists troll because they get pleasure out from it, and psychopaths do it for jealousy, revenge, or competition. There is, undoubtedly, need for more research into looking at aversive personalities and motivations for trolling on different internet sites.

7.3.2 Bullying

Bullying is a pervasive, widespread problem, affecting countless people, especially school-aged children, across the globe. Cyber-environment has allowed the bullies to extend their toxic influence outside of face-to-face contact, following the victims from school to their home environments via the internet. Cyberbullying is difficult to tackle, as the perpetrators are constantly finding new ways to torment their victims (e.g., new applications, social networking sites, websites). Online bullying can result in devastating consequences for the victims, suicide as an example of an extreme outcome (http://www.puresight.com/Real-Life-Stories/real-life-stories.html). The cyber-environment is used in impersonating, harassing and ostracizing others, fueled by motivations that range from revenge, boredom, and jealousy, to seeking approval from others. Different forms of bullying include posting embarrassing photos of the victim, making derogatory remarks, and threatening the victim publicly or in private. Bullying can also be more subtle, and include things like making sure that a person is aware of a social event that they were not invited to. Mounting evidence suggests that cyberbullies have similar kind of personality profiles as off-line bullies, scoring low on traits that normally prevent people from aggressing against others (e.g., empathy; Doane, Pearson, & Kelley, 2014).

Only a handful of studies have investigated how the Dark Triad traits influence cyberbullying in young people. In one such study, Pabian, De Backer, and Vandebosch (2015) sampled 324 14- to 18-year-old high school students in Netherlands, asking them about their use of Facebook as a device for bullying. They studied eight cyberbullying acts, including repeated negative comments, hacking into the victim's accounts, spreading rumors, and post embarrassing pictures and threats. The findings suggest that high school children who use Facebook more intensively and scored high on a psychopathy measure are the most likely cyberbullies. Goodboy and Martin (2015) reported similar kind of findings in an adult sample. In correlational analyses, all the Dark Triad traits were positively related to reports of using both visual (e.g., sending embarrassing videos/photographs about a person) and text-based (i.e., writing derogating comments on a victim's social media page) forms of bullying. However, when shared variance between the three traits was controlled for in regression analyses, only psychopathy emerged as a significant predictor. Both of these studies suggest that online bullying in both children and adults is most likely to be perpetrated by those who are high on trait psychopathy, but not necessarily on Machiavellianism or narcissism.

Do cyberbullies possess similar personality traits as off-line bullies? Online bullying is an easy, low-cost method of exerting dominance over the victim. Writing a denigrating post is only a few clicks away and has the potential to hurt the victim in front of wide audiences. Traditional bullying involves face-to-face contact with the victim, and the bully can see the reaction of the victim in real time. In the online environment, the reactions are less visible and indirect. Not many studies have compared the personality traits of online and off-line bullies to see if they have similar personalities. A study by van Geel and colleagues (van Geel, Goemans, Toprak, & Vedder, 2017) looked at the association between traditional bullying, cyberbullying, and personality in a large sample of adolescents and young adults in Netherlands. The personality profiles of traditional bullies were characterized by low agreeableness and high scores in psychopathy, Machiavellianism, and sadism. Online bullies had low agreeableness and high sadism scores. Although Machiavellianism and psychopathy had a positive correlation with cyberbullying, the relationship was not quite statistically significant. The results of this study suggest that online bullies may have different motivations than traditional bullies. In an off-line environment, one of the incentives for bullying is to manipulate and gain power over the victim, something that individuals high in psychopathy and Machiavellianism may be motivated to do. However, those who are high in sadism may be more enthused to bully due to no other reason but the pleasure they gain from hurting others. Perhaps the online environment is more conductive of meaningless bullying, perpetrated by those who are sadistic in nature. More traditional, off-line bullying could be more strategic in nature and provide a means for antisocial influence for those who are psychopathic and Machiavellian.

Sometimes bullying takes place in established relationships where the bully and the victim are friends with each other (see also Chapter 4 for "toxic friendships"). Indirect, subtle bullying in friendships is common and can happen through the use of the internet, especially social media. For example, posting photos of social gatherings sends a strong message of exclusion for a friend who was not invited to the event. A discussion forum post from in Mumsnet.com highlights the feelings of ostracism and loneliness that social media can create when an individual is excluded from a friendship group:

> *... then one night a few weeks after this started I noticed that Lucy had put some pictures on Facebook titled 'A great night out with great friends', and it turned out that all 3 of them had been out to the cinema then for a meal and I hadn't been invited. I was upset but didn't want to appear needy and so I didn't say anything to them all. I decided to pretend that it doesn't bother me but it really does ... All of their husbands have de-friended me on Facebook .... I know I should be getting over it by now but I noticed last night on FB they were all sharing poems on each others' walls about good friendships and valuing each other and I just felt sorry for myself. nuttynittynora; Mon 27-Jul-15; 09:03:08; https://www.mumsnet.com/Talk/relationships/2434873-Totally-excluded-from-group-of-friends-and-no-idea-why*

In Chapter 4, I discussed research on the Dark Triad and relational aggression in friendships. Most of the current research has focused on trait Machiavellianism, demonstrating that individuals high in this trait use subtle bullying tactics in order to manipulate their friends. One study by Loren Abell and Gayle Brewer (2014) looked at how Machiavellianism impacts online bullying between close friends in Facebook. They used a questionnaire that consisted of items measuring the frequency of Facebook activities such as ignoring the friend when they try to speak to the person on Facebook chat or writing something embarrassing about the friend on their Facebook status. They also measured the honesty of Facebook behaviors with items such as "I often update my status saying I am doing something exciting even though this is not true," or "I often send friend requests to people I don't know in order to increase my number of Facebook friends." Interestingly, the findings indicate that Machiavellian women use online bullying more than men do. Women who are more Machiavellian use subtle tactics of ignoring, excluding, and derogating their best friend on Facebook. Machiavellian women were also more inclined to "keep up their appearances," and exaggerate and lie about themselves on Facebook. This sex difference in online bullying of friends is interesting and indicates that Machiavellian women use social networking sites for manipulating and controlling their friends. This one study aside, there is a scarcity of research into the Dark Triad (and Tetrad), and online friendship strategies. It would be expected that individuals high in these traits use the online environment as an extension to the manipulation they exert in their friends in off-line too.

7.3.3 Cyberstalking

By nature, the cyberworld is an ideal place for perpetrating intrusion of privacy of others in the form of stalking. Stalking is obsessive behavior, classified as a criminal offense, where the perpetrator wants to gain the attention of the victim by exerting dominance over them. The victims often (but not always) have had some form of personal relationship with the stalker. Traditional stalking consists of a battery of behaviors including unwanted phone calls or text messages, showing up at the victim's home or workplace, sending unwanted gifts, and spying on the victim's life. The invention of the internet, especially social media, has provided more tools for the stalkers to help them to exercise terror over the victims.

Indeed, cyberstalking has become so common it now accounts for more stalking cases that face-to-face stalking (see McVeigh, 2011, for statistics in the United Kingdom). With regards to the effect that it has on the victim, it is as harmful as traditional stalking. Victims of cyberstalking and can result in high number of measures that the victim takes in order to protect themselves. Nobles, Reyns, Fox, and Fisher (2014) listed the self-protection strategies as "time off from work or school; changing or quitting a job or school; changing the way they went to work or school; avoiding relatives, friends, or holiday celebrations; changing usual activities outside of work or school; staying with friends or relatives or having them stay with you; altering appearance to be unrecognizable; taking self-defense or martial arts classes; getting pepper spray; obtaining a gun; acquiring any other kind of weapon; changing social security number; changing email address; changing telephone numbers; installing caller identification or call blocking systems; and changing or installing new locks or a security system" (p. 998). It is easy to see how persistent online stalking can have a dramatic influence on the individual's life, preventing them from carrying on their everyday activities without a fear.

The online dating environment is especially a fertile ground for cyberstalking. Much of cyberstalking involves persistent torment of current or former intimate partners. Sometimes, the victim may have met the stalker first in an online dating platform. A common story is that a woman meets a man on a dating website and may have a few dates before calling off the budding relationship. However, the other person may have different ideas about their connection with the casual date, resulting in delusional thoughts about the intimacy and importance of the relationship. The delusional stalker may start a campaign in the form of persistent online messaging, phone calls, and even following the victim to their home or workplace, sometimes with tragic consequences (see Patrick, 2017, for examples of real-life stories). Stalkers may have other motivations besides of deluded ideas of love, and some may torment their victims out of pure maliciousness or the need to dominate.

Despite the prevalence and seriousness of cyberstalking, there has been relatively little research on investigating the phenomena in scientific studies (Nobles et al., 2014). Even less is known about the online strategies of those who are at the higher end of the Dark Triad continuum. Studies on incarcerated offenders have found that overall, stalkers score lower on psychopathy than other types of offenders, probably due to the detached interpersonal nature of those high in this trait (e.g., Reavis, Allen, & Meloy, 2008). To put simply, psychopaths may not care enough to start obsessing about other people, which could make them less likely to perpetrate stalking. On the other hand, researchers have suggested that some features of narcissism may lead to obsession when the romantic advances are declined, which could make them more likely to stalk the object of their preoccupations (Wilson, Ermshar, & Welsh, 2006). Thus stalking perpetration may not be the same across all the Dark Triad traits.

Smoker and March (2017) constructed a questionnaire to measure the tendency to cyberstalk one's partner with acts such as checking their phone/computer histories, installing tracking apps on the partners phone to know where they are at all times, constantly checking their social media, and other obsessive acts that happen online. The results were interesting in terms of sex differences. Women were more likely than men to monitor their intimate partners in an online environment. The authors suggested than online stalking could be a low-cost, covert way for women to attain intimacy and maintain their relationship. They also found that irrespective of the sex of the participant, all of the Dark Tetrad traits had a significant, positive relationship with cyberstalking of intimate relationship partners. This indicates that aversive personality traits are important in understanding who uses modern technology in following and tracking their partners.

7.4 Cybercrime

Have you ever received an email from a lonely Russian lady looking for a friend? Or from a Nigerian prince who needs to deposit an investment with the help of your money? There is a high probability that you have. With the expansion of the internet, the dark side of the web has grown at the same rate. The internet provides an excellent platform for scamming, stealing, and causing harm, perpetrated by individuals as well as by organized criminal gangs. Cybercrimes range from hacking, spreading viruses, and laundering money to phishing, fraud, and terrorism. The scams vary from credible-looking bills with fake log-on details to announcements of winning money in a lottery. Some of the least credible ones are badly written sob stories about misfortune, illness, and the need to invest substantial amounts of money. The motivations behind the crimes can be intellectual curiosity (e.g., "how can I hack this system?"), maliciousness (e.g., "I want to spread viruses and harm others for fun"), and selfishness (e.g., "I want to make money out of scamming someone").

The Dark Triad is a very relevant, albeit relatively little studied personality trait in the propensity and success of internet crimes. Socially aversive personalities may have a moral compass that is set for self-gain and deviousness, rather than altruism or social norms. Shallow morality and lack of guilt facilitates criminal behavior, which can lead to online crimes as well as offline crimes.

One of the common cybercrimes intending to get sensitive information out of the victims is called "phishing." Curtis, Rajivan, Jones, and Gonzalez (2018) defined phishing as "... the most common form of cyberattack in which criminals (attackers) deceive people via socially-engineered strategies into installing harmful software or surrendering sensitive information" (p. 175). Successful phishing emails (i.e., those who get fast response from the victims) are authoritative in nature, communicate a failure, send notifications, express a shared interest, or pretend to be a friend (Rajivan & Gonzalez, 2018). There are individual differences in how good people are in constructing phishing messages. Testifying for the impulsive nature of this kind of cybercrime, when the sender gets higher, immediate rewards, they are likely to put more effort into future phishing emails. This type of instant gratification is typical of the Dark Triad, making it a promising personality trait for investigating phishing.

Successful phishing does not only require a credible message from the attacker, but also susceptible victim who will fall for the message. Curtis et al. (2018) created a two-part study in order to investigate how the Dark Triad influences both success of phishing as well as vulnerability to phishing attacks. In the first part of the research, they asked online participants to write phishing emails that both evade the spam filters and persuade the receiver to respond to the message. In the second part, a different set of participants were asked to imagine that they were helping an office manager to sort out her emails, deciding which ones to leave/respond to, and which ones to delete. Half of the emails were phishing emails from Study 1, and the other half were harmless (i.e., "ham") emails. The researchers found that none of the Dark Triad traits contributed to more successful or credible phishing. However, those who were higher in Machiavellianism put more effort into constructing the messages, whereas higher end of narcissism and psychopathy related to less effort. With regards to the Dark Triad and vulnerability to phishing attacks, end-user narcissism was related to greater acceptance of the phishing emails, especially if they were sent by narcissistic attackers. The results of this study indicate that socially antagonistic traits may not relate to success in phishing, but individuals who are high on socially scheming and manipulative trait Machiavellianism are willing to invest more time into trying to scam others.

Other studies have looked at individual Dark Triad components with regards to online scamming. For example, Seigfried-Spellar, Villacís-Vukadinović, and Lynam (2017) studied psychopathy and different computer crime behaviors in an internet sample. They found that those who scored higher on antagonism and disinhibition facets of psychopathy were more likely to have tried their luck with all the aspects of cybercrime (i.e., unauthorized access, monitoring network traffic, constricting viruses, defacing websites, identity frauds and thefts). Psychopathy is generally related to criminal behavior, and the results of this study indicate that criminal tendencies extend to the online environment as well.

7.5 Self-Presentation, Visibility, and Detection of the Dark Triad on Social Media

Social media websites (e.g., Twitter, Facebook, and Instagram) provide an invaluable tool for presenting oneself to wide audiences of friends, acquaintances, and even strangers. Researchers have been interested in studying whether the Dark Triad relates to an increased use of social media, as well as greater visibility in terms of updating status information and posting selfies (i.e., photographs that one has taken of oneself). In this section, the focus will be on how the Dark Triad relates to the frequency and style of social media use, the motivations behind it, as well as visible markers that may distinguish someone who is high on socially aversive personality traits.

7.5.1 Selfie Posting

One social media activity that would be expected to relate to the Dark Triad is the frequency that people post selfies of themselves on their social media sites. Indeed, taking and posting selfies has almost become an epitome of narcissism. Posing in front of the mobile phone camera, flirting at oneself, and posting the pictures on social media seems like an ideal way of getting admiration in order to perpetuate the inflated self-image narcissists have of themselves. The motivations for selfies may not always be driven by the need to get attention. For example, people may post selfies in order to keep in touch and communicate with friends and family, to record and archive one's life in form of an online diary, and for entertainment in order to pass time and have fun. In a study on a sample of people from Korea, Sung, Lee, Kim, and Choi (2016) found that selfie posting in narcissistic individuals is driven mainly by the motivation of getting attention, and to a lesser extent, by the need to communicate with others, and for combatting boredom (Sung et al.,

2016). In the same study, the authors found that narcissism was related to more frequent selfie posting, and the intention to post future selfies. These findings back up the idea that selfie posting provides means for narcissistic individuals to get the attention they crave from others.

There have been a few other studies on selfie-posting frequency and the Dark Triad. Fox and Rooney (2015) explored the influence of the Dark Triad and self-objectification (i.e., the tendency to see one's body as an object of attractiveness) on men's social media behavior. Their sample consisted of 1000 US men, recruited via advertising in a national magazine. The participants were asked about the time they spent each day on different social media websites, their frequency of taking and posting selfies in the past week, and the frequency of using editing (e.g., photoshopping techniques) in order to make themselves look more attractive. All the Dark Triad traits had positive correlations with all the measured social media behaviors. However, when controlling for the similarity between the traits, only narcissism had a positive relationship with editing the photos of oneself in order to look more presentable. Both narcissism and self-objectification were positive predictors of the time that an individual spent on social media sites on a daily bases. Finally, those US men who were higher on narcissism and psychopathy had a higher frequency of posting selfies on the social media. The findings of the Fox and Rooney (2015) study suggest that especially narcissism (with the desire for fame and admiration by masses of people) influences the visibility and frequency of using social media for self-advertising. The editing of the photos by more narcissistic men mirrors the findings in an off-line environment. In an earlier study, we found that those who were high on narcissism were more likely to manipulate their appearance in a deceptive way in order to attract potential mates (Jonason, Lyons, Baughman, and Vernon, 2014), and the results on photo editing online support the off-line literature on narcissism and deceptive self-enhancement. An interesting question is, then, whether women who are narcissistic have the same patterns of selfie posting as narcissistic men. This was investigated in a study on a sample of Turkish university students, with the intention to find out whether women who are narcissistic have same kind of selfie-posting behavior as men do (Arpaci, 2018). Selfie-posting attitudes (i.e., "posting selfies on social media is a good idea"), intentions (i.e., "I plan to post selfies on social media"), and behaviors (i.e., "I post selfies on social media") were all related to higher narcissism scores in men, but not in women. According to Arpaci (2018), the selfie-posting behavior in narcissistic men could be a tool for seeking social validation and creating an impression of importance and high social standing. It is possible that selfie-posting motivations relate to status-seeking behaviors associated with narcissism, something that future research should investigate further.

As you may remember from Chapter 1, narcissism is not a uniform personality trait but it consists of several subcomponents, some of which have been branded as adaptive, and others that are considered maladaptive. Different traits of narcissism may influence selfie-posting behavior in a unique manner. Weiser (2015) studied the three-factor model of narcissism with regards to selfie-posting frequency in a large sample of US residents. He found that the adaptive Leadership/Authority (dominance and perception of oneself as a great leader) and Grandiose Exhibitionism (vanity and desire to be admired) predicted a higher frequency of posting selfies. Interestingly, the socially toxic Entitlement/Exploitativeness facet (a sense that one deserves more than others, and willingness to exploit) did not have association with posting selfies. The author suggested that posting selfies relates to seeking for admiration, but also to conveying dominance an authority. It is possible that those high in the socially toxic Entitlement/Exploitativeness facet of narcissism use other social media behaviors (such as retaliation to negative comments from others) as more viable means to achieve their goals.

In two studies, McCain et al. (2016) investigated the Dark Triad in relation to a wide range of social media behaviors, including why, where, and when selfies are posted. They found that those selfies posted during the workday were more likely to be displayed by those high in narcissism, Machiavellianism, and psychopathy. However, only narcissism was related to posting more selfies from social events, or during one's time off (e.g., evenings and weekends). When asked about the motivations for posting selfies, all the Dark Triad traits were related to asserting that self-presentation is an important motivation. Other motivations included professional reasons (e.g., networking to make professional contacts), which were associated with narcissism and psychopathy (but interestingly, not with Machiavellianism). Further, selfie posting was reported as a positive experience for high narcissistic individuals, and as a negative experience for high psychopathy individuals.

Body image could be an important factor in explaining the relationship between selfie posting and personality. Wang et al. (2018) studied a sample of University students in China, asking them about their selfie-posting behavior on any social media site. Their results suggested that narcissistic individuals have a higher confidence in the attractiveness of their bodies, which leads to greater frequency of posting selfies on social media sites.

The authors suggested that selfie posting could be a self-regulatory strategy for narcissists, allowing them to maintain and improve their self-image by getting feedback from others. Indeed, it is possible that the positive body image associated with narcissism is partially nurtured by the selfie-taking culture.

7.5.2 Social Media Profiles and Status Updates

One way of understanding how personality is manifested in the online environment is to study the content of status updates and personal profiles on social networking sites. Status updates have become one of the most popular features on social networking websites such as Facebook. Status updates vary from funny personal anecdotes, political opinions, and declarations of love or dislike to talking about current or future events, states of mind, or future intentions. The content of the written updates can reveal important information about the individual's inner life, their desires and motivations. Researchers have started to use status updates as an interesting window to the world of those who are high on the Dark Triad traits.

The reason for updating a status is to get some kind of a response from others. People are different in how they react to other people's "likes" and comments regarding to their status and profile updates. Some are not too bothered about how much attention they get, and others get very angry and retaliatory if their social media presence is not acknowledged by their followers. Overall, receiving more responses to status updates results in greater happiness, increased self-esteem, and the feeling that others care about them (Zell & Moeller, 2018).

Zell and Moeller (2017) investigated University student's narcissism, and their reactions to other's responses with regards to their recent status updates. They looked at different aspects of narcissism: Entitlement/Exploitativeness, Grandiose exhibitionism, and Leadership/Authority. The authors found that participants who were high on Entitlement/Exploitativeness had a more intense desire to get response from others, and irrespective of the number of responses, they were still not happy with the amount of attention their updates received from others. This facet of narcissism also related to "retaliation" in the form of not liking/commenting on a friend's posts if the friend did not acknowledge their post. Maladaptive narcissism has a link to dissatisfaction with social media use, leaving the individual to crave for more.

Several studies have explored whether status updates have an association with one, or all of the Dark Triad traits. Narcissism has been one of the most popular traits in this regard, perhaps because narcissists may use their status update as a means for gaining validation and admiration from their followers. The expectation is that those who are narcissistic communicate in a manner that draws positive attention to them, resulting in "likes" of the posting. The Dark Triad (and especially narcissism) has also received research interest with regards of the content of Facebook status updates, as well as to the motivations for updating statuses.

Content and motivation for status updates was the focus of investigation by Marshall, Lefringhausen, and Ferenczi (2015), who looked at the influence of narcissism, the Big Five, and self-esteem on the Facebook updates in a sample of 555 US residents. They found that participants who scored highly on a narcissism measure had a higher frequency of posting about their achievements, and these posts were related to the motivation of using Facebook for gaining validation from others. They also had a higher frequency of posting about diet and exercise, which could be related to the importance of physical appearance for narcissistic individuals. Further, narcissism related to receiving more likes and comments after updating their statuses. Narcissistic updating about achievements seems to be reinforced by positive attention, which, in turn, leads to more updating. However, one notable shortcoming of this study was that the questionnaire relied on self-reported Facebook activity. It is entirely possible that those who are more narcissistic do not report the attention their posts get in an accurate manner, but exaggerate the number of likes that their statuses receive.

Is it possible to guess what type of personality a Facebook user has by glancing at their status updates? Garcia and Sikström (2014) sampled 304 US citizens in order to see if the Dark Triad predicts the content of status updates. Participants filled in personality measurements, and provided fifteen Facebook status updates. The findings suggest that narcissism, and even more so psychopathy predicted the types of statuses that people post. Both traits were associated with status updates that had words with negative emotional content. Those who were high on narcissism and psychopathy also posted updates that were odd and unusual in nature. One of the common complaints from users who want to leave Facebook is that they struggle to deal with the negativity from other users. It is an intriguing possibility that socially aversive personalities are the ones responsible for spawning negativity, making other users feel bad enough to stop using social media.

Nathan DeWall, Buffardi, Bonser, and Campbell (2011) were interested in the use of language by narcissistic social media users. More specifically, they wanted to look at the use of the singular first-person pronouns (e.g.,

I, me, mine). In face to face communication, narcissists are willing to brag about their achievements, and are overusing singular first person pronouns. The idea in this study was to see how narcissists try to get attention in an online environment, and whether it happens through provoking, sexy photographs, or through using language in a way that directs attention to the persona and their achievements. They analyzed the Facebook profile pages of undergraduate students and found that those who were narcissistic were using self-promoting strategies by either utilizing first-person singular pronouns, or if these were not used, by having a self-promoting and sexy profile picture. Thus narcissism on Facebook may be manifested by either an increased use of self-promoting pronouns, or by having an exaggeratingly eye-catching profile picture (in which case the self-promoting language is unnecessary).

Most of the studies on linguistic content of social media posting have been conducted using English-speaking participants. One exception to this is the research by Olga Bogolyubova, Panicheva, Tikhonov, Ivanov, and Ledovaya (2018), who were interested in Russian-speaking Facebook users and the semantic content of their posts. Their participants consisted of over 6000 Facebook users and 15,000 posts posted by those users. The three traits were strikingly different from each other with regards to the content of the posts. In Russian Facebook users, narcissism had a positive association with posting about social interaction with others, as well as posting about status or self-image. This reflects some of the features that have been identified in offline research too—those high in narcissism are less "dark" and more sociable than those high in Machiavellianism and psychopathy. Narcissism is related to an inflated self-view and strive for high status, which could result in overt posting about issues that are connected with self-image, status, and the need to maintain them. People who were higher in psychopathy were posting more about basic needs (e.g., need for food and money), politics, and authority. In line with the socially aloof, unemotional style related to Machiavellianism, Russian Facebook users high in this trait posted less about interacting with others, social relationships, or posts that were positive in their nature.

7.5.3 Detection of the Dark Triad on Social Media

Is it possible to detect narcissistic, psychopathic, or Machiavellian individuals by just having a glance at their social networking sites? Having a predatory, exploitative friend, colleague, or acquaintance is potentially harmful, and it would be expected that people have above-chance accuracy when trying to judge dark personality characters based on online presence. An added problem in detection is the possibility that manipulative individuals are presenting an idealized, rather than a truthful image of themselves. If people show a profile that is inconsistent with their actual personality, detection rates can remain low. However, research is more supportive of the "extended real life" hypothesis, which suggests that social media profiles are an extension of the actual personality (Back et al., 2010; Orehek & Human, 2017). If this is the case, just as in real life, people should be accurate in inferring the personality of someone on the bases of their cyberworld presence.

In a similar manner as in face-to-face context, there is a high consensus between self and observer ratings of some of the Dark Triad base on online profiles. Vander Molen, Kaplan, Choi, and Montoya (2018) collected Dark triad measures and Facebook profiles of 145 University students, and asked them also to rate other user's profiles for perceived levels of the Dark Triad. They found that only narcissism was predicted somewhat accurately, but the self-other agreement for Machiavellianism and psychopathy were not significant. The authors also analyzed the type of cues that lead to accurate identification of aversive personalities in Facebook profiles. For psychopathy, there were hardly any identifiable cues. It looks like high psychopathy individuals are less likely to be identified, and this could be due to the elusive profiles that don't give much out to the observers. Those who were high on Machiavellianism posted less written information about themselves and shared more information about future events. It is possible that high Machiavellian individuals are strategic in wanting people to know less about themselves, while wanting to appear to be important by sharing information. Narcissism had an association with posting information that had cues about self-enhancement (attractiveness, number of friends). The results of Vander Molen et al. (2018) indicate that narcissists are more likely to enhance their appearance and personalities, and this can lead to accurate identification of narcissism in the online environment. Although other studies referred to in the earlier section showed that all of the Dark Triad traits are associated with differences in their profiles and status updates, it could be that only the features related to narcissism can be identified by others based on their online behaviors. It would be interesting to see if online presence of psychopathic or Machiavellian individuals is recognized more accurately from other sites, such as Twitter, where information is presented in a much briefer format.

7.6 The Dark Triad and Online Mating Behaviors

When I started literature reviews into this section, I was surprised to find that there was very little research into how the Dark Triad relates to mating-related behaviors in the online environment. Majority of the off-line research on the Dark Triad has focused on mating-related behaviors, suggesting that especially narcissism and psychopathy are associated with a stronger drive for short-term relationships (see also Chapter 3). Online dating applications are used for seeking both long-term, serious relationships, as well as brief sexual encounters. Thus I was expecting to encounter a large body of research investigating how the Dark Triad manifests itself in seeking for mating opportunities in the online environment.

Research that has investigated individual differences in the use of online hook up apps such as Tinder has resulted in interesting findings. For example, those who have low sexual disgust (e.g., not being bothered by listening to other people having sex) and high sociosexuality (i.e., an increased interests in short-term sexual relationships) are more likely to use Tinder for the reason of finding casual sex partners (Sevi, Aral, & Eskenazi, 2017). Thus higher interest in casual sex may relate to taking the risk of getting acquainted to strangers in online environment. Future research should investigate how the Dark Triad influences strategies and motivations for using online dating apps, especially applications such as Tinder, which offer a possibility for an instant sexual hook-up with another user.

One interesting avenue for future research is online "sexting" behavior. Sexting includes sending, receiving, or forwarding sexually suggestive materials via text messages or as online communication. Sexting can take the form of unsolicited (i.e., not requested by the receiver) nude pictures to a potential dating partner. In the context of heterosexual dating, especially women who have tried online dating have experiences of receiving a nude picture of the potential date, often as the first (and last) point of communication. Women send nude pictures too, but this often happens after some kind of a relationship has already been formed with the online date, and often only after it has been requested. Most women tend to find unsolicited "dick picks" funny, offensive, and/or disgusting (Vitis & Gilmour, 2017), and although it may present a strategy for short-term mating in the sending males, the success of this kind of strategy is not clear. Out of the three traits, especially psychopathy is related to short-term mating interests, and it would be expected that this trait is also the more likely suspect when investigating personalities of people who send the pictures of their genitalia to others.

March and Wagstaff (2017) were interested in the role of the Dark Tetrad in sending others unsolicited nude pictures of oneself (measured by the frequency, own enjoyment, and perceived enjoyment of the recipients). They found that sex (being male), higher self-perceived value as a mate, and Machiavellianism were significant factors in sending unsolicited pictures of one's genitalia to others. The results of the study were surprising, as psychopathy did not play a role in sexting in the form of unsolicited nude pictures. The authors explained this by linking it to the strategic manipulation associated with Machiavellianism. They suggested that sending explicit images could be part of an aggressive mating strategy, where the individuals are trying their luck. Even if the success rate is low, the scattergun approach to sending images could relate to occasional stroke of luck.

7.7 Conclusion

In the recent decades, the explosion of the internet has led to a need to understand why aversive behaviors such as trolling, bullying, and stalking happens in an online environment, and who the perpetrators are. Further, the internet provides a valuable tool for investigating strategies of those who are at the higher end of the Dark Triad continuum. So far, research has found that although problematic internet use with addictive qualities is more typical to those who are high on psychopathy and narcissism, it may be that amount of time spent on applications such as social media is not necessarily bad for the individual, especially not for those who are high on grandiose narcissism. In the cyber-aggression literature, sadism and psychopathy have emerged as the most important traits, leading to stronger identities as a troll, and higher incidences of bullying and stalking. Narcissism, in turn, has the most relevance in social media, with a higher likelihood of posting selfies, getting angry if their posts are not acknowledged by others, and using more digital enhancement techniques in trying to make themselves look more appealing. In a similar way as in off-line environment, narcissists thrive from the attention they get in online social networking sites. One of the most fruitful area for future research is investigating why, how, and when dark personalities use the online environment in dating and mating. It is expected that individuals high in the Dark Triad use more coercive and manipulative tactics when searching for partners online, acting in a way that is not dissimilar to their off-line mating behaviors either.

Further Reading

Seigfried-Spellar, K. C., Villacís-Vukadinović, N., & Lynam, D. R. (2017). Computer criminal behavior is related to psychopathy and other antisocial behavior. *Journal of Criminal Justice*, *51*, 67–73.

Sung, Y., Lee, J. A., Kim, E., & Choi, S. M. (2016). Why we post selfies: Understanding motivations for posting pictures of oneself. *Personality and Individual Differences*, *97*, 260–265.

Trombly, D. R., & Zeigler-Hill, V. (2017). The dark triad and disordered gambling. *Current Psychology*, *36*, 740–746.

REFERENCES

Abell, L., & Brewer, G. (2014). Machiavellianism, self-monitoring, self-promotion and relational aggression on Facebook. *Computers in Human Behavior, 36*, 258–262.

Abell, L., & Brewer, G. (2017). Machiavellianism and Schadenfreude in women's friendships. *Psychological Reports*.

Abell, L., Brewer, G., Qualter, P., & Austin, E. (2016). Machiavellianism, emotional manipulation, and friendship functions in women's friendships. *Personality and Individual Differences, 88*, 108–113.

Abell, L., Lyons, M., & Brewer, G. (2014). The relationship between parental bonding, Machiavellianism and adult friendship quality. *Individual Differences Research, 12*(4-B), 191–197.

Abell, L., Qualter, P., Brewer, G., Barlow, A., Stylianou, M., Henzi, P., et al. (2015). Why Machiavellianism matters in childhood: the relationship between children's Machiavellian traits and their peer interactions in a natural setting. *Europe's Journal of Psychology, 11*, 484–493.

Adams, H. M., Luevano, V. X., & Jonason, P. K. (2014). Risky business: willingness to be caught in an extra-pair relationship, relationship experience, and the dark triad. *Personality and Individual Differences, 66*, 204–207.

Aghababaei, N., & Błachnio, A. (2015). Well-being and the dark triad. *Personality and Individual Differences, 86*, 365–368.

Aitken, S. J., Lyons, M., & Jonason, P. K. (2013). Dads or cads? Women's strategic decisions in the mating game. *Personality and Individual Differences, 55*, 118–122.

Akhtar, R., Ahmetoglu, G., & Chamorro-Premuzic, T. (2013). Greed is good? Assessing the relationship between entrepreneurship and subclinical psychopathy. *Personality and Individual Differences, 54*, 420–425.

Al-Dajani, N., Gralnick, T. M., & Bagby, R. M. (2016). A psychometric review of the Personality Inventory for DSM-5 (PID-5): current status and future directions. *Journal of Personality Assessment, 98*(1), 62–81.

Alalehto, T., & Azarian, R. (2018). When white collar criminals turn to fatal violence: the impact of narcissism and psychopathy. *Journal of Investigative Psychology and Offender Profiling*.

Alavi, M., Mei, T. K., & Mehrinezhad, S. A. (2018). The dark triad of personality and infidelity intentions: the moderating role of relationship experience. *Personality and Individual Differences, 128*, 49–54.

Anderson, J. L., Sellbom, M., Wygant, D. B., Salekin, R. T., & Krueger, R. F. (2014). Examining the associations between DSM-5 section III antisocial personality disorder traits and psychopathy in community and university samples. *Journal of Personality Disorders, 28*, 675–697.

Archer, J. (2004). Sex differences in aggression in real-world settings: a meta-analytic review. *Review of General Psychology, 8*, 291–322.

Arnulf, J. K., & Gottschalk, P. (2013). Heroic leaders as white-collar criminals: an empirical study. *Journal of Investigative Psychology and Offender Profiling, 10*, 96–113.

Arpaci, I. (2018). The moderating effect of gender in the relationship between narcissism and selfie-posting behavior. *Personality and Individual Differences, 134*, 71–74.

Ashby, H. U. (1978). An MMPI scale for narcissistic personality disorder. *Dissertation Abstracts International, 10*, 39 [University Microfilms No. 7907849, 5053-B].

Atari, M., & Chegeni, R. (2017). The dark triad and long-term mate preferences in Iranian women. *Personality and Individual differences*, *104*, 333–335.

Austin, E. J., Farrelly, D., Black, C., & Moore, H. (2007). Emotional intelligence, Machiavellianism and emotional manipulation: does EI have a dark side? *Personality and Individual Differences*, *43*, 179–189.

Azizli, N., Atkinson, B. E., Baughman, H. M., Chin, K., Vernon, P. A., Harris, E., et al. (2016). Lies and crimes: dark triad, misconduct, and high-stakes deception. *Personality and Individual Differences*, *89*, 34–39.

Babiak, P., & Hare, R. D. (2006). *Snakes in suits: when psychopaths go to work*. New York, NY: Regan Books.

Babiak, P., Neumann, C. S., & Hare, R. D. (2010). Corporate psychopathy: talking the walk. *Behavioral Sciences & The Law*, *28*, 74–193.

Back, M. D., Schmuckle, S. C., & Egloff, B. (2010). Why are narcissists so charming at first sight? Decoding the narcissism popularity link at zero acquaintance. *Journal of Personality and Social Psychology*, *98*, 132–145.

Back, M. D., Stopfer, J. M., Vazire, S., Gaddis, S., Schmukle, S. C., Egloff, B., et al. (2010). Facebook profiles reflect actual personality, not self-idealization. *Psychological Science*, *21*(3), 372–374.

Backman, H., Laajasalo, T., Jokela, M., & Aronen, E. T. (2018). Interpersonal relationships as protective and risk factors for psychopathy: a follow-up study in adolescent offenders. *Journal of Youth and Adolescence*, *47*, 1022–1036.

Barelds, D. P., Dijkstra, P., Groothof, H. A., & Pastoor, C. D. (2017). The dark triad and three types of jealousy: its' relations among heterosexuals and homosexuals involved in a romantic relationship. *Personality and Individual Differences*, *116*, 6–10.

Baughman, H. M., Dearing, S., Giammarco, E., & Vernon, P. A. (2012). Relationships between bullying behaviours and the dark triad: a study with adults. *Personality and Individual Differences*, *52*, 571–575.

Baughman, H. M., Jonason, P. K., Lyons, M., & Vernon, P. A. (2014). Liar liar pants on fire: cheater strategies linked to the dark triad. *Personality and Individual Differences*, *71*, 35–38.

Baughman, H. M., Jonason, P. K., Veselka, L., & Vernon, P. A. (2014). Four shades of sexual fantasies linked to the dark triad. *Personality and Individual Differences*, *67*, 47–51.

Baumeister, R. F., Catanese, K. R., & Wallace, H. M. (2002). Conquest by force: a narcissistic reactance theory of rape and sexual coercion. *Review of General Psychology*, *6*, 92–135.

Bertl, B., Pietschnig, J., Tran, U. S., Stieger, S., & Voracek, M. (2017). More or less than the sum of its parts? Mapping the dark triad of personality onto a single dark core. *Personality and Individual Differences*, *114*, 140–144.

Blanchard, A., Lyons, M., & Centifanti, L. (2016). Baby was a black sheep: digit ratio (2D:4D), maternal bonding and primary and secondary psychopathy. *Personality and Individual Differences*, *99*, 67–71.

Blanchard, A., Lyons, M., & Centifanti, L. (2016). An effective way to deal with predators is to taste terrible: primary and secondary psychopathy and mate preference. *Personality and Individual Differences*, *92*, 128–134.

Bland, R. C., Newman, S. C., Dyck, R. J., & Orn, H. (1990). Prevalence of psychiatric disorders and suicide attempts in a prison population. *The Canadian Journal of Psychiatry*, *35*, 407–413.

Blickle, G., Schlegel, A., Fassbender, P., & Klein, U. (2006). Some personality correlates of business white-collar crime. *Applied Psychology*, *55*, 220–233.

Blickle, G., & Schütte, N. (2017). Trait psychopathy, task performance, and counterproductive work behavior directed toward the organization. *Personality and Individual Differences*, *109*, 225–231.

Blickle, G., Schütte, N., & Genau, H. A. (2018). Manager psychopathy, trait activation, and job performance: a multi-source study. *European Journal of Work and Organizational Psychology*, 1–12.

Blinkhorn, V., Lyons, M., & Almond, L. (2015). The ultimate femme fatale? Narcissism predicts serious and aggressive sexually coercive behaviour in females. *Personality and Individual Differences*, *87*, 219–223.

Blinkhorn, V., Lyons, M., & Almond, L. (2016). Drop the bad attitude! Narcissism predicts acceptance of violent behaviour. *Personality and Individual Differences*, *98*, 157–161.

Boddy, C. R. (2011). The corporate psychopaths theory of the global financial crisis. In *Corporate psychopaths* (pp. 163–166). UK: Palgrave Macmillan.

Boddy, C. R. (2014). Corporate psychopaths, conflict, employee affective well-being and counterproductive work behaviour. *Journal of Business Ethics*, *12*, 107–121.

Boddy, C. R., Ladyshewsky, R., & Galvin, P. (2010). Leaders without ethics in global business: corporate psychopaths. *Journal of Public Affairs*, *10*, 121–138.

Boduszek, D., Debowska, A., & Willmott, D. (2017). Latent profile analysis of psychopathic traits among homicide, general violent, property, and white-collar offenders. *Journal of Criminal Justice*, *51*, 17–23.

Bogolyubova, O., Panicheva, P., Tikhonov, R., Ivanov, V., & Ledovaya, Y. (2018). Dark personalities on Facebook: harmful online behaviors and language. *Computers in Human Behavior*, *78*, 151–159.

Braun, S. (2017). Leader narcissism and outcomes in organizations: a review at multiple levels of analysis and implications for future research. *Frontiers in Psychology*, *8*, 773.

Brewer, G., & Abell, L. (2015a). Machiavellianism and sexual behavior: motivations, deception and infidelity. *Personality and Individual Differences*, *74*, 186–191.

Brewer, G., & Abell, L. (2015b). Machiavellianism in long-term relationships: competition, mate retention and sexual coercion. *Scandinavian Journal of Psychology*, *56*(3), 357–362.

Brewer, G., Abell, L., & Lyons, M. (2013). It's not just a man-thing: testing sex as a moderator between peer attachment and Machiavellianism, competition and selfdisclosure. *Individual Differences Research*, *11*, 114–120.

Brewer, G., Abell, L., & Lyons, M. (2014). Machiavellianism, competition and self-disclosure in friendship. *Individual Differences Research*, *12*, 1–7.

Brewer, G., Bennett, C., Davidson, L., Ireen, A., Phipps, A. J., Stewart-Wilkes, D., et al. (2018). Dark triad traits and romantic relationship attachment, accommodation, and control. *Personality and Individual Differences*, *120*, 202–208.

Brewer, G., Carter, G. L., Lyons, M., & Green, J. (2018). Sensation-seeking in women does not affect their preference for dark triad male faces. *Personality and Individual Differences*, *130*, 92–95.

Brewer, G., Christiansen, P., Dorozkinaite, D., Ingleby, B., O'Hagan, L., Williams, C., et al. (2018). A drunk heart speaks a sober mind: alcohol does not influence the selection of short-term partners with dark triad traits. *Personality and Individual Differences*.

Brewer, G., Hunt, D., James, G., & Abell, L. (2015). Dark triad traits, infidelity and romantic revenge. *Personality and Individual Differences*, *83*, 122–127.

Brown, E. C., & Guy, R. F. (1983). The effects of sex and Machiavellianism on self-disclosure patterns. *Social Behavior and Personality*, *11*, 93–96.

Buck, K. (2018). *Fast-food worker spits in customer's dinner then says "I want to go home"* https://metro.co.uk/2018/03/25/fast-food-worker-spits-in-customers-dinner-then-says-i-want-to-go-home-7415669/.

Buckels, E. E., Jones, D. N., & Paulhus, D. L. (2013). Behavioral confirmation of everyday sadism. *Psychological Science*, *24*, 2201–2209.

Buckels, E. E., Trapnell, P. D., & Paulhus, D. L. (2014). Trolls just want to have fun. *Personality and Individual Differences*, *67*, 97–102.

Buonanno, P., Drago, F., Galbiati, R., & Vertova, P. (2014). How much should we trust crime statistics? A comparison between EU and US. *European Journal of Law and Economics*, 1–15.

Burton, K. A., Adams, J. M., Hart, W., Grant, B., Richardson, K., & Tortoriello, G. (2017). You remind me of someone awesome: narcissistic tolerance is driven by perceived similarity. *Personality and Individual Differences*, *104*, 499–503.

Buunk, A. P., & Fisher, M. (2009). Individual differences in intrasexual competition. *Journal of Evolutionary Psychology*, 7(1), 37–48.

Byrnes, J. P., Miller, D. C., & Schafer, W. D. (1999). Gender differences in risk taking: a meta-analysis. *Psychological Bulletin*, *125*, 367–383.

Cai, H., Kwan, V. S., & Sedikides, C. (2012). A sociocultural approach to narcissism: the case of modern China. *European Journal of Personality*, *26*, 529–535.

Cain, N. M., Pincus, A. L., & Ansell, E. B. (2008). Narcissism at the crossroads: phenotypic description of pathological narcissism across clinical theory, social/personality psychology, and psychiatric diagnosis. *Clinical Psychology Review*, *28*, 638–656.

Cairncross, M., Veselka, L., Schermer, J. A., & Vernon, P. A. (2013). A behavioral genetic analysis of alexithymia and the dark triad traits of personality. *Twin Research and Human Genetics*, *16*, 690–697.

Caligor, E., Levy, K. N., & Yeomans, F. E. (2015). Narcissistic personality disorder: diagnostic and clinical challenges. *American Journal of Psychiatry*, *172*, 415–422.

Campbell, A. (1995). A few good men: evolutionary psychology and female adolescent aggression. *Ethology and Sociobiology*, *16*, 99–123.

Campbell, W. K. (2005). *When you love a man who loves himself: how to deal with a oneway relationship*. Chicago: Sourcebooks Casablanca.

Caponecchia, C., Sun, A. Y., & Wyatt, A. (2012). 'Psychopaths' at work? Implications of lay persons' use of labels and behavioural criteria for psychopathy. *Journal of Business Ethics*, *107*, 399–408.

Carlson, E. N., & DesJardins, N. M. L. (2015). Do mean guys always finish first or just say that they do? Narcissists' awareness of their social status and popularity over time. *Personality and Social Psychology Bulletin*, *41*, 901–917.

Carter, G. L., Campbell, A. C., & Muncer, S. (2014). The dark triad: beyond a 'male' mating strategy. *Personality and Individual Differences*, *56*, 159–164.

Carter, G. L., Lyons, M., & Brewer, G. (2018). Lifetime offspring and the dark triad. *Personality and Individual Differences*, *132*, 79–83.

Carter, G. L., Montanaro, Z., Linney, C., & Campbell, A. C. (2015). Women's sexual competition and the dark triad. *Personality and Individual Differences*, *74*, 275–279.

Carton, H., & Egan, V. (2017). The dark triad and intimate partner violence. *Personality and Individual Differences*, *105*, 84–88.

Castille, C. M., Kuyumcu, D., & Bennett, R. J. (2017). Prevailing to the peers' detriment: organizational constraints motivate Machiavellians to undermine their peers. *Personality and Individual Differences*, *104*, 29–36.

Chabrol, H., Bouvet, R., & Goutaudier, N. (2017). The dark tetrad and antisocial behavior in a community sample of college students. *Journal of Forensic Psychology Research and Practice*, *17*, 295–304.

Chabrol, H., Melioli, T., Van Leeuwen, N., Rodgers, R., & Goutaudier, N. (2015). The dark tetrad: identifying personality profiles in high-school students. *Personality and Individual Differences*, *83*, 97–101.

Chabrol, H., Van Leeuwen, N., Rodgers, R., & Séjourné, N. (2009). Contributions of psychopathic, narcissistic, Machiavellian, and sadistic personality traits to juvenile delinquency. *Personality and Individual Differences*, *47*, 734–739.

Chatterjee, A., & Hambrick, D. C. (2007). It's all about me: narcissistic chief executive officers and their effects on company strategy and performance. *Administrative Science Quarterly*, *52*, 351–386.

Cheng, J., Danescu-Niculescu-Mizil, C., Leskovec, J., & Bernstein, M. (2017). Anyone can become a troll. *American Scientist, 105*(3), 152–155.

Chin, K., Atkinson, B. E., Raheb, H., Harris, E., & Vernon, P. A. (2017). The dark side of romantic jealousy. *Personality and Individual Differences, 115*, 23–29.

Christian, E., Sellbom, M., & Wilkinson, R. B. (2018). Is psychopathy associated with deficits in bonding in an adult noninstitutionalized sample? The association between intimate social network size, attachment behavior, and psychopathy. *Journal of Social and Personal Relationships*.

Christie, R., & Geis, F. L. (1970). *Studies in Machiavellianism*. New York: Academic Press.

Christov-Moore, L., Simpson, E. A., Coudé, G., Grigaityte, K., Iacoboni, M., & Ferrari, P. F. (2014). Empathy: gender effects in brain and behavior. *Neuroscience & Biobehavioral Reviews, 46*, 604–627.

Clark, L. A. (2007). Assessment and diagnosis of personality disorder: perennial issues and an emerging reconceptualization. *Annual Review of Psychology, 58*, 227–257.

Collins, N. L., & Miller, L. C. (1994). Self-disclosure and liking: a meta-analytic review. *Psychological Bulletin, 116*, 457–475.

Coyne, S. M., & Archer, J. (2004). Indirect aggression in the media: a content analysis of British television programs. *Aggressive Behavior, 30*, 254–271.

Craker, N., & March, E. (2016). The dark side of Facebook®: the dark tetrad, negative social potency, and trolling behaviours. *Personality and Individual Differences, 102*, 79–84.

Crysel, L. C., Crosier, B. S., & Webster, G. D. (2013). The dark triad and risk behavior. *Personality and Individual Differences, 54*, 35–40.

Curtis, S. R., Rajivan, P., Jones, D. N., & Gonzalez, C. (2018). Phishing attempts among the dark triad: patterns of attack and vulnerability. *Computers in Human Behavior*.

Czar, K. A., Dahlen, E. R., Bullock, E. E., & Nicholson, B. C. (2011). Psychopathic personality traits in relational aggression among young adults. *Aggressive Behavior, 37*, 207–214.

Czarna, A. Z., Dufner, M., & Clifton, A. D. (2014). The effects of vulnerable and grandiose narcissism on liking-based and disliking-based centrality in social networks. *Journal of Research in Personality, 50*, 42–45.

Czarna, A. Z., Leifeld, P., Śmieja, M., Dufner, M., & Salovey, P. (2016). Do narcissism and emotional intelligence win us friends? Modeling dynamics of peer popularity using inferential network analysis. *Personality and Social Psychology Bulletin, 42*, 1588–1599.

Czibor, A., & Bereczkei, T. (2012). Machiavellian people's success results from monitoring their partners. *Personality and Individual Differences, 53*, 202–206.

De Bruyn, E. H., & Cillessen, A. H. (2006). Popularity in early adolescence: prosocial and antisocial subtypes. *Journal of Adolescent Research, 21*, 607–627.

Demetrioff, S., Porter, S., & Baker, A. (2017). I know how you feel: the influence of psychopathic traits on the ability to identify micro-expressions. *Psychology, Crime & Law, 23*, 274–290.

DeWall, C. N., Buffardi, L. E., Bonser, I., & Campbell, W. K. (2011). Narcissism and implicit attention seeking: evidence from linguistic analyses of social networking and online presentation. *Personality and Individual Differences, 51*(1), 57–62.

Doane, A. N., Pearson, M. R., & Kelley, M. L. (2014). Predictors of cyberbullying perpetration among college students: an application of the theory or reasoned action. *Computers in Human Behavior, 36*, 154–162.

Domelsmith, D. E., & Dietch, J. T. (1978). Sex differences in the relationship between Machiavellianism and self-disclosure. *Psychological Reports, 42*, 715–721.

Drislane, L. E., Patrick, C. J., Sourander, A., Sillanmäki, L., Aggen, S. H., Elonheimo, H., et al. (2014). Distinct variants of extreme psychopathic individuals in society at large:

evidence from a population-based sample. *Personality Disorders: Theory, Research, and Treatment*, *5*, 154–163.

Drouin, M., Miller, D., Wehle, S. M., & Hernandez, E. (2016). Why do people lie online? "Because everyone lies on the internet" *Computers in Human Behavior*, *64*, 134–142.

Dubois, D., Rucker, D. D., & Galinsky, A. D. (2015). Social class, power, and selfishness: when and why upper and lower class individuals behave unethically. *Journal of Personality and Social Psychology*, *108*, 436–449.

Dufner, M., Egloff, B., Hausmann, C. M., Wendland, L. M., Neyer, F. J., & Back, M. D. (2015). Narcissistic tendencies among actors: craving for admiration, but not at the cost of others. *Social Psychological and Personality Science*, *6*, 447–454.

Dutton, K. (2012). *The wisdom of psychopaths*. Random House.

Edens, J. F., Colwell, L. H., Desforges, D. M., & Fernandez, K. (2005). The impact of mental health evidence on support for capital punishment: are defendants labeled psychopathic considered more deserving of death? *Behavioral Sciences & the Law*, *23*, 603–625.

Edwards, B. G., Albertson, E., & Verona, E. (2017). Dark and vulnerable personality trait correlates of dimensions of criminal behavior among adult offenders. *Journal of Abnormal Psychology*, *126*, 921–927.

Egan, V., Chan, S., & Shorter, G. W. (2014). The dark triad, happiness and subjective well-being. *Personality and Individual Differences*, *67*, 17–22.

Einarsen, S., & Nielsen, M. B. (2015). Workplace bullying as an antecedent of mental health problems: a five-year prospective and representative study. *International Archives of Occupational and Environmental Health*, *88*, 131–142.

Eisenbarth, H., Hart, C. M., & Sedikides, C. (2018). Do psychopathic traits predict professional success? *Journal of Economic Psychology*, *64*, 130–139.

Ellison, W. D., Levy, K. N., Cain, N. M., Ansell, E. B., & Pincus, A. L. (2013). The impact of pathological narcissism on psychotherapy utilization, initial symptom severity, and early-treatment symptom change: a naturalistic investigation. *Journal of Personality Assessment*, *95*(3), 291–300.

Fehr, B., Samsom, D., & Paulhus, D. L. (1992). The construct of Machiavellianism: twenty years later. In C. D. Spielberger & J. N. Butcher (Eds.), 9. *Advances in personality assessment* (pp. 77–116). Hillsdale, NJ: Erlbaum.

Felson, J. (2014). What can we learn from twin studies? A comprehensive evaluation of the equal environments assumption. *Social Science Research*, *43*, 184–199.

Feresin, E. (2011). *Italian court reduces murder sentence based on neuroimaging data. Nature news blog*. http://blogs.nature.com/news/2011/09/italian_court_reduces_murder_s.html.

Figueredo, A. J., Gladden, P. R., Sisco, M. M., Patch, E. A., & Jones, D. N. (2015). The unholy trinity: the dark triad, coercion, and Brunswik-symmetry. *Evolutionary Psychology*, *13*, 435–454.

Fix, R. L., & Fix, S. T. (2015). Trait psychopathy, emotional intelligence, and criminal thinking: predicting illegal behavior among college students. *International Journal of Law and Psychiatry*, *42*, 183–188.

Flexon, J. L., Meldrum, R. C., & Piquero, A. R. (2016). Low self-control and the victim–offender overlap: a gendered analysis. *Journal of Interpersonal Violence*, *31*, 2052–2076.

Flora, C. (2016). Bad Friends. Aeon. https://aeon.co/essays/when-a-friendship-turns-sour-more-than-feelings-get-hurt.

Forzano, F., Borry, P., Cambon-Thomsen, A., Hodgson, S. V., Tibben, A., De Vries, P., et al. (2010). Italian appeal court: a genetic predisposition to commit murder? *European Journal of Human Genetics*, *18*, 519–521.

Foster, J. D., Misra, T. A., & Reidy, D. E. (2009). Narcissists are approach-oriented toward their money and their friends. *Journal of Research in Personality*, *43*, 764–769.

Foulkes, L., McCrory, E. J., Neumann, C. S., & Viding, E. (2014a). Inverted social reward: associations between psychopathic traits and self-report and experimental measures of social reward. *PLoS One*, *9*(8)e106000.

Foulkes, L., Seara-Cardoso, A., Neumann, C. S., Rogers, J. S., & Viding, E. (2014b). Looking after number one: associations between psychopathic traits and measures of social motivation and functioning in a community sample of males. *Journal of Psychopathology and Behavioral Assessment, 36*, 22–29.

Fowler, J. H., Settle, J. E., & Christakis, N. A. (2011). Correlated genotypes in friendship networks. *Proceedings of the National Academy of Sciences of the United States of America, 108*, 1993–1997.

Fox, J., & Rooney, M. C. (2015). The dark triad and trait self-objectification as predictors of men's use and self-presentation behaviors on social networking sites. *Personality and Individual Differences, 76*, 161–165.

Frances, A., & Halon, R. (2013). The uses and misuses of the DSM in forensic settings. *Psychological Injury and Law, 6*(4), 336–344.

Furnham, A., Richards, S. C., & Paulhus, D. L. (2013). The dark triad of personality: a 10 year review. *Social and Personality Psychology Compass*, 7, 199–216.

Garcia, D., & Sikström, S. (2014). The dark side of Facebook: semantic representations of status updates predict the dark triad of personality. *Personality and Individual Differences, 67*, 92–96.

Giacomin, M., & Jordan, C. H. (2016). The wax and wane of narcissism: grandiose narcissism as a process or state. *Journal of Personality, 84*, 154–164.

Giammarco, E. A., & Vernon, P. A. (2014). Vengeance and the dark triad: the role of empathy and perspective taking in trait forgivingness. *Personality and Individual Differences, 67*, 23–29.

Gibb, Z. G., & Devereux, P. G. (2014). Who does that anyway? Predictors and personality correlates of cyberbullying in college. *Computers in Human Behavior, 38*, 8–16.

Gnambs, T., & Appel, M. (2018). Narcissism and social networking behavior: a meta-analysis. *Journal of Personality, 86*(2), 200–212.

Goetz, C. D., & Meyer, K. B. (2018). Mate value discrepancies, the dark triad and relationship satisfaction: a Euclidean distances approach. *Evolutionary Psychological Science*, 1–7.

Goncalves, M. K., & Campbell, L. (2014). The dark triad and the derogation of mating competitors. *Personality and Individual Differences, 67*, 42–46.

Goodboy, A. K., & Martin, M. M. (2015). The personality profile of a cyberbully: examining the dark triad. *Computers in Human Behavior, 49*(1–4).

Gottfredson, M. R., & Hirschi, T. (1990). *A general theory of crime*. Stanford University Press.

Gottschalk, P. (2018). Characteristics of white-collar crime. In *Investigating White-Collar Crime* (pp. 1–12). Cham: Springer.

Greenberg, E. (2017). *The survival guide for living with a narcissist*. https://www.psychologytoday.com/blog/understanding-narcissism/201710/the-survival-guide-living-narcissist.

Greitemeyer, T. (2015). Everyday sadism predicts violent video game preferences. *Personality and Individual Differences, 75*, 19–23.

Greitemeyer, T., & Sagioglou, C. (2016). Subjective socioeconomic status causes aggression: a test of the theory of social deprivation. *Journal of Personality and Social Psychology, 111*, 178–194.

Grigg, D. W. (2010). Cyber-Aggression: definition and concept of cyberbullying. *Australian Journal of Guidance and Counselling, 20*, 143–156.

Grigoras, M., & Wille, B. (2017). Shedding light on the dark side: associations between the dark triad and the DSM-5 maladaptive trait model. *Personality and Individual Differences, 104*, 516–521.

Halpern, D., Valenzuela, S., & Katz, J. E. (2016). "Selfie-ists" or "Narci-selfiers"? A cross-lagged panel analysis of selfie taking and narcissism. *Personality and Individual Differences, 97*, 98–101.

Hamilton, K. R., Felton, J. W., Risco, C. M., Lejuez, C. W., & MacPherson, L. (2014). Brief report: the interaction of impulsivity with risk-taking is associated with early alcohol use initiation. *Journal of Adolescence, 37*, 1253–1256.

Hare, R. D. (1991). *The Hare Psychopathy Checklist–Revised (PCL–R)*. Toronto, ON: Multi-Health Systems.

Hare, R. D. (2003). *The Psychopathy Checklist–Revised*. Toronto, ON: Multi-Health systems.

Harris, G. T., & Rice, M. E. (2006). Treatment of psychopathy. *Handbook of Psychopathy*, 555–572.

Harris, K., & Vazire, S. (2016). On friendship development and the big five personality traits. *Social and Personality Psychology Compass*, *10*, 647–667.

Hart, W., Richardson, K., & Tortoriello, G. K. (2018). Meet your public relations team: people with dark traits may help you manage your image. *Personality and Individual Differences*, *134*, 164–173.

Hartwig, M., Granhag, P. A., Strömwall, L. A., & Andersson, L. O. (2004). Suspicious minds: criminal's ability to detect deception. *Psychology, Crime and Law*, *10*, 83–95.

Hawley, P. H. (2003). Prosocial and coercive configurations of resource control in early adolescence: a case for the well-adapted Machiavellian. *Merrill-Palmer Quarterly*, *49*, 279–309.

Hendin, H. M., & Cheek, J. M. (1997). Assessing hypersensitive narcissism: a reexamination of Murray's Narcism Scale. *Journal of Research in Personality*, *31*, 588–599.

Henrich, J., Heine, S. J., & Norenzayan, A. (2010). Most people are not WEIRD. *Nature*, *466*(7302), 29.

Hesse, M. (2009). Portrayal of psychopathy in the movies. *International Review of Psychiatry*, *21*, 207–212.

Hmieleski, K. M., & Lerner, D. A. (2016). The dark triad and nascent entrepreneurship: an examination of unproductive versus productive entrepreneurial motives. *Journal of Small Business Management*, *54*, 7–32.

Hodson, G., Hogg, S. M., & MacInnis, C. C. (2009). The role of "dark personalities" (narcissism, Machiavellianism, psychopathy), big five personality factors, and ideology in explaining prejudice. *Journal of Research in Personality*, *43*, 686–690.

Hogue, M., Levashina, J., & Hang, H. (2013). Will I fake it? The interplay of gender, Machiavellianism, and self-monitoring on strategies for honesty in job interviews. *Journal of Business Ethics*, *117*, 399–411.

Holtzman, N. S. (2011). Facing a psychopath: detecting the dark triad from emotionally-neutral faces, using prototypes from the Personality Faceaurus. *Journal of Research in Personality*, *45*, 648–654.

Holtzman, N. S., & Donnellan, M. B. (2015). The roots of Narcissus: old and new models of the evolution of narcissism. In *Evolutionary perspectives on social psychology* (pp. 479–489): Springer International Publishing.

Holtzman, N. S., & Strube, M. J. (2010). Narcissism and attractiveness. *Journal of Research in Personality*, *44*, 133–136.

Holtzman, N. S., & Strube, M. J. (2011). The intertwined evolution of narcissism and short-term mating: an emerging hypothesis. In *The handbook of narcissism and narcissistic personality disorder: theoretical approaches, empirical findings, and treatments* (pp. 210–220).

Holtzman, N. S., & Strube, M. J. (2013). People with dark personalities tend to create a physically attractive veneer. *Social Psychological and Personality Science*, *4*, 461–467.

Hunter, J. E., Gerbing, D. W., & Boster, F. J. (1982). Machiavellian beliefs and personality: construct invalidity of the Machiavellianism dimension. *Journal of Personality and Social Psychology*, *43*, 1293.

Ilmarinen, V. J., Lönnqvist, J. E., & Paunonen, S. (2016). Similarity-attraction effects in friendship formation: honest platoon-mates prefer each other but dishonest do not. *Personality and Individual Differences*, *92*, 153–158.

Ináncsi, T., Láng, A., & Bereczkei, T. (2016). A darker shade of love: Machiavellianism and positive assortative mating based on romantic ideals. *Europe's Journal of Psychology*, *12*, 137.

International Telecommunication Union, (2015). *The world in 2015.* Retrieved from https://www.itu.int/en/ITU-D/Statistics/Documents/facts/ICTFactsFigures2015.pdf. Accessed 3 September 2015.

Jakobwitz, S., & Egan, V. (2006). The dark triad and normal personality traits. *Personality and Individual Differences, 40*, 331–339.

Jauk, E., Freudenthaler, H. H., & Neubauer, A. C. (2016). The dark triad and trait versus ability emotional intelligence. *Journal of Individual Differences, 37*, 112–118.

Jauk, E., Neubauer, A. C., Mairunteregger, T., Pemp, S., Sieber, K. P., & Rauthmann, J. F. (2016). How alluring are dark personalities? The dark triad and attractiveness in speed dating. *European Journal of Personality, 30*, 125–138.

Jonason, P. K., Abboud, R., Tomé, J., Dummett, M., & Hazer, A. (2017). The dark triad traits and individual differences in self-reported and other-rated creativity. *Personality and Individual Differences, 117*, 150–154.

Jonason, P. K., Baughman, H. M., Carter, G. L., & Parker, P. (2015). Dorian Gray without his portrait: psychological, social, and physical health costs associated with the dark triad. *Personality and Individual Differences, 78*, 5–13.

Jonason, P. K., Foster, J. D., Egorova, M. S., Parshikova, O., Csathó, Á., Oshio, A., et al. (2017). The dark triad traits from a life history perspective in six countries. *Frontiers in Psychology, 8*, 1476.

Jonason, P. K., Girgis, M., & Milne-Home, J. (2017). The exploitive mating strategy of the dark triad traits: tests of rape-enabling attitudes. *Archives of Sexual Behavior, 46*, 697–706.

Jonason, P. K., Icho, A., & Ireland, K. (2016). Resources, harshness, and unpredictability: the socioeconomic conditions associated with the dark triad traits. *Evolutionary Psychology, 14*.

Jonason, P. K., Koehn, M. A., Okan, C., & O'Connor, P. J. (2018). The role of personality in individual differences in yearly earnings. *Personality and Individual Differences, 121*, 170–172.

Jonason, P. K., Koenig, B. L., & Tost, J. (2010). Living a fast life. *Human Nature, 21*, 428–442.

Jonason, P. K., & Krause, L. (2013). The emotional deficits associated with the dark triad traits: cognitive empathy, affective empathy, and alexithymia. *Personality and Individual Differences, 55*, 532–537.

Jonason, P. K., Li, N. P., & Buss, D. M. (2010). The costs and benefits of the dark triad: implications for mate poaching and mate retention tactics. *Personality and Individual Differences, 48*, 373–378.

Jonason, P. K., Li, N. P., Webster, G. D., & Schmitt, D. P. (2009). The dark triad: facilitating a short-term mating strategy in men. *European Journal of Personality, 23*, 5–18.

Jonason, P. K., Luevano, V. X., & Adams, H. M. (2012). How the dark triad traits predict relationship choices. *Personality and Individual Differences, 53*, 180–184.

Jonason, P. K., Lyons, M., Baughman, H. M., & Vernon, P. A. (2014). What a tangled web we weave: the dark triad traits and deception. *Personality and Individual Differences, 70*, 117–119.

Jonason, P. K., Lyons, M., & Bethell, E. (2014). The making of Darth Vader: parent–child care and the dark triad. *Personality and Individual Differences, 67*, 30–34.

Jonason, P. K., Lyons, M., Bethell, E. J., & Ross, R. (2013). Different routes to limited empathy in the sexes: examining the links between the dark triad and empathy. *Personality and Individual Differences, 54*, 572–576.

Jonason, P. K., Lyons, M., & Blanchard, A. (2015). Birds of a "bad" feather flock together: the dark triad and mate choice. *Personality and Individual Differences, 78*, 34–38.

Jonason, P. K., & O'Connor, P. J. (2017). Cutting corners at work: an individual differences perspective. *Personality and Individual Differences, 107*, 146–153.

Jonason, P. K., & Schmitt, D. P. (2012). What have you done for me lately? Friendship-selection in the shadow of the dark triad traits. *Evolutionary Psychology, 10*(3).

Jonason, P. K., Slomski, S., & Partyka, J. (2012). The dark triad at work: how toxic employees get their way. *Personality and Individual Differences, 52*, 449–453.

Jonason, P. K., & Tost, J. (2010). I just cannot control myself: the dark triad and self-control. *Personality and Individual Differences, 49*, 611–615.

Jonason, P. K., Valentine, K. A., Li, N. P., & Harbeson, C. L. (2011). Mate-selection and the dark triad: facilitating a short-term mating strategy and creating a volatile environment. *Personality and Individual Differences, 51*, 759–763.

Jonason, P. K., & Webster, G. D. (2010). The dirty dozen: a concise measure of the dark triad. *Psychological Assessment, 22*(2), 420.

Jonason, P. K., Webster, G. D., Schmitt, D. P., Li, N. P., & Crysel, L. (2012). The antihero in popular culture: life history theory and the dark triad personality traits. *Review of General Psychology, 16*, 192.

Jonason, P. K., Wee, S., & Li, N. P. (2015). Competition, autonomy, and prestige: mechanisms through which the dark triad predict job satisfaction. *Personality and Individual Differences, 72*, 112–116.

Jonason, P. K., Wee, S., Li, N. P., & Jackson, C. (2014). Occupational niches and the dark triad traits. *Personality and Individual Differences, 69*, 119–123.

Jonason, P. K., Zeigler-Hill, V., & Baldacchino, J. (2017). Before and after: personality pathology, childhood conditions, and life history outcomes. *Personality and Individual Differences, 116*, 38–43.

Jones, D. A. (2009). Getting even with one's supervisor and one's organization: relationships among types of injustice, desires for revenge, and counterproductive work behaviors. *Journal of Organizational Behavior, 30*, 525–542.

Jones, D. N. (2014). Risk in the face of retribution: psychopathic individuals persist in financial misbehavior among the dark triad. *Personality and Individual Differences, 67*, 109–113.

Jones, D. N., & Figueredo, A. J. (2013). The core of darkness: uncovering the heart of the dark triad. *European Journal of Personality, 27*, 521–531.

Jones, D. N., & Paulhus, D. L. (2011). The role of impulsivity in the dark triad of personality. *Personality and Individual Differences, 51*, 679–682.

Jones, D. N., & Paulhus, D. L. (2014). Introducing the short dark triad (SD3) a brief measure of dark personality traits. *Assessment, 21*, 28–41.

Jones, D. N., & Paulhus, D. L. (2017). Duplicity among the dark triad: three faces of deceit. *Journal of Personality and Social Psychology, 113*, 329–342.

Jones, D. N., & Weiser, D. A. (2014). Differential infidelity patterns among the Dark Triad. *Personality and Individual Differences, 57*, 20–24.

Judge, T. A., Higgins, C. A., Thoresen, C. J., & Barrick, M. R. (1999). The big five personality traits, general mental ability, and career success across the life span. *Personnel Psychology, 52*, 621–652.

Judge, T. A., LePine, J. A., & Rich, B. L. (2006). Loving yourself abundantly: relationship of the narcissistic personality to self and other perceptions of workplace deviance, leadership, and task and contextual performance. *Journal of Applied Psychology, 91*, 762–776.

Kahn, J. (2012). *Can you call a 9-year old a psychopathy*. https://www.nytimes.com/2012/05/13/magazine/can-you-call-a-9-year-old-a-psychopath.html.

Kardum, I., Hudek-Knezevic, J., Mehic, N., & Pilek, M. (2018). The effects of similarity in the dark triad traits on the relationship quality in dating couples. *Personality and Individual Differences, 131*, 38–44.

Kardum, I., Hudek-Knezevic, J., Schmitt, D. P., & Covic, M. (2017). Assortative mating for dark triad: evidence of positive, initial, and active assortment. *Personal Relationships, 24*, 75–83.

Kavanagh, P. S., Signal, T. D., & Taylor, N. (2013). The dark triad and animal cruelty: dark personalities, dark attitudes, and dark behaviors. *Personality and Individual Differences*, *55*, 666–670.

Khan, R., Brewer, G., Kim, S., & Centifanti, L. C. M. (2017). Students, sex, and psychopathy: borderline and psychopathy personality traits are differently related to women and men's use of sexual coercion, partner poaching, and promiscuity. *Personality and Individual Differences*, *107*, 72–77.

Kiire, S. (2017). Psychopathy rather than Machiavellianism or narcissism facilitates intimate partner violence via fast life strategy. *Personality and Individual differences*, *104*, 401–406.

Kircaburun, K., Demetrovics, Z., & Tosuntaş, Ş. B. (2018). Analyzing the links between problematic social media use, dark triad traits, and self-esteem. *International Journal of Mental Health and Addiction*, 1–12.

Knight, N. M., Dahlen, E. R., Bullock-Yowell, E., & Madson, M. B. (2018). The HEXACO model of personality and dark triad in relational aggression. *Personality and Individual Differences*, *122*, 109–114.

Koladich, S. J., & Atkinson, B. E. (2016). The dark triad and relationship preferences: a replication and extension. *Personality and Individual Differences*, *94*, 253–255.

Konrath, S., Corneille, O., Bushman, B. J., & Luminet, O. (2014). The relationship between narcissistic exploitativeness, dispositional empathy, and emotion recognition abilities. *Journal of Nonverbal Behavior*, *38*, 129–143.

Kowalski, C. M., Kwiatkowska, K., Kwiatkowska, M. M., Ponikiewska, K., Rogoza, R., & Schermer, J. A. (2018). The dark triad traits and intelligence: Machiavellians are bright, and narcissists and psychopaths are ordinary. *Personality and Individual Differences*, *135*, 1–6.

Kowalski, C. M., Vernon, P. A., & Schermer, J. A. (2017). Vocational interests and dark personality: are there dark career choices? *Personality and Individual Differences*, *104*, 43–47.

Krick, A., Tresp, S., Vatter, M., Ludwig, A., Wihlenda, M., & Rettenberger, M. (2016). The relationships between the dark triad, the moral judgment level, and the students' disciplinary choice: self-selection, indoctrination, or both? *Journal of Individual Differences*, *37*, 24–30.

Küfner, A. C., Nestler, S., & Back, M. D. (2013). The two pathways to being an (un-) popular narcissist. *Journal of Personality*, *81*, 184–195.

Lamkin, J., Campbell, W. K., & Miller, J. D. (2015). An exploration of the correlates of grandiose and vulnerable narcissism in romantic relationships: homophily, partner characteristics, and dyadic adjustment. *Personality and Individual Differences*, *79*, 166–171.

Lamkin, J., Maples-Keller, J. L., & Miller, J. D. (2018). How likable are personality disorder and general personality traits to those who possess them? *Journal of Personality*, *86*, 173–185.

Lavner, J. A., Lamkin, J., Miller, J. D., Campbell, W. K., & Karney, B. R. (2016). Narcissism and newlywed marriage: partner characteristics and marital trajectories. *Personality Disorders: Theory, Research, and Treatment*, 7(2), 169.

LeBreton, J. M., Shiverdecker, L. K., & Grimaldi, E. M. (2018). The dark triad and workplace behavior. *Annual Review of Organizational Psychology and Organizational Behavior*, *5*, 387–414.

Lee, K., & Ashton, M. C. (2005). Psychopathy, Machiavellianism, and narcissism in the Five-Factor Model and the HEXACO model of personality structure. *Personality and Individual Differences*, *38*, 1571–1582.

Lee, K., & Ashton, M. C. (2014). The dark triad, the big five, and the HEXACO model. *Personality and Individual Differences*, *67*, 2–5.

Lee, K., Ashton, M. C., Wiltshire, J., Bourdage, J. S., Visser, B. A., & Gallucci, A. (2013). Sex, power, and money: prediction from the dark triad and honesty–humility. *European Journal of Personality*, *27*, 169–184.

Lee, R. T., & Brotheridge, C. M. (2006). When prey turns predatory: workplace bullying as a predictor of counteraggression/bullying, coping, and well-being. *European Journal of Work and Organizational Psychology, 15*, 352–377.

Leising, D., Rogers, K., & Ostner, J. (2009). The undisordered personality: normative assumptions underlying personality disorder diagnoses. *Review of General Psychology, 13*, 230–241.

Lemay, E. P., Jr., & Wolf, N. R. (2016). Human mate poaching tactics are effective: evidence from a dyadic prospective study on opposite-sex "friendships". *Social Psychological and Personality Science*, 7, 374–380.

Levenson, M. R., Kiehl, K. A., & Fitzpatrick, C. M. (1995). Assessing psychopathic attributes in a noninstitutionalized population. *Journal of Personality and Social Psychology, 68*, 151–158.

Li, C., Sun, Y., Ho, M. Y., You, J., Shaver, P. R., & Wang, Z. (2016). State narcissism and aggression: the mediating roles of anger and hostile attributional bias. *Aggressive Behavior, 42*, 333–345.

Lilienfeld, S. O., Waldman, I. D., Landfield, K., Watts, A. L., Rubenzer, S., & Faschingbauer, T. R. (2012). Fearless dominance and the US presidency: implications of psychopathic personality traits for successful and unsuccessful political leadership. *Journal of Personality and Social Psychology, 103*, 489–505.

Lingnau, V., Fuchs, F., & Dehne-Niemann, T. E. (2017). The influence of psychopathic traits on the acceptance of white-collar crime: do corporate psychopaths cook the books and misuse the news? *Journal of Business Economics, 87*, 1193–1227.

Linton, D. K., & Power, J. L. (2013). The personality traits of workplace bullies are often shared by their victims: is there a dark side to victims? *Personality and Individual Differences, 54*, 738–743.

Litten, V., Roberts, L. D., Ladyshewsky, R. K., Castell, E., & Kane, R. (2018). The influence of academic discipline on empathy and psychopathic personality traits in undergraduate students. *Personality and Individual Differences, 123*, 145–150.

Lopes, B., & Yu, H. (2017). Who do you troll and why: an investigation into the relationship between the dark triad personalities and online trolling behaviours towards popular and less popular Facebook profiles. *Computers in Human Behavior, 77*, 69–76.

Love, A. B., & Holder, M. D. (2014). Psychopathy and subjective well-being. *Personality and Individual Differences, 66*, 112–117.

Lukaszewski, A. W. (2015). Parental support during childhood predicts life history-related personality variation and social status in young adults. *Evolutionary Psychological Science, 1*, 131–140.

Lyons, M., & Aitken, S. (2010). Machiavellian friends? The role of Machiavellianism in friendship formation and maintenance. *Journal of Social, Evolutionary, and Cultural Psychology, 4*, 194–202.

Lyons, M., & Blanchard, A. (2016). "I could see, in the depth of his eyes, my own beauty reflected": women's assortative preference for narcissistic, but not for Machiavellian or psychopathic male faces. *Personality and Individual Differences, 97*, 40–44.

Lyons, M., & Brockman, C. (2017). The dark triad, emotional expressivity and appropriateness of emotional response: fear and sadness when one should be happy? *Personality and Individual Differences, 104*, 466–469.

Lyons, M., Croft, A., Fairhurst, S., Varley, K., & Wilson, C. (2017). Seeing through crocodile tears? Sex-specific associations between the dark triad traits and lie detection accuracy. *Personality and Individual Differences, 113*(1-4).

Lyons, M., Healy, N., & Bruno, D. (2013). It takes one to know one: relationship between lie detection and psychopathy. *Personality and Individual Differences, 55*(6), 676–679.

Lyons, M., & Jonason, P. K. (2015). Dark triad, tramps, and thieves. *Journal of Individual Differences, 36*, 215–220.

Lyons, M., & Simeonov, L. (2016). The undesirable dark triad? Women dislike dark triad male faces across different mating context and socio-ecological conditions. *Personality and Individual Differences*, *90*, 338–341.

Lyons, M. T., Marcinkowska, U. M., Helle, S., & McGrath, L. (2015). Mirror, mirror, on the wall, who is the most masculine of them all? The dark triad, masculinity, and women's mate choice. *Personality and Individual Differences*, *74*, 153–158.

Maaß, U., Lämmle, L., Bensch, D., & Ziegler, M. (2016). Narcissists of a feather flock together: narcissism and the similarity of friends. *Personality and Social Psychology Bulletin*, *42*, 366–384.

Magidson, J. F., Collado-Rodriguez, A., Madan, A., Perez-Camoirano, N. A., Galloway, S. K., Borckardt, J. J., et al. (2012). Addressing narcissistic personality features in the context of medical care: integrating diverse perspectives to inform clinical practice. *Personality Disorders: Theory, Research, and Treatment*, *3*(2), 196.

Maibom, H. L. (2008). The mad, the bad, and the psychopath. *Neuroethics*, *1*, 167–184.

Malesza, M., & Ostaszewski, P. (2016). The utility of the dark triad model in the prediction of the self-reported and behavioral risk-taking behaviors among adolescents. *Personality and Individual Differences*, *90*, 7–11.

Maples, J. L., Lamkin, J., & Miller, J. D. (2014). A test of two brief measures of the dark triad: the dirty dozen and short dark triad. *Psychological Assessment*, *26*, 326.

March, E., Grieve, R., Marrington, J., & Jonason, P. K. (2017). Trolling on Tinder® (and other dating apps): examining the role of the dark tetrad and impulsivity. *Personality and Individual Differences*, *110*, 139–143.

March, E., & Wagstaff, D. L. (2017). Sending nudes: sex, self-rated mate value, and trait Machiavellianism predict sending unsolicited explicit images. *Frontiers in Psychology*, *8*, 2210.

Marcinkowska, U. M., Helle, S., & Lyons, M. T. (2015). Dark traits: sometimes hot, and sometimes not? Female preferences for dark triad faces depend on sociosexuality and contraceptive use. *Personality and Individual Differences*, *86*, 369–373.

Marcinkowska, U. M., Lyons, M. T., & Helle, S. (2016). Women's reproductive success and the preference for dark triad in men's faces. *Evolution and Human Behavior*, *37*, 287–292.

Marshall, T. C., Lefringhausen, K., & Ferenczi, N. (2015). The big five, self-esteem, and narcissism as predictors of the topics people write about in Facebook status updates. *Personality and Individual Differences*, *85*, 35–40.

Martel, M. M. (2013). Sexual selection and sex differences in the prevalence of childhood externalizing and adolescent internalizing disorders. *Psychological Bulletin*, *139*, 1221–1259.

Massar, K., Winters, C. L., Lenz, S., & Jonason, P. K. (2017). Green-eyed snakes: the associations between psychopathy, jealousy, and jealousy induction. *Personality and Individual Differences*, *115*, 164–168.

Massen, J. J., & Koski, S. E. (2014). Chimps of a feather sit together: chimpanzee friendships are based on homophily in personality. *Evolution and Human Behavior*, *35*, 1–8.

Mathieu, C., & Babiak, P. (2015). Tell me who you are, I'll tell you how you lead: beyond the full-range leadership model, the role of corporate psychopathy on employee attitudes. *Personality and Individual Differences*, *87*, 8–12.

Mathieu, C., Neumann, C., Babiak, P., & Hare, R. D. (2015). Corporate psychopathy and the full-range leadership model. *Assessment*, *22*, 267–278.

Mathieu, C., Neumann, C. S., Hare, R. D., & Babiak, P. (2014). A dark side of leadership: corporate psychopathy and its influence on employee well-being and job satisfaction. *Personality and Individual Differences*, *59*, 83–88.

McCain, J. L., Borg, Z. G., Rothenberg, A. H., Churillo, K. M., Weiler, P., & Campbell, W. K. (2016). Personality and selfies: narcissism and the dark triad. *Computers in Human Behavior*, *64*, 126–133.

McCain, J. L., & Campbell, W. K. (2016). Narcissism and social media use: a meta-analytic review. *Psychology of Popular Media Culture*.

McCuish, E. C., Corrado, R. R., Hart, S. D., & DeLisi, M. (2015). The role of symptoms of psychopathy in persistent violence over the criminal career into full adulthood. *Journal of Criminal Justice, 43*, 345–356.

McDonald, M. M., Donnellan, M. B., & Navarrete, C. D. (2012). A life history approach to understanding the dark triad. *Personality and Individual Differences, 52*, 601–605.

McHoskey, J. W. (2001). Machiavellianism and personality dysfunction. *Personality and Individual Differences, 31*, 791–798.

McHoskey, J. W., Worzel, W., & Szyarto, C. (1998). Machiavellianism and psychopathy. *Journal of Personality and Social Psychology, 74*, 192–210.

McVeigh, K. (2011). https://www.theguardian.com/uk/2011/apr/08/cyberstalking-study-victims-men.

Mealey, L. (1995). The sociobiology of sociopathy: an integrated evolutionary model. *Behavioral and Brain Sciences, 18*, 523–541.

Međedović, J., & Petrović, B. (2015). The dark tetrad. *Journal of Individual Differences, 36*, 228–236.

Ménard, K. S., & Pincus, A. L. (2012). Predicting overt and cyber stalking perpetration by male and female college students. *Journal of Interpersonal Violence, 27*(11), 2183–2207.

Miller, H. A., Bouffard, J. A., & DeHaan, C. A. (2017). The role of psychopathic traits in female sexual coercion. *Violence and Victims, 32*, 479–492.

Miller, J. D., Dir, A., Gentile, B., Wilson, L., Pryor, L. R., & Campbell, W. K. (2010). Searching for a vulnerable dark triad: comparing factor 2 psychopathy, vulnerable narcissism, and borderline personality disorder. *Journal of Personality, 78*, 1529–1564.

Miller, J. D., Hoffman, B. J., Gaughan, E. T., Gentile, B., Maples, J., & Keith Campbell, W. (2011). Grandiose and vulnerable narcissism: a nomological network analysis. *Journal of Personality, 79*, 1013–1042.

Milosevic, A., & Ledgerwood, D. M. (2010). The subtyping of pathological gambling: a comprehensive review. *Clinical Psychology Review, 30*, 988–998.

Moffitt, T. E., Arseneault, L., Belsky, D., Dickson, N., Hancox, R. J., Harrington, H., et al. (2011). A gradient of childhood self-control predicts health, wealth, and public safety. *Proceedings of the National Academy of Sciences, 108*(7), 2693–2698.

Mogilski, J. K., Wade, T. J., & Welling, L. L. (2014). Prioritization of potential mates' history of sexual fidelity during a conjoint ranking task. *Personality and Social Psychology Bulletin, 40*, 884–897.

Monaghan, C., Bizumic, B., & Sellbom, M. (2018). Nomological network of two-dimensional Machiavellianism. *Personality and Individual Differences, 130*, 161–173.

Morey, L. C., Waugh, M. H., & Blashfield, R. K. (1985). MMPI scales for DSM-III personality disorders: their derivation and correlates. *Journal of Personality Assessment, 49*, 245–251.

Moroz, S., Chen, S., Daljeet, K. N., & Campbell, L. (2018). The dark triad and break-up distress. *Personality and Individual Differences, 132*, 52–59.

Muñoz, L. C., Kerr, M., & Bsic, N. (2008). A matter of perspective: the peer relationships of youths with psychopathic personality traits. *Criminal Justice and Behavior, 35*, 212–227.

Muñoz, L. C., Khan, R., & Cordwell, L. (2011). Sexually coercive tactics used by university students: a clear role for primary psychopathy. *Journal of Personality Disorders, 25*, 28–40.

Muris, P., Meesters, C., & Timmermans, A. (2013). Some youths have a gloomy side: correlates of the dark triad personality traits in non-clinical adolescents. *Child Psychiatry & Human Development, 44*, 658–665.

Muris, P., Merckelbach, H., Otgaar, H., & Meijer, E. (2017). The malevolent side of human nature: a meta-analysis and critical review of the literature on the dark triad (Narcissism, Machiavellianism, and Psychopathy). *Perspectives on Psychological Science, 12*, 183–204.

Murphy, J. M. (1976). Psychiatric labeling in cross-cultural perspective. *Science, 141*, 1019–1028.

Murphy, S. C., von Hippel, W., Dubbs, S. L., Angilletta, M. J., Jr., Wilson, R. S., Trivers, R., et al. (2015). The role of overconfidence in romantic desirability and competition. *Personality and Social Psychology Bulletin, 41*, 1036–1052.

Nagler, U. K., Reiter, K. J., Furtner, M. R., & Rauthmann, J. F. (2014). Is there a "dark intelligence"? Emotional intelligence is used by dark personalities to emotionally manipulate others. *Personality and Individual Differences, 65*, 47–52.

Nascimento, B. S., Hanel, P. P., Monteiro, R. P., Gouveia, V. V., & Little, A. C. (2018). Sociosexuality in Brazil: validation of the SOI-R and its correlates with personality, self-perceived mate value, and ideal partner preferences. *Personality and Individual Differences, 124*, 98–104.

Nathanson, C., Paulhus, D. L., & Williams, K. M. (2006). Personality and misconduct correlates of body modification and other cultural deviance markers. *Journal of Research in Personality, 40*, 779–802.

Neo, B., Sellbom, M., Smith, S. F., & Lilienfeld, S. O. (2016). Of boldness and badness: insights into workplace malfeasance from a triarchic psychopathy model perspective. *Journal of Business Ethics*, 1–19.

Nobles, M. R., Reyns, B. W., Fox, K. A., & Fisher, B. S. (2014). Protection against pursuit: a conceptual and empirical comparison of cyberstalking and stalking victimization among a national sample. *Justice Quarterly, 31*, 986–1014.

Nolfe, G., Petrella, C., Blasi, F., Zontini, G., & Nolfe, G. (2007). Psychopathological dimensions of harassment in the workplace (mobbing). *International Journal of Mental Health, 36*, 67–85.

Noser, A. E., Zeigler-Hill, V., & Besser, A. (2014). Stress and affective experiences: the importance of dark personality features. *Journal of Research in Personality, 53*, 158–164.

O'Riordan, C., & O'Connell, M. (2014). Predicting adult involvement in crime: personality measures are significant, socio-economic measures are not. *Personality and Individual Differences, 68*, 98–101.

O'Boyle, E. H., Jr., Forsyth, D. R., Banks, G. C., & McDaniel, M. A. (2012). A meta-analysis of the dark triad and work behavior: a social exchange perspective. *Journal of Applied Psychology, 97*, 557–579.

O'Brien, M. L. (1987). Examining the dimensionality of pathological narcissism: factor analysis and construct validity of the O'Brien Multiphasic Narcissism Inventory. *Psychological Reports, 61*, 499–510.

O'connor, E. M., & Simms, C. M. (1990). Self-revelation as manipulation: the effects of sex and Machiavellianism on self-disclosure. *Social Behavior and Personality, 18*, 95–99.

Ogloff, J. R., Talevski, D., Lemphers, A., Wood, M., & Simmons, M. (2015). Co-occurring mental illness, substance use disorders, and antisocial personality disorder among clients of forensic mental health services. *Psychiatric Rehabilitation Journal, 38*, 16–23.

O'meara, A., Davies, J., & Hammond, S. (2011). The psychometric properties and utility of the Short Sadistic Impulse Scale (SSIS). *Psychological Assessment, 23*, 523–531.

Orehek, E., & Human, L. J. (2017). Self-expression on social media: do tweets present accurate and positive portraits of impulsivity, self-esteem, and attachment style? *Personality and Social Psychology Bulletin, 43*, 60–70.

Pabian, S., De Backer, C. J., & Vandebosch, H. (2015). Dark triad personality traits and adolescent cyber-aggression. *Personality and Individual Differences, 75*, 41–46.

Pailing, A., Boon, J., & Egan, V. (2014). Personality, the dark triad and violence. *Personality and Individual Differences, 67*, 81–86.

Palmer, J. C., Komarraju, M., Carter, M. Z., & Karau, S. J. (2017). Angel on one shoulder: can perceived organizational support moderate the relationship between the dark triad traits and counterproductive work behavior? *Personality and Individual Differences, 110*, 31–37.

Patrick, C. J., Fowles, D. C., & Krueger, R. F. (2009). Triarchic conceptualization of psychopathy: developmental origins of disinhibition, boldness, and meanness. *Development and Psychopathology, 21*, 913–938.

Patrick, W. (2017). How to spot a stalker? When casual dating is dangerous. *Psychology Today*. https://www.psychologytoday.com/gb/blog/why-bad-looks-good/201711/how-spot-the-stalker-when-casual-dating-is-dangerous.

Patton, C. L., Smith, S. F., & Lilienfeld, S. O. (2018). Psychopathy and heroism in first responders: traits cut from the same cloth? *Personality Disorders: Theory, Research, and Treatment, 9*, 354–368.

Paulhus, D. L., Neumann, C. S., & Hare, R. D. (2009). *Manual for the self-report psychopathy scale*. Toronto, ON: Multi-Health systems.

Paulhus, D. L., Westlake, B. G., Calvez, S. S., & Harms, P. D. (2013). Self-presentation style in job interviews: the role of personality and culture. *Journal of Applied Social Psychology, 43*, 2042–2059.

Paulhus, D. L., & Williams, K. M. (2002). The dark triad of personality: narcissism, Machiavellianism, and psychopathy. *Journal of Research in Personality, 36*, 556–563.

Perri, F. S. (2011). White-collar criminals: the 'Kinder, Gentler' offender? *Journal of Investigative Psychology and Offender Profiling, 8*, 217–241.

Petrides, K. V., Vernon, P. A., Schermer, J. A., & Veselka, L. (2011). Trait emotional intelligence and the dark triad traits of personality. *Twin Research and Human Genetics, 14*, 35–41.

Pfeiffer, S. M., & Wong, P. T. (1989). Multidimensional jealousy. *Journal of Social and Personal Relationships, 6*, 181–196.

Piff, P. K. (2014). Wealth and the inflated self: class, entitlement, and narcissism. *Personality and Social Psychology Bulletin, 40*(1), 34–43.

Pilch, I., & Turska, E. (2015). Relationships between Machiavellianism, organizational culture, and workplace bullying: emotional abuse from the target's and the perpetrator's perspective. *Journal of Business Ethics, 128*, 83–93.

Pincus, A. L., Ansell, E. B., Pimentel, C. A., Cain, N. M., Wright, A. G. C., & Levy, K. N. (2009). Initial construction and validation of the Pathological Narcissism Inventory. *Psychological Assessment, 21*, 365–379.

Pincus, A. L., Cain, N. M., & Wright, A. G. (2014). Narcissistic grandiosity and narcissistic vulnerability in psychotherapy. *Personality Disorders: Theory, Research, and Treatment, 5*, 439–443.

Pincus, A. L., Dowgwillo, E. A., & Greenberg, L. S. (2016). Three cases of narcissistic personality disorder through the lens of the DSM-5 alternative model for personality disorders. *Practice Innovations, 1*, 164–177.

Plouffe, R. A., Saklofske, D. H., & Smith, M. M. (2017). The assessment of sadistic personality: preliminary psychometric evidence for a new measure. *Personality and Individual Differences, 104*, 166–171.

Porter, S., Fairweather, D., Drugge, J., Hervé, H., Birt, A., & Boer, D. P. (2000). Profiles of psychopathy in incarcerated sexual offenders. *Criminal Justice and Behavior, 27*, 216–233.

Próspero-Luis, J., Moreira, P. S., Paiva, T. O., Teixeira, C. P., Costa, P., & Almeida, P. R. (2017). Psychopathy, criminal intentions, and abnormal appraisal of the expected outcomes of theft. *Legal and Criminological Psychology, 22*, 314–331.

Raine, A., Laufer, W. S., Yang, Y., Narr, K. L., Thompson, P., & Toga, A. W. (2012). Increased executive functioning, attention, and cortical thickness in white-collar criminals. *Human Brain Mapping, 33*, 2932–2940.

Rajivan, P., & Gonzalez, C. (2018). Creative persuasion: a study on adversarial behaviors and strategies in phishing attacks. *Frontiers in Psychology, 9*, 135.

Rantala, M. J., Moore, F. R., Skrinda, I., Krama, T., Kivleniece, I., Kecko, S., et al. (2012). Evidence for the stress-linked immunocompetence handicap hypothesis in humans. *Nature Communications*, *3*, 694.

Raskin, R., & Hall, C. S. (1981). The Narcissistic Personality Inventory: alternative form reliability and further evidence of construct validity. *Journal of Personality Assessment*, *45*(2), 159–162.

Raskin, R., & Terry, H. (1988). A principal-components analysis of the Narcissistic Personality Inventory and further evidence of its construct validity. *Journal of Personality and Social Psychology*, *54*, 890–902.

Rasmussen, K. R., & Boon, S. D. (2014). Romantic revenge and the dark triad: a model of impellance and inhibition. *Personality and Individual Differences*, *56*, 51–56.

Rauthmann, J. F. (2012). The dark triad and interpersonal perception: similarities and differences in the social consequences of narcissism, Machiavellianism, and psychopathy. *Social Psychological and Personality Science*, *3*, 487–496.

Rauthmann, J. F. (2013). Investigating the MACH–IV with item response theory and proposing the trimmed MACH. *Journal of Personality Assessment*, *95*, 388–397.

Rauthmann, J. F., Kappes, M., & Lanzinger, J. (2014). Shrouded in the veil of darkness: Machiavellians but not narcissists and psychopaths profit from darker weather in courtship. *Personality and Individual Differences*, *67*, 57–63.

Rauthmann, J. F., & Kolar, G. P. (2013). The perceived attractiveness and traits of the dark triad: narcissists are perceived as hot, Machiavellians and psychopaths not. *Personality and Individual Differences*, *54*, 582–586.

Reavis, J. A., Allen, E. K., & Meloy, J. R. (2008). Psychopathy in a mixed gender sample of adult stalkers. *Journal of Forensic Sciences*, *53*, 1214–1217.

Richardson, E. N., & Boag, S. (2016). Offensive defenses: the mind beneath the mask of the dark triad traits. *Personality and Individual Differences*, *92*, 148–152.

Ro, E., Nuzum, H., & Clark, L. A. (2017). Antagonism trait facets and comprehensive psychosocial disability: comparing information across self, informant, and interviewer reports. *Journal of Abnormal Psychology*, *126*, 890–897.

Robinson, S. L., & Bennett, R. J. (1995). A typology of deviant workplace behaviors: a multidimensional scaling study. *Academy of Management Journal*, *38*, 555–572.

Rogoza, R., & Cieciuch, J. (2018). Dark triad traits and their structure: an empirical approach. *Current Psychology*, 1–16.

Ross, S. R., Lutz, C. J., & Bailley, S. E. (2004). Psychopathy and the five factor model in a noninstitutionalized sample: a domain and facet level analysis. *Journal of Psychopathology and Behavioral Assessment*, *26*, 213–223.

Rotkirch, A., Lyons, M., David-Barrett, T., & Jokela, M. (2014). Gratitude for help among adult friends and siblings. *Evolutionary Psychology*, *12*(4).

Roulin, N., & Bourdage, J. S. (2017). Once an impression manager, always an impression manager? Antecedents of honest and deceptive impression management use and variability across multiple job interviews. *Frontiers in Psychology*, *8*.

Rulseh, A., Edens, J. F., & Cox, J. (2017). Triarchic model personality traits and their impact on mock juror perceptions of a white-collar criminal defendant. *Journal of Personality Assessment*, *99*, 453–464.

Russell, R. J., & Wells, P. A. (1991). Personality similarity and quality of marriage. *Personality and Individual Differences*, *12*, 407–412.

Ryan, T., Chester, A., Reece, J., & Xenos, S. (2014). The uses and abuses of Facebook: a review of Facebook addiction. *Journal of Behavioral Addictions*, *3*, 133–148.

Sadeh, N., Javdani, S., Jackson, J. J., Reynolds, E. K., Potenza, M. N., Gelernter, J., et al. (2010). Serotonin transporter gene associations with psychopathic traits in youth vary as a function of socioeconomic resources. *Journal of Abnormal Psychology*, *119*, 604–609.

Sakellaropoulo, M., & Baldwin, M. W. (2007). The hidden sides of self esteem: two dimensions of implicit self-esteem and their relation to narcissistic reactions. *Journal of Experimental Social Psychology, 43*, 995–1001.

Salked, E. (2018). *Directors feel 'betrayed' after employee steals almost £78,000 from Waterlooville company's funds - and spends it on new clothes and holiday*. https://www.portsmouth.co.uk/news/crime/directors-feel-betrayed-after-employee-steals-almost-78-000-from-waterlooville-company-s-funds-and-spends-it-on-new-clothes-and-holiday-1-8424308.

Schneider, B. (1987). The people make the place. *Personnel Psychology, 40*, 437–453.

Sedikides, C., Rudich, E. A., Gregg, A. P., Kumashiro, M., & Rusbult, C. (2004). Are normal narcissists psychologically healthy? Self-esteem matters. *Journal of Personality and Social Psychology, 87*, 400–416.

Seigfried-Spellar, K. C., & Lankford, C. M. (2018). Personality and online environment factors differ for posters, trolls, lurkers, and confessors on Yik Yak. *Personality and Individual Differences, 124*, 54–56.

Seigfried-Spellar, K. C., Villacís-Vukadinović, N., & Lynam, D. R. (2017). Computer criminal behavior is related to psychopathy and other antisocial behavior. *Journal of Criminal Justice, 51*, 67–73.

Selfhout, M., Burk, W., Branje, S., Denissen, J., Van Aken, M., & Meeus, W. (2010). Emerging late adolescent friendship networks and big five personality traits: a social network approach. *Journal of Personality, 78*, 509–538.

Semenyna, S. W., & Honey, P. L. (2015). Dominance styles mediate sex differences in dark triad traits. *Personality and Individual Differences, 83*, 37–43.

Serota, K. B., & Levine, T. R. (2015). A few prolific liars: variation in the prevalence of lying. *Journal of Language and Social Psychology, 34*, 138–157.

Sest, N., & March, E. (2017). Constructing the cyber-troll: psychopathy, sadism, and empathy. *Personality and Individual Differences, 119*, 69–72.

Sevi, B., Aral, T., & Eskenazi, T. (2017). Exploring the hook-up app: low sexual disgust and high sociosexuality predict motivation to use Tinder for casual sex. *Personality and Individual Differences*.

Seyfarth, R. M., & Cheney, D. L. (2012). The evolutionary origins of friendship. *Annual Review of Psychology, 63*, 153–177.

Sheehan, L., Nieweglowski, K., & Corrigan, P. (2016). The stigma of personality disorders. *Current Psychiatry Reports, 18*, 11.

Singleton, R. A., & Vacca, J. (2007). Interpersonal competition in friendships. *Sex Roles, 57*, 617–627.

Smith, C. V., Hadden, B. W., Webster, G. D., Jonason, P. K., Gesselman, A. N., & Crysel, L. C. (2014). Mutually attracted or repulsed? Actor–partner interdependence models of dark triad traits and relationship outcomes. *Personality and Individual Differences, 67*, 35–41.

Smith, M. B., Hill, A. D., Wallace, J. C., Recendes, T., & Judge, T. A. (2018). Upsides to dark and downsides to bright personality: a multidomain review and future research agenda. *Journal of Management, 44*, 191–217.

Smith, M. B., & Webster, B. D. (2017). A moderated mediation model of Machiavellianism, social undermining, political skill, and supervisor-rated job performance. *Personality and Individual Differences, 104*, 453–459.

Smith, S. F., & Lilienfeld, S. O. (2013). Psychopathy in the workplace: the knowns and unknowns. *Aggression and Violent Behavior, 18*, 204–218.

Smith, S. F., Watts, A., & Lilienfeld, S. (2014). On the trail of the elusive successful psychopath. *Psychological Assessment, 15*, 340–350.

Smoker, M., & March, E. (2017). Predicting perpetration of intimate partner cyberstalking: gender and the dark tetrad. *Computers in Human Behavior, 72*, 390–396.

Sparr, L. F. (2009). Personality disorders and criminal law: an international perspective. *Journal of the American Academy of Psychiatry and the Law*, *37*, 168–181.

Spurk, D., Keller, A. C., & Hirschi, A. (2016). Do bad guys get ahead or fall behind? Relationships of the dark triad of personality with objective and subjective career success. *Social Psychological and Personality Science*, 7, 113–121.

Statista. (2017). *Social media statistics & facts*. Retrieved from https://www.statista.com/topics/1164/social-networks/. Accessed April 2018.

Stattin, H., & Magnusson, D. (1989). The role of early aggressive behavior in the frequency, seriousness, and types of later crime. *Journal of Consulting and Clinical Psychology*, *57*, 710–718.

Stead, R., Fekken, G. C., Kay, A., & McDermott, K. (2012). Conceptualizing the dark triad of personality: links to social symptomatology. *Personality and Individual Differences*, *53*, 1023–1028.

Stein, J. (2016). *How trolls are ruining the internet*. http://time.com/4457110/internet-trolls/.

Stenason, L., & Vernon, P. A. (2016). The dark triad, reinforcement sensitivity and substance use. *Personality and Individual Differences*, *94*, 59–63.

Stone, M. H. (2007). Violent crimes and their relationship to personality disorders. *Personality and Mental Health*, *1*, 138–153.

Strickland, C. M., Drislane, L. E., Lucy, M., Krueger, R. F., & Patrick, C. J. (2013). Characterizing psychopathy using DSM-5 personality traits. *Assessment*, *20*, 327–338.

Struckman-Johnson, C., Struckman-Johnson, D., & Anderson, P. B. (2003). Tactics of sexual coercion: when men and women don't take no for an answer. *Journal of Sex Research*, *40*, 76–86.

Suedfeld, P., & Landon, P. B. (1978). Approaches to treatment. In R. D. Hare & D. Schalling (Eds.), *Psychopathic behavior: Approaches to research* (pp. 347–376). Chichester: John Sright & Sons Ltd.

Suler, J. (2004). The online disinhibition effect. *Cyberpsychology & Behavior*, 7(3), 321–326.

Sumner, C., Byers, A., Boochever, R., & Park, G. J. (2012). Predicting dark triad personality traits from twitter usage and a linguistic analysis of tweets. In December) (Ed.), *2012 11th international conference on machine learning and applications (ICMLA)*. vol. 2 (pp. 386–393): IEEE.

Sung, Y., Lee, J. A., Kim, E., & Choi, S. M. (2016). Why we post selfies: understanding motivations for posting pictures of oneself. *Personality and Individual Differences*, *97*, 260–265.

Szabó, Z. P., Czibor, A., Restás, P., & Bereczkei, T. (2018). "The darkest of all" The relationship between the dark triad traits and organizational citizenship behavior. *Personality and Individual Differences*.

Szepsenwol, O., Simpson, J. A., Griskevicius, V., & Raby, K. L. (2015). The effect of unpredictable early childhood environments on parenting in adulthood. *Journal of Personality and Social Psychology*, *109*, 1045–1067.

Tanzilli, A., Colli, A., Muzi, L., & Lingiardi, V. (2015). Clinician emotional response toward narcissistic patients: a preliminary report. *Research in Psychotherapy: Psychopathology, Process and Outcome*, *18*(1), 1–9.

Templer, K. J. (2018). Dark personality, job performance ratings, and the role of political skill: an indication of why toxic people may get ahead at work. *Personality and Individual Differences*, *124*, 209–214.

ten Brinke, L., Kish, A., & Keltner, D. (2018). Hedge fund managers with psychopathic tendencies make for worse investors. *Personality and Social Psychology Bulletin*, *44*(2), 214–223.

Tokarev, A., Phillips, A. R., Hughes, D. J., & Irwing, P. (2017). Leader dark traits, workplace bullying, and employee depression: exploring mediation and the role of the dark core. *Journal of Abnormal Psychology*, *126*, 911–920.

Tortoriello, G. K., Hart, W., Richardson, K., & Tullett, A. M. (2017). Do narcissists try to make romantic partners jealous on purpose? An examination of motives for deliberate jealousy-induction among subtypes of narcissism. *Personality and Individual Differences, 114*, 10–15.

Trivers, R. L. (1971). The evolution of reciprocal altruism. *The Quarterly Review of Biology, 46*, 35–57.

Trombly, D. R., & Zeigler-Hill, V. (2016). The dark triad and disordered gambling. *Current Psychology*, 1–7.

Trombly, D. R., & Zeigler-Hill, V. (2017). The dark triad and disordered gambling. *Current Psychology, 36*(4), 740–746.

Twenge, J. M., & Campbell, W. K. (2009). *The narcissism epidemic: living in the age of entitlement.* Simon and Schuster.

Twenge, J. M., & Foster, J. D. (2008). Mapping the scale of the narcissism epidemic: increases in narcissism 2002–2007 within ethnic groups. *Journal of Research in Personality, 42*, 1619–1622.

Ullrich, S., Farrington, D. P., & Coid, J. W. (2008). Psychopathic personality traits and life-success. *Personality and Individual Differences, 44*, 162–171.

van den Eijnden, R. J., Lemmens, J. S., & Valkenburg, P. M. (2016). The social media disorder scale. *Computers in Human Behavior, 61*, 478–487.

van Geel, M., Goemans, A., Toprak, F., & Vedder, P. (2017). Which personality traits are related to traditional bullying and cyberbullying? A study with the big five, dark triad and sadism. *Personality and Individual Differences, 106*, 231–235.

van Osch, Y., Blanken, I., Meijs, M. H., & van Wolferen, J. (2015). A group's physical attractiveness is greater than the average attractiveness of its members: the group attractiveness effect. *Personality and Social Psychology Bulletin, 41*, 559–574.

Vander Molen, R. J., Kaplan, S., Choi, E., & Montoya, D. (2018). Judgments of the dark triad based on Facebook profiles. *Journal of Research in Personality, 73*, 150–163.

Vazire, S., Naumann, L. P., Rentfrow, P. J., & Gosling, S. D. (2008). Portrait of a narcissist: manifestations of narcissism in physical appearance. *Journal of Research in Personality, 42*, 1439–1447.

Vedel, A. (2016). Big five personality group differences across academic majors: a systematic review. *Personality and Individual Differences, 92*, 1–10.

Vedel, A., & Thomsen, D. K. (2017). The dark triad across academic majors. *Personality and Individual Differences, 116*, 86–91.

Vernon, P. A., Villani, V. C., Vickers, L. C., & Harris, J. A. (2008). A behavioral genetic investigation of the dark triad and the big 5. *Personality and Individual Differences, 44*, 445–452.

Vigil-Colet, A. (2007). Impulsivity and decision making in the balloon analogue risk-taking task. *Personality and Individual Differences, 43*, 37–45.

Viljoen, J. L., MacDougall, E. A., Gagnon, N. C., & Douglas, K. S. (2010). Psychopathy evidence in legal proceedings involving adolescent offenders. *Psychology, Public Policy, and Law, 16*, 254–283.

Vitis, L., & Gilmour, F. (2017). Dick pics on blast: a woman's resistance to online sexual harassment using humour, art and Instagram. *Crime, Media, Culture, 13*(3), 335–355.

Vize, C. E., Collison, K. L., Miller, J. D., & Lynam, D. R. (2018). Examining the effects of controlling for shared variance among the dark triad using meta-analytic structural equation modelling. *European Journal of Personality, 32*, 46–61.

Vize, C. E., Lynam, D. R., Collison, K. L., & Miller, J. D. (2018). Differences among dark triad components: a meta-analytic investigation. *Personality Disorders: Theory, Research, and Treatment, 9*, 101–111.

Volmer, J., Koch, I. K., & Göritz, A. S. (2016). The bright and dark sides of leaders' dark triad traits: effects on subordinates' career success and well-being. *Personality and Individual Differences, 101*, 413–418.

Wai, M., & Tiliopoulos, N. (2012). The affective and cognitive empathic nature of the dark triad of personality. *Personality and Individual Differences*, *52*, 794–799.

Waling, A., & Pym, T. (2017). 'C' mon, no one wants a 'dick pic': exploring the cultural framings of the 'dick pic' in contemporary online publics. *Journal of Gender Studies*, 1–16.

Walker, D., & Vul, E. (2014). Hierarchical encoding makes individuals in a group seem more attractive. *Psychological Science*, *25*, 230–235.

Walters, N. T., & Horton, R. (2015). A diary study of the influence of Facebook use on narcissism among male college students. *Computers in Human Behavior*, *52*, 326–330.

Wang, Y., Xie, X., Wang, X., Wang, P., Nie, J., & Lei, L. (2018). Narcissism and selfie-posting behavior: the mediating role of body satisfaction and the moderating role of attitude toward selfie-posting behavior. *Current Psychology*, 1–8.

Watson, P. J. (2005). Complexity of narcissism and a continuum of self-esteem regulation. *Personality Disorders*, 336–338.

Watts, A. L., Lilienfeld, S. O., Smith, S. F., Miller, J. D., Campbell, W. K., Waldman, I. D., et al. (2013). The double-edged sword of grandiose narcissism implications for successful and unsuccessful leadership among US Presidents. *Psychological Science*.

Weeks, G. R., Gambescia, N., & Jenkins, R. E. (2004). Treating infidelity. Therapeutic dilemmas and effective strategies. *Tijdschrift voor Psychiatrie*, *46*, 875.

Weiser, E. B. (2015). # Me: narcissism and its facets as predictors of selfie-posting frequency. *Personality and Individual Differences*, *86*, 477–481.

Welker, K. M., Lozoya, E., Campbell, J. A., Neumann, C. S., & Carré, J. M. (2014). Testosterone, cortisol, and psychopathic traits in men and women. *Physiology & Behavior*, *129*, 230–236.

Westerlaken, K. M., & Woods, P. R. (2013). The relationship between psychopathy and the full range leadership model. *Personality and Individual Differences*, *54*, 41–46.

Westhead, J., & Egan, V. (2015). Untangling the concurrent influences of the dark triad, personality and mating effort on violence. *Personality and Individual Differences*, *86*, 222–226.

Wetzel, E., Brown, A., Hill, P., Chung, J. M., Robins, R. W., & Roberts, B. W. (2017). The narcissism epidemic is dead; long live the narcissism epidemic. *Psychological Science*, *28*, 1833–1847.

Wetzel, E., Roberts, B. W., Fraley, R. C., & Brown, A. (2016). Equivalence of Narcissistic Personality Inventory constructs and correlates across scoring approaches and response formats. *Journal of Research in Personality*, *61*, 87–98.

Willis, M., Birthrong, A., King, J. S., Nelson-Gray, R. O., & Latzman, R. D. (2017). Are infidelity tolerance and rape myth acceptance related constructs? An association moderated by psychopathy and narcissism. *Personality and Individual Differences*, *117*, 230–235.

Wilson, J. S., Ermshar, A. L., & Welsh, R. K. (2006). Stalking as paranoid attachment: a typological and dynamic model. *Attachment & Human Development*, *8*(2), 139–157.

Wilson, M., & Daly, M. (1985). Competitiveness, risk taking, and violence: the young male syndrome. *Ethology and Sociobiology*, *6*, 59–73.

Wilson, M. S., & McCarthy, K. (2011). Greed is good? Student disciplinary choice and self-reported psychopathy. *Personality and Individual Differences*, *51*, 873–876.

Wilson, R. E., Harris, K., & Vazire, S. (2015). Personality and friendship satisfaction in daily life: do everyday social interactions account for individual differences in friendship satisfaction? *European Journal of Personality*, *29*, 173–186.

Wisse, B., Barelds, D. P., & Rietzschel, E. F. (2015). How innovative is your employee? The role of employee and supervisor dark triad personality traits in supervisor perceptions of employee innovative behavior. *Personality and Individual Differences*, *82*, 158–162.

Wisse, B., & Sleebos, E. (2016). When the dark ones gain power: perceived position power strengthens the effect of supervisor Machiavellianism on abusive supervision in work teams. *Personality and Individual Differences*, *99*, 122–126.

Wissing, B. G., & Reinhard, M. A. (2017). The dark triad and the PID-5 maladaptive personality traits: accuracy, confidence and response bias in judgments of veracity. *Frontiers in Psychology*, *8*, 1549.

Wong, S. C., & Olver, M. E. (2015). Risk reduction treatment of psychopathy and applications to mentally disordered offenders. *CNS Spectrums*, *20*(3), 303–310.

Woodworth, M., & Porter, S. (2002). In cold blood: characteristics of criminal homicides as a function of psychopathy. *Journal of Abnormal Psychology*, *111*, 436–445.

Wright, G. R., Berry, C. J., & Bird, G. (2012). "You can't kid a kidder": association between production and detection of deception in an interactive deception task. *Frontiers in Human Neuroscience*, *6*, 87.

Wright, G. R., Berry, C. J., Catmur, C., & Bird, G. (2015). Good liars are neither 'dark' nor self-deceptive. *PloS One*, *10*(6)e0127315.

Wright, J. P., Morgan, M. A., Almeida, P. R., Almosaed, N. F., Moghrabi, S. S., & Bashatah, F. S. (2017). Malevolent forces: self-control, the dark triad, and crime. *Youth Violence and Juvenile Justice*, *15*, 191–215.

Wu, T., & Barnes, J. C. (2013). Two dopamine receptor genes (DRD2 and DRD4) predict psychopathic personality traits in a sample of American adults. *Journal of Criminal Justice*, *41*, 188–195.

Yochelson, S., & Samenow, S. (1993). *The criminal personality: a profile for change*. Vol. 1. Jason Aronson.

Yost, M. R., & Zurbriggen, E. L. (2006). Gender differences in the enactment of sociosexuality: an examination of implicit social motives, sexual fantasies, coercive sexual attitudes, and aggressive sexual behavior. *Journal of Sex Research*, *43*, 163–173.

Zachar, P., Krueger, R. F., & Kendler, K. S. (2016). Personality disorder in DSM-5: an oral history. *Psychological Medicine*, *46*, 1–10.

Zeigler-Hill, V., Besser, A., Morag, J., & Campbell, W. K. (2016). The dark triad and sexual harassment proclivity. *Personality and Individual Differences*, *89*, 47–54.

Zell, A. L., & Moeller, L. (2017). Narcissism and "likes": entitlement/exploitativeness predicts both desire for and dissatisfaction with responses on Facebook. *Personality and Individual Differences*, *110*, 70–73.

Zell, A. L., & Moeller, L. (2018). Are you happy for me... on Facebook? The potential importance of "likes" and comments. *Computers in Human Behavior*, *78*, 26–33.

Zhang, H., Ou, A. Y., Tsui, A. S., & Wang, H. (2017). CEO humility, narcissism and firm innovation: a paradox perspective on CEO traits. *The Leadership Quarterly*, *28*, 585–604.

Zhang, W., Zou, H., Wang, M., & Finy, M. S. (2015). The role of the dark triad traits and two constructs of emotional intelligence on loneliness in adolescents. *Personality and Individual Differences*, *75*, 74–79.

Index

Note: Page numbers followed by *f* indicate figures and *t* indicate tables.

Made in the USA
Monee, IL
13 September 2026

63138367R00122